The Poetry of Wang Wei

CHINESE LITERATURE IN TRANSLATION

Editors

Irving Yucheng Lo
Joseph S. M. Lau
Leo Ou-fan Lee

The Poetry of
WANG WEI

NEW TRANSLATIONS
AND COMMENTARY

Pauline Yu

INDIANA UNIVERSITY PRESS
Bloomington

Manufactured in the United States of America

Library of Congress Cataloging in Publication Data

Wang Wei, 701–761.
    The poetry of Wang Wei.

    (Chinese literature in translation)
    Bibliography: p.
    Includes index.
    I. Yu, Pauline, 1949–   II. Title.   III. Series.
PL2676.A285   895.1'13   79–3623
ISBN 0–253–17772–3   1 2 3 4 5 84 83 82 81 80
ISBN 0–253–20252–3 (pbk.)

Contents

CHAPTER FOUR: *Buddhist Poems*   112

Preface

Wang Wei occupies a curious position in twentieth-century Chinese and Western literary scholarship. On the one hand, despite his generally acknowledged status as one of the major poets of the Tang dynasty (618–907), the period of greatest poetic florescence in China, he has been the subject of few extensive critical studies in any language. There are several possible reasons for this relative lack of secondary material. In the first place, his poems possess a surface simplicity, the immediate appeal of apparently precise visual imagery, and a calm appreciation of nature which seem to leave little for the reader to interpret. Yet, paradoxically, on second glance his work reveals disturbingly elusive philosophical underpinnings, grounded in Buddhist metaphysics, and the difficulty of grappling with these concepts and relating them to his poetry may have discouraged critical analysis. But the most likely reason for this neglect, in China at least, is the dominant tradition of didactic criticism—Confucian and now Marxist—which uses the work to write the biography, evaluates both on extraliterary grounds, and focuses on poets who reflect and criticize contemporary social and political conditions in their poetry.

Yet, on the other hand, translations of Wang Wei's poetry, most of them dating from the last decade or so, outnumber those of any other Chinese poet. Again, several reasons could be adduced to explain this relative proliferation: the quietude of many of his nature poems, appealing to subcultures of the late sixties in the West; his reliance on concrete imagery, which translates rather well; the infrequency of obscure allusions in much of his work; his comparatively straightforward diction and syntax; and the quite manageable size of his corpus—approximately four hundred poems. But this last factor may also be responsible for one of the major failings of recent translations: since Wang Wei's nature poems represent what seems to be a significant proportion of a small body of poetry, it has been too easy to use them as the sum of his poetic world.

This volume is a response to both situations, an attempt to fill the critical gap and also to provide a more comprehensive view of Wang Wei's poetry. Thus my first chapter suggests a comparative framework for interpreting his work as a whole, and the introductions to each subsequent group of poems offer my own exegeses of them, based on that approach. At the same time, however, it has been my aim to present a broader sampling of his poems than has been translated into English before and to allow those works to stand, as much as possible, on their own. Although all translation must unavoidably involve an act of interpretation, I have not consciously been guided by any doctrinaire theories or programs. Juggling with the often conflicting goals of literalness and literacy, fidelity and felicity, can never be done to everyone's satisfaction, but I have tried to retain the original word order and spareness of diction while still producing a reasonably fluent English version. Although no effort has been made to reproduce rhyme schemes, I have generally followed Arthur Waley's example and given as many stresses to an English line as there are syllables in the original text.

It is my hope that this book will prove of interest to readers of Western and Chinese poetry alike, and the annotation has been directed equally to both. Much background information will undoubtedly seem superfluous or sketchy to sinologists; on the other hand, the Chinese texts in Appendix I are provided primarily for their convenience. To keep footnotes to a minimum, all page references to a source after the first mention are given in the text itself. In line with the decision of major periodicals and press agencies in both China and the United States following the establishment of diplomatic relations between the two countries, I have employed the *pinyin* system of romanization, with but three exceptions: the cities of Peking and Taipei, and all forms of the word "Tao" ("Way"). However, for those readers who may be more familiar with the older Wade-Giles system, Appendix II provides an alphabetically arranged list of names, titles, terms, etc., in both forms, as well as the Chinese characters for them.

Fortunately, textual variants do not pose serious problems for Wang Wei. I have based my translations on the standard 1736 edition of his complete works annotated by Zhao Diancheng and have indicated those few instances where I have chosen a variant reading. References given with each poem specify both the *juan* (fascicle) and page number in the *Sibu beiyao* edition (Rpt. Taipei: Zhonghua, 1966), as well as the volume and page number in the punctuated reprinting (Peking: Zhonghua, 1961).

Earlier translations of poems 64, 68, 80, 111, 132, 141, and 148 were published in *The Denver Quarterly*, Vol. 12, No. 2 (Summer 1977), pp. 353–55. Poems 41 and 133, as well as other material scattered throughout this study, appeared in my review article "Wang Wei: Recent Studies and Translations," *Chinese Literature: Essays, Articles, Reviews*, Vol. I, No. 2 (July 1979), pp. 219–40. Portions of the

Critical Introduction have been revised from my article "Chinese and Symbolist Poetic Theories," *Comparative Literature*, Vol. XXX, No. 4 (Fall 1978), pp. 291–312. I wish to thank the editors of these journals for permission to reprint this material.

A number of people have been helpful in the completion of this volume, and I am grateful to them all. The guidance of Professor James J. Y. Liu has been invaluable: he directed my study of Chinese poetry and poetics during my graduate years at Stanford University and encouraged both my interest in Wang Wei and my choice of critical methodology. Painstakingly reading all of my translations, he has saved me from many embarrassing errors and clumsy wordings. I would also like to thank Professor Irving Y. Lo of Indiana University; his patient and careful reading of the manuscript and his many suggestions and corrections were extremely valuable. I am grateful to Marsha Wagner for sharing her thought-provoking work on Wang Wei with me; to my husband, Ted Huters, for his encouragement and counsel; and to our daughter, Emily, for waiting until I had finished writing to be born. And finally, I would like to acknowledge the American Association of University Women and Stanford University, whose Dissertation and Postdoctoral Fellowships, respectively, provided me with financial assistance during the writing and revision of this study.

ONE

Critical Introduction

THE poetry of Wang Wei creates a world of harmony and integration. Its imagery is nonmimetically suggestive yet seems visually precise; it prefers intuition over logic, and ambiguity and paradoxes over distinctions; and it is typically reluctant to assert an overtly subjective presence. All of these features help to shape a poetic universe where subject and object, emotion and scene are mutually implicated and fused, and where apparent contradictions in attitudes, themes, or imagery are ultimately resolved.

These traits were advocated by an important tradition of Chinese literary criticism which James J. Y. Liu has called "metaphysical," some of whose representatives consequently saw in Wang Wei's work the fulfillment of their ideals. I agree with Liu that before applying wholesale the methods and standards of Western criticism to Chinese literature, we should examine the theories of the Chinese themselves.[1] Yet these very notions do reappear in the writings of nineteenth- and twentieth-century Western poets, suggesting that the poetry of Wang Wei may be regarded as an illuminating embodiment of their poetics as well. Furthermore, I believe that a methodology drawing on twentieth-century phenomenological criticism, with its possible affinities to both Chinese and Symbolist conceptions of literature, may be the most appropriate and least foreign approach to his poetry. Thus before discussing and presenting Wang Wei's poems themselves, I would like to provide an introduction in this chapter first to the Chinese and then to the modern Western poetic theories which offer us the most congenial frame of reference in which to understand his work and whose terminology, at the same time, may be clarified by the example of his poems.

I.

Chinese metaphysical theories begin with the notion that literature (by which is meant chiefly poetry) is the manifestation of the Tao ("Way"), the principle of the universe immanent in the totality of all being. This doctrine is postulated on the assumption that a fundamental correspondence exists between the patterns (*wen*) and workings of the universe and those of human culture, such as writing (also *wen*). At this point I should note that the term "metaphysical" in this context is somewhat misleading, implying as it does the existence of a suprasensory realm that lies beyond and is superior to the level of physical beings; on the contrary, the Tao is seen by both Confucians and Taoists to be totally immanent in this world, at the same time that it transcends any individual phenomenon. This belief is grounded in the notion fundamental to all strains of Chinese thought that the universe is a spontaneously self-generating organism in which everything exists in an orderly, mutually implicating, correlative harmony with everything else.[2]

Two implications immediately come to mind. In the first place, this world view would seem to preclude the development of certain theories of literature that the West has come to take for granted. The concept of mimesis (art as imitation), for example, was based by the Greeks on the assumption of a dichotomy between this world and another transcendent one. Plato, of course, used this fact to denigrate and condemn art in Book X of *The Republic* as an illusory copy twice removed from the true realm of timeless Forms, yet Aristotle, while interested in rehabilitating concrete reality and reasserting the value of art, was even more insistent that imitation is both a basic human instinct and the primary activity of the artist (*Poetics*, chs. IV and I). The existence of Plato's Forms remained unquestioned, although for Aristotle they only took on reality when actualized through concrete matter.[3] While Judeo-Christian cosmology may have altered some of the terminology, this Platonic dualism persisted in the West, in the notion, for example, that events in this world are but a *figura* of those in another.[4] Given the fundamentally monistic tendency of traditional Chinese thought, the lack of a fully developed theory of mimesis—postulated as it is on such a dichotomy—should not be surprising.

Yet another influence of world view on literary criticism can be seen in the absence of Chinese theories stressing either the writer's radical creativity or the work's absolute autonomy. Both of these notions can be traced ultimately to the assumption of the universe as a *created* one. The relative unconcern with originality, for example, can be explained by the lack of any canonical work that would provide a model, and thus an implicit sanction, for creation *ex nihilo*; these the

West can find in the description of God's activities in the Book of Genesis, or even in the Greek concept of a *logos* or demiurge, a will external to creation yet necessary for its existence.[5] The Chinese cosmos was viewed as an uncreated one, and theories were, if anything, more likely to advocate imitation of exemplary works of the past rather than creation anew, for the Confucian conviction remained persistent that history was the story of a decline from a golden age. Everything, therefore, had already been said. More recently, the Western model of the creator–work relationship has provided the underpinning for conceptions of the autonomy of the work of art. Anglo-American New Critical notions of the poem as *sui generis*, an organic, autotelic heterocosm, in particular, are based implicitly on parallels between the artist and God, the creator of a world in itself.[6] This concept could not be fully developed in a culture that neither posited such a model of creation nor divorced art from the total realm of human activity.

In addition to discouraging the development of certain theories of literature familiar to the West, the cosmological foundations of what have been called the metaphysical theories are by no means unique to that one strain, but also underlie the other major tendencies of the Chinese critical tradition. The *Great Preface (Da xu)* to the *Classic of Poetry (Shi jing)*, for example, adapts ideas from earlier classical texts and declares:

> Poetry is where the intent of the heart/mind (*xin*) goes: what in the heart is intent is poetry when emitted in words. An emotion moves within and takes form in words. If words are insufficient, then one sighs; if sighing is insufficient, then one prolongs it [the emotion] in song; if prolonging through song is insufficient, then one unconsciously dances it with hands and feet.
>
> Emotions are emitted in sounds, and when sounds form a pattern, that is called music. The music of a well-governed world is peaceful and happy, its government harmonious; the music of a disorderly world is resentful and angry, its government perverse; the music of a defeated state is mournful and longing, its people in difficulty. Thus in regulating success and failure, moving heaven and earth, and touching spirits and gods, nothing comes closer than poetry.[7]

Although this passage may seem to juxtapose a number of non sequiturs, the notion of organic correlations between the human and natural worlds and the individual and society does resolve many of the contradictions. The nascent expressive theory—that poetry is the expression of emotions—assumes that what is internal can find some externally correspondent form or action. The deterministic and pragmatic theories that follow—that poetry both reflects and effects political order—are also logical extensions of a view of the universe as a network of associations, particularly strong during the Han dynasty, when the *Great Preface* was probably written (ca. first century A.D.). The Confucian belief in the universal morality of human nature, the cosmos, and the Tao further supports the argument here that literature can simultaneously reveal feelings, provide a gauge of governmental stability, and serve as a practical, didactic tool.

The conviction of a fundamental connection between the internal and the external, man and nature, remained strong in other early Chinese critical texts. Lu Ji's (261–303) *Rhymeprose on Literature* (*Wen fu*) begins with the assertion that the writer "stands at the center of the universe":

> He moves with the four seasons, sighing at transience, and looks at the myriad objects, contemplating their complexity.
> He laments the falling leaves during autumn's vigor and delights in the tender branches of fragrant spring.[8]

As Archibald MacLeish has pointed out, "To Lu Chi the begetting of a poem involves not a single electric pole thrust deep into the acids of the self but a pair of poles—a man and the world opposite. A poem begins, in the Wen Fu, not in isolation but in relationship."[9] Poetry is thus engendered, according to Lu Ji, by the response of the writer to the world around him, and that he can be moved in this way at all implies the existence of preexisting links between them.

Similar statements suggesting a sensory-emotional stimulus-response model of writing also appear in Liu Xie's (ca. 465–523) more comprehensive work, *The Literary Mind: Dragon-Carvings* (*Wenxin diaolong*). In his sixth chapter, "Elucidating Poetry" (*Ming shi*), for example, he explains that "Man is endowed with seven emotions, which are moved in response to objects. When moved by objects one sings of one's intent totally spontaneously."[10] Later, in chapter 27, he echoes the *Great Preface* in writing that "Emotions are moved and take form in words; reason emerges and literature appears: for in following the hidden to reach the manifest, one matches the external to the internal" (6/505). And chapter 46 develops this correlative thinking even further, giving specific examples of how, "when things move, the heart/mind is also stirred"; emotions will vary in accord with seasonal and atmospheric changes, since all phenomena are mutually resonant: "Things all call to one another—how can man remain at rest?" (10/693). The notion of correspondences pervades Liu Xie's entire work, whose "anatomy" of literature posits a number of organic relationships among universe, writer, language, and literary work, and within the work itself as well. As he observes in the chapter on "Style and Nature" (*Ti xing*): "What is manifest and what is within always tally with each other. Is this not the enduring property of nature and the general principle of talent and spirit?" (6/506).

The analogical assumptions characteristic of Chinese thought thus also underlie what James J. Y. Liu has termed "pragmatic," "deterministic," and "expressive" theories of literature; the "metaphysical" strain, however, pursued the implications of such notions at a less concrete level, strongly influenced by both Taoism and Chan (better known in its Japanese pronunciation, Zen) Buddhism. Several ideas characteristic of this tradition can be derived from the work attributed to Zhuangzi (369?–286? B.C.) and referred to by his name. This Taoist philosopher offers several words of advice on how best to get along in the world: one should follow the course of things and not engage in purposeful striving or intellection, but instead forget oneself to merge with the Tao. One will then no longer make distinctions among worldly things, between such states as life and death, nor between one's self and the universe: "Heaven and earth were born at the same time I was, and the ten thousand things are one with me."[11] This state of integrality is best exemplified by the parable at the end of the chapter in which this statement appears, where Zhuangzi dreams that he is a butterfly, but on awakening cannot determine if it was really he that dreamt of being a butterfly or vice versa.

Because both perceptual and conceptual modes of cognition are incomplete and necessarily imply a separation between self and object, the knower and the known, Zhuangzi rejects them and advocates instead a kind of intuitive apprehension, listening with the empty "spirit":

> Don't listen with your ears, listen with your mind. No, don't listen with your mind, but listen with your spirit. Listening stops with the ears, the mind stops with recognition, but spirit is empty and waits on all things. The Way gathers in emptiness alone. Emptiness is the fasting of the mind. ("In the World of Men" [*Ren jian shi*, 9/4/26]; trans. Watson, pp. 57–58)

And he frequently likens this emptiness or nondifferentiating selflessness to a mirror:

> When a man does not dwell in self, then things will of themselves reveal their forms to him. His movement is like that of water, his stillness like that of a mirror, his responses like those of an echo. Blankeyed, he seems to be lost; motionless, he has the limpidity of water. Because he is one with it, he achieves harmony; should he reach out for it, he would lose it. ("The World" [*Tian xia*, 93/33/56]; trans. Watson, p. 372)

This apparently spontaneous and passive mirroring cannot, however, be achieved without effort, for Zhuangzi includes several anecdotes about craftsmen whose skill is perfected through prolonged concentration and practice alone; only then can they perform with a seemingly unstudied ease.

Although Zhuangzi himself does not discuss poetry, such notions as mystical union with the Way, intuitive cognition of and selfless (or impersonal) identification with things, realization of relativity and flux, and refusal to make distinctions all proved fruitful for later literary critics. Both the *Rhymeprose on Literature* and *The Literary Mind*, for example, bear the imprint of Taoist thinking. In the former work, after opening with a discussion of the writer's interaction with and response to physical phenomena and the literary tradition, Lu Ji describes a process which rejects sensory perception for an obliteration of self-awareness:

> At first he shuts off sight and turns back hearing,
> Pondering deeply, questioning on all sides. . . .
> He cleanses his mind completely to condense his thoughts. (p. 255)

This different mode of cognition transcends both time and space:

> His spirit gallops to the eight reaches of the universe,
> His mind roams for a myriad miles. . . .
> He floats on the celestial pool, peacefully flowing,
> And dives into the nether spring, deeply submerged. . . .
> He views past and present in an instant,
> Touching the four seas in a twinkling. (pp. 255–56)

Lu Ji's description of the poet's activity also employs the Taoist notion of being as evolving from nonbeing: "He imposes on nonbeing to demand being, / Knocking on silence in search of music" (p. 259). Although this passage may appear to contain a conception of creation *ex nihilo*, it does not in fact present the writer as a purposeful producer: poetry does not come from the poet but rather from the nonbeing and silence of both the cosmos itself and his own state of mental emptiness. Nor is he the one who actually forges something from nothing, since being and music come rather as an answer to his "knock"; he is simply setting a process in motion, and the work in turn will continue to participate in the natural, endless workings of the universe. A later passage, in fact, alludes to the fifth section of the Taoist classic, the *Dao de jing*, which compares heaven and earth to a bellows whose emptiness is the source of unending activity: "[Literature] like the bellows is inexhaustible / And grows together with heaven and earth" (p. 271). And finally, although much of the

Rhymeprose deals with aspects of the literary process that the writer can polish and manipulate—Lu Ji's stated purpose, after all, had been "To tell of the splendid writings of past authors and to discuss the reasons behind literary success and failure" (p. 252)—his concluding passages assert rather its ineffable qualities. He alludes to an anecdote in the *Zhuangzi* ("The Way of Heaven" [*Tian dao*, 50/13/66]), about an artisan who knows that the secrets of his craft cannot be communicated to others:

> Like dancers following rhythms by flicking their sleeves
> Or singers answering strings by casting their voices:
> This is what wheelwright Pian could never speak of;
> Nor could the finest language ever explain it. (p. 270)

And a long section near the end of the *Rhymeprose* introduces that element of artistic activity that most clearly eludes both explanation and conscious control—inspiration itself (p. 273).

Although the bulk of *The Literary Mind* is devoted to more concrete aspects of writing—the interaction between emotions and objects, the organic relationship between form and content, the nature and history of various genres, the role of learning and craftsmanship, and specific felicities and faults—Liu Xie like Lu Ji employs Taoist notions to discuss the intuitive elements of the literary process. Chapter 26 on "Spiritual Thinking" (*Shen si*), in particular, describes a period immediately before writing when the poet stills his mind in union with the cosmic principle. It opens with an allusion to a passage in the *Zhuangzi* about an ancient prince who said: "My body is here beside these rivers and seas, but my mind is back there beside the palace towers of Wei" ("Giving Away a Throne" [*Rang wang*, 79/ 28/56]; trans. Watson, p. 317). In the original text this is an implicit criticism of a ruler unable to forget mundane glories, but Liu Xie uses it as an example of a kind of "spiritual" thinking or intuitive contemplation that can transcend both time and space. This is achieved, he writes, during a state of mental emptiness: "Thus in shaping his literary thinking, one should value vacuity and tranquility, cleanse the five viscera, and purify the quintessential spirit" (6/493). When the writer couples this with profound learning and broad experience, he can achieve the intuitive spontaneity of the master craftsmen in the *Zhuangzi* (like Lu Ji, Liu Xie gives the wheelwright Pian as a classic example) and leave no traces of conscious artistry: "Once spiritual thinking is set in motion, a myriad paths spring forth together; the place of rules and standards becomes meaningless and there is no sign of carving [i.e., deliberate effort]." Furthermore, he will attain not a simple, passive mirroring of external objects but a fusion of self and world: "When he climbs mountains his emotions will fill the mountains, and when he views the ocean his ideas will flow through the ocean" (6/493–94).

Even more than Lu Ji, throughout his work Liu Xie emphasizes the need for the harmonious integration of elements in the literary process—such as personality and genre, substance and adornment, emotions and objects, inner and outer realities in general—but he introduces another concept that was to become essential in metaphysical aesthetics. Whereas the earlier author had worried that "the meaning will not correspond to the objects and the text will not reach the meaning" (p. 252), echoing the statement in a commentary on the *Classic of Changes* (*Yi jing*), attributed to Confucius, that "Writing does not exhaust speech; speech does not exhaust the meaning,"[12] Liu Xie transforms this potential inadequacy into a positive transcendence of language. In chapter 40, for example, he defines a certain excellence as that of "the mysterious, the important meaning beyond the text" and writes further that "when the mysterious is the form, the meaning lodges beyond the text, hidden echoes penetrate indirectly, and concealed beauties emerge unobtrusively" (8/632). A later statement in chapter 46 praises a similar incommensurability of description and emotion: "One whose [description of] physical appearances ends but who [produces] a lingering emotion has thoroughly comprehended [the secret of writing]" (10/694).

A conviction as to the necessity of transcending language was common, of course, to both the indigenous Taoist and the Buddhist thought which had recently arrived in China from India. Probably the best-known statement to this effect can be found in the *Zhuangzi*:

> The fish trap exists because of the fish; once you've gotten the fish you can forget the trap. The rabbit snare exists because of the rabbit; once you've gotten the rabbit, you can forget the snare. Words exist because of meaning; once you've gotten the meaning, you can forget the words. Where can I find a man who has forgotten words so I can have a word with him? ("External Things" [*Wai wu*, 75/26/48]; trans. Watson, p. 302)

What characterizes the metaphysical tradition, however, is the transformation of this insufficiency of the verbal to the nonverbal into a quality of the highest poetry, one which can successfully evoke emotions or meanings that persist beyond the text itself. Although occasional assertions in this vein do occur earlier, and not only in *The Literary Mind*,[13] this idea did not begin to be developed until the Tang dynasty. Thus in his *Discussion of Literature and Meaning* (*Lun wen yi*), Wang Changling (698–757) states that "Only if the final line [of a poem] causes the thoughts to extend on endlessly will it be fine."[14]

This work is linked to the metaphysical tradition in several other respects. Like Lu Ji and Liu Xie, Wang Changling presents the writing process as beginning with a state of mental tranquility in which "one must forget the self and not be constrained" (p. 129), so that thoughts can arise spontaneously and produce a desired impression of naturalness. In other sections Wang describes a more active stage in which the poet must concentrate his mind and attempt to penetrate his object, and he also emphasizes the need to master rules and tricks of the trade, but the thrust of his discussion points toward an ideal mutual interaction between self and world which dissolves subject–object distinctions and results in an evocative work with no traces of laborious effort. Although the *Discussion* does not cite any passages from Wang Wei's work, focusing instead on examples drawn from earlier texts, these are precisely the qualities for which his poetry is known.

The monk Jiaoran (fl. 760) advocates similar aesthetic standards in his *Poetic Styles* (*Shi shi*), where he speaks, for example, of a "meaning beyond the text"[15] evident in the poetry of Xie Lingyun (385–433), of whom he happened to be a tenth-generation descendant. Like Wang Changling and earlier critics in this tradition, he recognizes the necessity of conscious artistry while praising the impression of effortless ease. He explains this ideal combination in his *Discussion of Poetry* (*Shi yi*):

> Someone has said: "In poetry one should not belabor one's thinking; if one belabors one's thinking, then one will lose the quality of naturalness." This is not so at all. Indeed, one must unravel one's thoughts amid difficulties, pluck what is marvelous from beyond phenomena, for soaring, animated verses, and describe obscure and mysterious ideas. For a rare pearl must be taken from the chin of a black dragon— how much more [difficult] is writing that penetrates the nether regions and embodies transformations? Yet what one values is that once the piece is finished, it has the appearance of effortlessness, as if it had been achieved with no thought at all.[16]

It is in the works of Sikong Tu (837–908) that we find the earliest extensive development of a theory of literature based on Taoist and Buddhist notions of the transcendence of self and language. In his series of poems entitled *The Twenty-four Moods of Poetry* (*Ershisi shi pin*), for example, he employs a tetrasyllabic verse form and image-laden, nondiscursive, highly elliptical language to embody various poetic moods or styles. Whether interpreted as containing advice to the poet on how to write or as depicting an ideal poet or poem, each poem in the sequence also describes itself indirectly; there is, however, no order to the series and the differences between some of the "moods" are well-nigh imperceptible. Unifying the whole is a conception of poetry as manifesting the writer's identification with the cosmic principle or Tao. Sikong Tu sees the poet as achieving a state of mental purity that casts off worldly and logical distinctions, purposive seeking, and coercion, so that he can intuitively apprehend the essence of natural phenomena, identify and flow with the Way informing them. Echoing earlier critics, Sikong Tu writes that this fusion enables the writer to transcend the boundaries of sensuous perception and endows him with a corresponding creative power. The beginning of his tenth poem, "Natural and Spontaneous" (*Ziran*), presents this process:

> Stoop to get it, there it is:
> Don't go seeking everywhere.
> Move along with the whole Tao
> And a hand's touch creates spring.[17]

Reminiscent of Zhuangzi, the first two lines here advise against forceful or teleological movement, a warning that recurs frequently in the group of poems. By following the Way, however, the poet can both cause something to possess a natural vitality and also create with absolute effortlessness. Other poems repeat this notion; in "Unrestrained and Virile" (*Haofang*, no. 12), for example, he writes:

> Follow the Tao, return to the spirit
> And everywhere you will be untrammeled. . . .
> Once you are filled with the true power,
> The myriad beings are at your side." (p. 44)

And the eighth poem, "Vigorous and Strong" (*Jingjian*), concludes with a similar testament to the productive powers of union with the cosmos:

> Stand together with heaven and earth,
> Your spirit transforming together with them.
> If you truly meet with this,
> You may avail yourself of it forever. (p. 36)

What results is a poetry that goes beyond a simple mimetic representation of phenomena. Thus in his first poem, "Powerful and Grand" (*Xionghun*), after describing the invigorating power of union with the Tao that enables the poet to evoke the myriad phenomena in the boundless realm of the imagination, Sikong Tu writes:

> Leap beyond the external appearance
> To reach the center of the circle—
> Hold it without coercion,
> It will come without end. (p. 22)

Here he suggests that the successful poetic image involves transcendence—by leaping beyond external description or by reaching "the center of the circle."[18] A poetic image which goes beyond a forced precision or a limited perspective will evoke an indeterminate, boundless meaning. In his twentieth poem, "Presentation" (*Xingrong*), Sikong Tu reformulates this conception of the image and supplies some examples:

> Solely gather spiritual simplicity
> And soon the pure truth will return,
> Like seeking the shadows in water
> Or writing the glories of spring.
> Winds' and clouds' shifting shapes,
> Flowers' and grasses' vividness,
> Oceans' rolling billows,
> Mountains' precipitous crags—
> All resemble the great Tao,
> Mysteriously bonded even to dust.
> Leave the substance, reach the image
> To approximate this kind of poet. (p. 59)

Although the disyllabic title is usually translated as "description," I have chosen to avoid that word because of its implication of external detail, which is precisely the opposite of the issue here. The poem opens with a statement that an inner purity is a necessary prerequisite for the poet to apprehend intuitively the spirit beyond phenomena, and the following two similes may refer to the nature of his encounter—intangible and miraculous—or to its possible effects. In the next four lines Sikong Tu provides some examples of essences of phenomena, abstract qualities transcending concrete detail. When the poet can apprehend and identify with the Tao immanent in them, he can manifest that union as an image of boundless meaning.

The poet, then, should be indirect and provocative, as the ninth poem of the group, "Resplendent Beauty" (*Jili*), puts it: "Thick ornateness ends up dry; / The thin and subtle is often profound" (p. 38). And ultimately, Sikong Tu's emphasis on this suggestive mode of presentation leads him to advocate the transcendence of language itself, as in "Concealed and Implied" (*Hanxu*, no. 11): "Without writing a single word, / Completely capture the spirit of it" (p. 42). Two of his letters develop this notion further. Writing to a certain Wang Ji (fl. 891), for instance, he notes: "Dai Rongzhou [Dai Shulun (732–89)] said: 'Poets' scenes, such as: "At Lantian when the sun is warm, smoke arises from fine jade," can be gazed at from afar but cannot be placed in front of one's eyebrows and lashes.' An image beyond the image, a scene beyond the scene—can these be easily verbalized?"[19]

Just as the perception of images in a poem is incommensurate with that of a concrete landscape, so any reader's actualization of a poetic scene in his own imagination will go beyond that of the poem as verbal artifact.[20] Another letter discussing poetry and addressed to a certain Master Li examines the same notion of transcendence in different terms:

> Prose is difficult, and poetry is even more difficult. From antiquity to the present there have been many metaphors for this, but I think that one must distinguish among flavors in order to discuss poetry. South of the Yangzi River and the five mountain ranges [i.e., in southern China], of those things that enhance the taste, if they are pickled in vinegar, it is not that they are not sour, but they stop at being sour and that is all. If they are salted in brine, it is not that they are not salty, but they stop at being salty and that is all. People of China [proper] will satisfy their hunger and stop eating because they know that something beyond saltiness and sourness, an exquisite beauty, is lacking.

As the more civilized population recognizes the need to go beyond mere sourness or saltiness, so the ideal poet should transcend the limits of words: when one's imagery is "immediate but not fleeting, far-reaching but inexhaustible, then one can speak of having gone beyond rhyme." With highly suggestive language, Sikong Tu concludes, the poet can exploit the symbolic and ineffable nature of language itself to open up a "meaning beyond flavor" (pp 68–69).

Sikong Tu's correspondence also contains some scattered opinions of specific poets in which he suggests that Wang Wei's poetry was the embodiment of these ideals. Writing to another poet, Wang Jia, for example, he praises Wang Wei highly, along with the later poet Wei Yingwu (773–828), for "their flavor is pure and peerless, like the penetrability of clear water" (p. 73). And in his letter to Master Li he remarks that these two poets are "pure and dispassionate, fine and delicate, yet there is an inherent 'style' within, and how can that hinder [them from also being] vigorous and forthright?" (p. 68). Although these statements are perhaps cryptic at best, by recalling his discussions of an ideal type of poetry in the *Twenty-four Moods* and in his correspondence we may surmise that what he appreciated about Wang Wei's work was a vigorous yet limpid subtlety and suggestiveness.

Guo Shaoyu has described both Jiaoran and Sikong Tu as representatives of the "Poet-Buddha school" (*Shi fo pai*), spokesmen for the poetics implicit in Wang Wei, who left no critical writings himself.[21] In fact, of course, the influence on Sikong Tu's ideas can be attributed as much to Taoism as to Buddhism, and similar theories can be found in the works of later critics who were not necessarily advocates of the poet's style or writing from a specifically Buddhist perspective. The notion of evoking a meaning unexhausted by language proved particularly popular during the Song dynasty. Thus Ouyang Xiu (1007–72) records a remark by his friend Mei Yaochen (1002–60) to the effect that

> Although poets may emphasize meaning, it is also difficult to come up with the right language. If one has fresh ideas and skilled diction and can say things in a way that no one has done before, that is good. One must be able to give form to scenes that are difficult to describe, such that they seem to be right before one's eyes, and to suggest an inexhaustible meaning that appears beyond the words themselves—only that can be called the utmost.[22]

The Southern Song poet Yang Wanli (1127–1206) resumes Sikong Tu's "flavor" metaphor to discuss the evocative, open-ended quality of the text that enables different modes of apprehension on the part of different readers:

> In reading books one must know the flavor beyond flavor. If one does not know the flavor beyond flavor and says, "I can read books," one is mistaken. There is a poem in the *Airs of the States* [*Classic of Poetry*, poem no. 35] which goes: "Who says the sow-thistle is bitter? / It is as sweet as shepherd's purse." I take this as the method for reading books. For when one eats the world's bitterest thing but obtains the world's sweetest thing, then although the act of eating is the same as with other men, what one obtains is different. What one shares with others is the flavor; what one does not share is the not-flavor.[23]

And the lyricist Jiang Kui (ca. 1155–1221) expresses a similar opinion:

> In language one values suggestiveness. Dongpo [Su Shi (1037–1101)] has said: "When words come to an end but the meaning is inexhaustible, those are the most accomplished words under heaven." Shangu [Huang Tingjian (1045–1105)] was even more concerned about this. When a zither plays "The Pure Temple" [*Classic of Poetry*, poem no. 266], one sings and three sigh in echo: how far-reaching! Can later students of poetry not regard this as fundamental? If a verse has no superfluous words and a work has no excessive diction, that is not the best of the best. But if a verse has a lingering flavor and a work has a lingering meaning, that is the best of the best.[24]

Later in the same work he states that there are four types of "supreme marvelousness" (*gao miao*) in poetry: reason, meaning, imagination, and naturalness.

> To be blocked and then to truly understand is called the supreme marvelousness of reason. To go beyond meaning itself is called the supreme marvelousness of meaning. To describe the mysterious and ob-

scure as if one were seeing to the bottom of a clear pond is called the supreme marvelousness of imagination. What is neither unusual nor strange and is stripped of literary ornament, such that one knows its subtle excellence but does not know its cause—that is called the supreme marvelousness of naturalness. (p. 440/4a)

Jiang Kui also stresses the importance of mastering learning and rules, but these remarks present in a nutshell the metaphysical tradition's interest in the ineffable nature of the poetic process and of poetry itself.

His contemporary Yan Yu, or Yen Canglang (fl. 1180–1235), however, is more frequently associated with the types of theories first developed fully by Sikong Tu. Yan Yu is best known for a statement in his *Canglang's Remarks on Poetry* (*Canglang shihua*) that "Discussing poetry is like discussing Chan,"[25] and for using terms from Buddhism—such as Greater and Lesser Vehicle, Northern and Southern traditions, Dharma or law, and enlightenment—to analyze the Chinese poetic tradition. He was not the first to make such analogies: in his history of Chinese literary criticism Guo Shaoyu cites several passages from the works of earlier poets, such as Han Ju (1086–1135) and Wu Ke (ca. 1126), that liken the study of poetry to that of Chan, the way of poetry to the Dharma, and the writing of poetry to sitting in meditation (pp. 214–15). These were comparisons that were characteristic of the Jiangxi school in general, associated with Huang Tingjian, which emphasized the importance of rules and method, to be mastered through a meditation on the works of great poets of the past. Yan Yu, however, turns from these critics' focus on archaism and imitation (although he does not reject such concerns) to a consideration of somewhat more intangible matters. Like Sikong Tu, he posits an ideal poetry as emanating from a fusion with the Way, which enables the poet to suggest the reality lying beyond both phenomena themselves and words: "In poetry the highest achievement consists of one thing: entering the spirit. If poetry enters the spirit, that is perfection, the utmost, and nothing can be added to it. Only Li [Bo (701–62)] and Du [Fu (712–70)] attain it" (p. 6). The phrase "entering the spirit" suggests an intuitive apprehension of the essence of things and recalls Sikong Tu's advice to "Leap beyond the external appearance / To reach the center of the circle," i.e., to penetrate the outward form of objects in order to grasp and evoke their more ineffable qualities.

Yan Yu then draws on Buddhist vocabulary to describe this special awareness:

In general the way of Chan rests in marvelous awakening alone, and the way of poetry also rests in marvelous awakening. Furthermore, Meng Xiangyang's [Meng Haoran (689–740)] strength of learning was far below that of Han Tuizhi [Han Yu (768–824)], yet the superiority of his poetry to Tuizhi's lies solely in the fact that its entire flavor is one of marvelous awakening. (p. 10)

In other words, although Yan Yu's *Remarks* are actually principally concerned with practical advice on how to write and evaluate poetry, he also recognizes the necessity of a suprarational mode of cognition. It may be that the two approaches implicate each other, as the twentieth-century writer Qian Zhongshu has argued: "One must perfect the five methods and only then can one order the styles; one must order the nine styles and only then can one enter the spirit."[26]

Like earlier critics in the metaphysical tradition, Yan Yu advocates a poetry that is suggestive and unforced. One of his "Rules for Poetry" (*shi fa*), for example, declares: "Avoid directness of language, shallowness of meaning, exposure of the pulse [structure], and shortness of flavor; be neither dilatory nor forced with your tones and rhymes" (p. 114). But his most famous description of an ideal poetry occurs in the first section of his *Remarks*. After alluding to the fish trap passage in the *Zhuangzi* to assert that "What is called not treading on the path of reason nor falling into the net of words is supreme," he continues:

> The people of the high Tang [eighth century] all relied on inspired interest alone, like the antelope which hangs by its horns without a trace to be followed. Thus their marvelousness consists of a crystalline penetrability that cannot be gathered together, like sound in air, color in appearances, the moon in water, an image in the mirror—the words come to an end but the meaning is inexhaustible. (p. 24)

This passage employs traditional Buddhist metaphors of illusoriness to describe a vague, indefinable, yet paradoxically immediately apprehensible quality of the highest poetry: like the antelope which hangs by its horns and thus leaves no tracks, it displays no traces of conscious artistry or concern with technique.[27] Thus for Yan Yu, the best poets achieve such a mastery of emotions that feelings and scenes are integrated and an obtrusive subjectivity cannot hinder the immediacy of a poem, and such a mastery of language that their very art lies in concealing that art and in transcending the limits of verbal description itself. This series of similes, then, encapsulates three fundamental aesthetic qualities advocated by the metaphysical critics: the impression of an intuitive vision and effortless ease that resembles a moment of sudden enlightenment; a method of indirectness and evocation; and an apparent impersonality.

In view of these standards, it may seem strange that Yan Yu singled out Li Bo and Du Fu as the only two poets to have "entered the spirit," and that he only mentions Wang Wei twice, in passing, in the course of his *Remarks*. To be sure, he praises Meng Haoran, whose work is generally associated with that of Wang Wei, both in the passage comparing him favorably to Han Yu cited above and in a later section that passes judgment on individual poets: "Meng Haoran's poetry, when chanted at length, sounds like the [first two notes of the pentatonic scale] *gong* and *shang* of bells and stones" (p. 180). And the first of his two "general categories" of poetry would also seem to characterize that style: "free and easy, and deeply expressive and exhaustive" (p. 6). Yan Yu's preference for Du Fu in particular, however, can be explained by recalling the interest of his *Remarks* as a whole in assessing the Chinese poetic tradition and establishing exemplary models and methods for latter-day poets. Not only does Yan Yu agree with the judgment of many of his contemporaries that Du Fu embodies all poetic tendencies of the past ("Shaoling's poetry is modeled on the Han and Wei and takes materials from the Six Dynasties. As for the marvelousness of his accomplishments, he is what former generations called a Synthesizer of Great Achievements" [p. 157][28]), he also recognizes his value as an example to imitate. In comparing Du Fu and Li Bo, Yan Yu writes: "Shaoling's poetic method is like Sun [Wu's] and Wu [Qi's]; [Li] Taibo's poetic method is like Li Guang's. Shaoling is like a master who keeps to the rules" (p. 156). Precisely because Du Fu resembles the famous generals of the past who went by the books, he is more useful than Li Bo, whose "strategies," like Li Guang's, were somewhat unorthodox. Yan Yu no doubt found Wang Wei's elusiveness even less susceptible to analysis and thus less suitable as a practical model.[29]

The influence of *Canglang's Remarks on Poetry* proved far-reaching, encouraging the development of extremely formalistic and archaistic theories of literature as well as the continuation of metaphysical ideas. During the Ming dynasty the former tendency predominated, while the latter strain focused on discussions of a necessary integration between internal emotion (*qing*) and external scene (*jing*). This notion, of course, was based on the assumption mentioned earlier of fundamental correlations between internal and external reality already implicit in the earliest Chinese critical texts, although not made explicit until somewhat later. For example, Wang Changling in his *Discussion of Literature and Meaning* advocates a harmonious balance between ideas or meaning and physical objects:

> In poetry one values fusing the title and central meaning together without limit; the scenic objects that one sees and one's pleasant thoughts should be presented together. If one speaks one's meaning in a direct, one-sided way, the poem will lack subtlety and flavor, and if there is overabundant talk of the scene, not bound with meaning, then even if it is well-organized it will be flavorless. Scenes of dusk and dawn and

the atmosphere of the four seasons should all be connected with mean-
ing and given an order: if one speaks of them together with meaning,
that is miraculous. (p. 138)

Sikong Tu employs similar vocabulary in his letter to Wang Jia, where
he praises the pentasyllabic regulated verse form for lending itself to
such an integration: "Its strong point lies in combining thought and
circumstances" (p. 73). And Jiang Kui makes a fragmentary remark
in his *Discourse on Poetry* to the effect that "There is scene within the
meaning and meaning within the scene" (p. 440/3a).

Two of the Seven Latter Masters of the Ming dynasty continue
to discuss poetry along these lines. Xie Zhen (1495–1575) shifts the
focus from meaning or thought to emotion in speaking of its relation-
ship to the scene:

> Writing poetry is based on emotion and scene. Alone, neither is com-
> plete, nor do the two oppose one another. . . . One should use one's
> strength to cause the internal and the external to be as one, so that
> there is no separation between what comes out of and what goes into
> the heart/mind. Scene is the matchmaker of poetry and emotion is the
> embryo of poetry: when they merge to become a poem, then just a few
> words will gather up a myriad forms and an all-embracing primordial
> spirit will arise that will overflow without limits.[30]

When the poet can transcend the duality between self and world, he
will be able to partake of the creative and invigorating force of the
cosmic principle, as Sikong Tu had also claimed ("Move along with
the whole Tao / And a hand's touch creates spring"). And as Yan Yu
had asserted that the resulting poetry would have limited words but
inexhaustible meaning, so Xie Zhen notes that its force "will overflow
without limits." Similarly, Wang Shizhen (1526–90) advocates this fu-
sion of subject and object, in a passage which is actually a critique of
sterile imitation of the ancients: "When feeling and scene are mirac-
ulously united, when one's personal style is naturally supreme,
when one does not serve antiquity and does not fall into a narrow
path, that is the utmost."[31] And as Guo Shaoyu points out (p. 326),
Wang Shizhen also made a point of elevating Wang Wei to the status
of Li Bo and Du Fu. Indeed, this very notion of a fusion of emotion
and scene is a particularly apt criterion for evaluating a poet who
most characteristically suggests inner states through the presentation
of natural objects.

It is in the writings of the Qing dynasty Wang Shizhen
(1634–1711) that the metaphysical theories once again find their full
expression. He touches on such concepts as union with the Tao, in-
tuitive apprehension of the essence of phenomena, fusion of emotion
and scene, and discusses the resulting qualities of a poetry that is

highly elusive, evocative, and seemingly effortless. It communicates
the ineffable, encourages the participation of the reader, and tran-
scends the limits of mimetic description, purely personal emotion,
and, ultimately, language itself. Wang Shizhen was most strongly in-
fluenced by both Sikong Tu and Yan Yu. Citations from the former's
Twenty-four Moods of Poetry and his correspondence appear frequently
in Wang's *Remarks on Poetry (Daijingtang shihua)*, compiled by a dis-
ciple. In one instance, for example, he writes:

> Sikong Biaosheng [Tu] wrote a classification of poetry into a total of
> twenty-four [moods]. There is one called "Placid and Subtle" [*Chong-
> dan*, no. 2], which says: "Encountering it is not difficult, / Pursue it and
> it grows more scarce"; there is one called "Natural and Spontaneous,"
> which says: "Stoop to get it—there it is; / Don't go seeking every-
> where"; and there is one called "Refreshing and Rare" [*Qingqi*, no. 16],
> which says: "Spirit comes from the ancient and rare, / Tranquil and
> ungraspable." These are the highest moods.[32]

And the adjoining comment quotes both a poem and the citation
from Dai Shulun:

> Biaosheng's discussion of poetry has twenty-four moods. The eight
> words I like most are: "Without writing a single word, / Completely
> capture the spirit of it" [from "Concealed and Implied"]. He also says
> "Brightly gleaming flowing water, / Flourishing growth of distant
> spring" ["Delicate Fullness" (*Xiannong*, no. 3)]. These two remarks de-
> scribe the state of poetry in an extremely marvelous way. They are just
> what Dai Rongzhou meant in those eight words: "At Lantian when the
> sun is warm, smoke arises from fine jade." (3/3b)

References to Yan Yu's *Remarks on Poetry* also abound in Wang
Shizhen's writings. Like the Song dynasty critic, Wang uses the
Buddhist metaphor of enlightenment to suggest an intuitive appre-
hension of reality which eliminates the duality between self and
world: "Discarding the raft and climbing ashore is what practitioners
of Chan consider to be the state of awakening and what poets con-
sider to be the state of transformation. Poetry and Chan reach the
same level and there is no distinction between them" (3/6b). The
metaphor of Chan meditation, which eliminates all subject-object dis-
tinctions, can also describe the poet's potential transcendence of lan-
guage: "The Tang poets' pentasyllabic quatrains frequently enter
Chan and can miraculously 'catch the meaning and forget the
words'" (3/1b). Here he alludes, as did Yan Yu, to the fish trap pas-
sage in the *Zhuangzi* to suggest the paradoxical verbal expression of
a fundamentally nonverbal union with the Tao. In another section
Wang praises three passages in particular:

In Yan Canglang's discussion of poetry I have singled out the two words "marvelous awakening," the statement about "not treading on the path of reason nor falling into the net of words," and also "an image in the mirror, the moon in water, the antelope hangs by its horns without a trace to be followed," etc. These all disclose secrets hitherto unrevealed by other men. (2/7a)

He also uses these same images from the earlier text to describe his own concepts, such as that of an intuitive apprehension of reality: "An image in the mirror, the moon in water, the color in appearances, the antelope hangs by its horns without a trace to be followed—this is inspired understanding" (3/4b). With this "inspired understanding" or "inspired encounter," the poet can transcend both perceptual and conceptual modes of cognition to acquire an intuitive knowledge of phenomena and the Way, a notion similar to that of Yan Yu's "entering the spirit." Elsewhere Wang borrows another phrase from the same passage to write: "Regulated verses have a spiritual resonance whose naturalness cannot be gathered together" (3/2b).

The term "spiritual resonance" (*shenyun*) is the one for which Wang Shizhen is best known—his followers, in fact, were labeled the "*shenyun* school"—but it is quite difficult to translate. Richard J. Lynn has argued that it

> signifies three essential concepts . . . . : *yün* surely refers to personal tone—the interior world of individual poetic consciousness. *Shen*, on the other hand, refers not to just one but two things: the poet's intuitive vision, his cognition, of the world around him, and his intuitive control over the poetic medium. (p. 248)

In other words, it describes the poet's relationship to both the universe and the activity of writing, as well as to the work itself—as James J. Y. Liu phrases it in *Chinese Theories of Literature*, "an ineffable personal tone or flavor in one's poetry" (p. 45)—manifested in an oblique rather than directly subjective manner. It may also, as the above quotation would suggest, refer to qualities of the poem less tied to questions of personality, an ungraspable, natural resonance with the world it embodies or with any potential reader.

In any case, Wang Shizhen parts company with Yan Yu in his opinions about which poets in particular embody these various ideals. Thus although he writes that "Yan Canglang used Chan as a metaphor for poetry, and I deeply agree with what he said: the pentasyllabic [verse form] best approaches it," he continues: "For example, in the Wang River quatrains of Wang [Wei] and Pei [Di], each word enters Chan" (3/6b). And whereas Yan Yu had felt that only Du

Fu and Li Bo's poetry "entered the spirit," Wang Shizhen agrees with
Sikong Tu's esteem of Wang Wei and his "school": "Among Tang writ-
ers the poems of Wang Mojie [Wei], Meng Haoran, Liu Shenxu (fl.
730), Chang Jian (fl. 749), and Wang Changling all speak of Chan" (3/
6a). Wang Wei, in particular, is praised for his ability to transcend the
realm of physical appearances, of conventional temporal-spatial lim-
itations:

> Generations have said that Wang Youcheng [Wei] painted bananas in
> the snow: his poetry is exactly the same. For example, take "On the
> Nine Rivers how many times have the maple trees turned green? / The
> entire strip of Yangzhou and the Five Lakes is white."[33] In the following
> couplet he mentions Lanling township, Fuchun district, and Shitou
> city—all of these place names are vast distances apart and do not be-
> long together. In general, the poetry and painting of the ancients only
> considered inspired understanding and reaching with the spirit. (3/1b).

Perhaps the most striking index of Wang Shizhen's appreciation of
this type of poetry is his anthology, the *Samādhi Collection of Tang Wor-
thies (Tang xian sanmei ji)*, the background behind whose compilation
he explains in his *Remarks on Poetry*:

> Yan Canglang in discussing poetry said: "The people of the high Tang
> all relied on inspired interest alone, like the antelope which hangs by
> its horns without a trace to be followed. Their crystalline penetrability
> cannot be gathered together, like sound in air, color in appearances,
> the moon in water, an image in the mirror—the words come to an end
> but the meaning is inexhaustible." Sikong Biaosheng in discussing po-
> etry also said: "The flavor lies beyond sourness and saltiness." During
> the *wuchen* year of Kangxi reign period [1688] at the end of spring, I
> took up the poetry of the Kaiyuan and Tianbao [713–55, i.e., the high
> Tang] masters and read them each day and had a different apprehen-
> sion of what these two men said. I copied out what was of especially
> intriguing interest and transcendent meaning—from Wang Youcheng
> on down there were forty-two men—to make up the *Samādhi Collection
> of Tang Worthies* in three short fascicles. I did not copy out anything
> from Li Bo or Du Fu. (4/4a)

The absence of the two last-mentioned poets is notable indeed; of the
approximately 450 poems in the collection, over one hundred are by
Wang Wei and ninety by Meng Haoran. Their style of poetry, then,
seems to have embodied most completely the ideals of the metaphys-
ical tradition as interpreted by Wang Shizhen.[34]

In sum, this conception of literature was grounded in Taoist,
and later Buddhist, notions of transcending the duality between sub-
jective consciousness and objective reality. For these critics poetry

embodies this intuitive union in an analogously intuitive manner: it relies on suggestive images which evoke qualities or essences of things rather than precise mimetic description or discursive, propositional language, and thus creates an open-endedness which extends the bounds of any poem to the actualizations of all possible readers. Because the poet can integrate emotion and scene, he can similarly transcend the limits of individual thoughts and feelings by objectifying them in an apparently impersonal manner; each poet's manner, however, characterizes his work.

But we should recall that, in one important respect at least, the metaphysical critics and Taoist-Buddhist precepts necessarily went their separate ways. Zhuangzi, for example, may have talked of a total, self-forgetting, receptive mirroring of the myriad phenomena, but Zhuangzi was not talking about poetry. Wai-lim Yip neglects this fact when, citing the Taoist philosopher, he states that "Wang Wei is Phenomenon itself: no trace of conceptualization" and that he is thus a poet of

> pure experience—experience in which we have no interference of intellectual knowledge. Intellectual knowledge, often involving linguistic means of rationalization, tends to force the materials at hand into an abstraction or abstractions rather than to yield to the concreteness of things. Pure experience means to receive the immediate presentation of things; intellectual interference necessarily distorts Phenomenon.[35]

Just as these critics implicitly rejected the Taoist-Buddhist denigration of language by affirming the worth of poetry, so, although they valued a poetry which seems naturally inspired rather than deliberately crafted, and although such a poetry (as Wang Wei's) may be fond of images of processes occurring spontaneously in ignorance, they by no means denied the importance of erudition and effort in the actual writing process. Their metaphors of selfless contemplation and intuitive apprehension of phenomena refer to a period preceding the actual production, though the poet's goal should be to create a poetry that appears to arise naturally from that period, concealing all traces of its artistry. Burton Watson points out this crucial distinction when he writes that Wang Wei

> gives the impression of viewing the landscape with perfect Buddhist passivity, not seeking to see anything at all, but merely allowing whatever may lie within the scope of vision to register upon his mind. Concealing the care he has taken to create such an impression, he would have us believe that he is a mirror, that favorite symbol in both Taoist and Buddhist literature, reflecting existence without partiality or prejudice.[36]

Not only does this passage stress an important feature of Wang Wei's poetry, but that very feature also marks his work as the fulfillment of the Chinese metaphysical critics' ideals.

II.

Many of the theories of poetry discussed above, amplified by various corollaries and expressed in slightly different terminology, reappeared centuries later in the writings of Symbolist and post-Symbolist poets. My intention here is certainly not to argue the case for influence, for, with the possible exception of Ezra Pound and certain contemporary American poets, that would be impossible to prove, if indeed it were even valid. Rather, I feel that a study in comparative poetics, putting aside the question of direct relation, possesses value in its own right, and for several reasons. In the first place, it requires us, before we can even begin the study, to isolate comparable features in the traditions under examination. This is particularly difficult for both the Chinese metaphysical and the Symbolist critics, for their ideas themselves are couched in highly poetic language, often metaphors of metaphors, paradoxical, or downright contradictory. If we do discover topics for discussion, however, we can then go on to point out certain similarities that may cut across historical and cultural boundaries, while the comparison at the same time will bring out important differences. In this particular case, the writings of these Western poets develop the critical terminology already hinted at by the Chinese metaphysical tradition and thus may provide a larger and clearer frame of reference from which to view Wang Wei's poetry. And conversely, I believe that Wang Wei's work is a fulfillment of several key Symbolist aims, and that his practice may, in fact, illuminate their theories.

Perhaps the most strikingly similar notion maintained by both the Chinese metaphysical and the Symbolist critics is that of a non-representational, suggestive poetry. We have seen how Sikong Tu, Yan Yu, and Wang Shizhen, for example, all advocated transcending the limits of external description to evoke an intangible spirit or essence of an object; such a poetry can have a "meaning beyond flavor," reverberating infinitely though the words may come to an end. Several years ago Northrop Frye pointed out that the Symbolists also used the word "as a symbol which turns away from its sign-meaning in the material world, not to point to something in the spiritual world, for this would still make it representational, but to awaken other words to suggest or evoke something in the spiritual world."[37] Mallarmé was probably the most eloquent spokesman for this poetics of suggestion. In his well-known comments to Jules Huret on the evolution of literature during the nineteenth century, he writes that his contemporaries approach the ideal of poetry more closely than did the earlier Parnassians, because they have chosen allusiveness over direct presentation of objects.

> [T]he Parnassians take the thing in its entirety and show it: in so doing they lack mystery; they withdraw from [readers'] minds that delectable joy in believing that they are creating. To *name* an object is to suppress three-fourths of the enjoyment of a poem, which comes from guessing little by little: to *suggest* it, there's the dream. It is the perfect employment of this mystery that constitutes the symbol: to evoke little by little an object to show a state of the soul, or, inversely, to choose an object and disengage a state of the soul from it, by a series of decipherings.[38]

And in "Crisis of Poetry" ("Crise de vers") he writes that an object so suggested, rather than mimetically represented, almost "disappears" as essence replaces concreteness:

> For what good is the marvel of transposing a fact of nature in its almost vibratory disappearance according to the game of the word, if not so that what emanates from it, without the bother of a close or concrete recollection, is the pure notion.
> I say: a flower! and beyond the forgetfulness to which my voice banishes any contour, and something quite different from known calices, musically raises itself, an idea itself and sweet, the one absent from all bouquets. (p. 368)

The flower "absent from all bouquets" thus exists only as the word, and Mallarmé then states that poetry restores to language its virtuality, its power to create a nonrepresentational reality. The "reminiscence" of the object evoked, he continues, "bathes in a new atmosphere" (ibid.).

This "new atmosphere" is the "musicalized" poetic universe of which Valéry speaks in "Poetry and Abstract Thought" ("Poésie et pensée abstraite"). He describes the poetic state as one in which neither external objects nor internal feelings appear as ordinarily apprehended, but rather in quite novel relationships, "resonating" or "corresponding harmonically" with one another—terms which recall the Chinese assumption of a universe of mutual correlations. And Valéry goes on to assert that it is the business of the poet not to experience this state himself but to evoke it in the reader. In fact, he even describes the poem as "a sort of machine for producing the poetic state by means of words." As Yang Wanli had observed that poetic flavors would differ in the mouths of different readers, so Valéry notes that "The effect of this machine is uncertain, because nothing is sure in matters of actions on minds."[39]

This conception of an evocable poetic universe also underlies the methodology of phenomenological criticism, which starts from the premise that a work of art is a schematic structure with points of indeterminacy that await concretization by individual readers.[40] Thus the work's openness invites the participation of the reader who, nevertheless, can never definitely "complete" it. What is interesting here is that this openness of meaning, though explicitly advocated by the Chinese metaphysical critics, results in the case of the Symbolists from what appears to be quite the opposite intention. Motivated by their opposition to any didactic, descriptive, or representational function of literature, they sought to divorce the language of poetry from the language of prose. With such techniques as convoluted syntax, ambiguous reference of articles and pronouns, and unusual usage of verbs as infinitives or participles, they attempted to renew the creative act of language in an apparently opaque, self-referential poetry free of the clichés and expectations normally necessary for communication. As Hugo Friedrich has written of Mallarmé, "he speaks in order to be no longer understood."[41] Yet what is crucial here is that while Mallarmé and other Symbolists may not have wanted to be "understood," to write a logically discursive, paraphrasable, finite poetry, they ultimately do not block the reader's access to the poem, all claims to an elitist or hermetic poetry notwithstanding. On the contrary, their work actually invites the reader to participate in its infinite potentiality. As Friedrich later phrases it (p. 179), understanding (*Verstehen*) is replaced by further creation (*Weiterdichten*).

This opposition to rational understanding leads to a second affinity between Symbolist and Chinese theories: the preference for embodiment over assertion, the intuitively apprehended image over logically structured, propositional discourse. Thus, as I have just mentioned, modern poets tried to differentiate the language of poetry from the language of prose, to create a distinctively poetic medium by such means as syntactic ambiguity and dislocation. Valéry, for example, frequently contrasts prose and poetry on the basis of their differing ends—communication versus evocation—and laments the fact that the poet, unlike the musician, does not have an exclusive, nonutilitarian medium immediately available to him. This desire for poetry to approach a nonverbal music was perhaps best expressed in the famous opening line of Verlaine's "Art poétique": "Music first, before everything"; the poem also urges poets to recognize the indissolubility of sound and sense (as does Valéry) and capitalize on the sensuous aspects of words. Similarly, Wallace Stevens writes that poetic truth "cannot be arrived at by the reason alone, [it is] a truth that the poet recognizes by *sensation*."[42]

For the Symbolists, this poetic truth is embodied in images

which are related by association and juxtaposition rather than by logical sequence. As they recognize the immanence of sense in sound, so they posit the image itself as no longer the ornament of some propositional statement, but the condensed meaning itself. They refuse to explain the image or symbol as merely relevant to some "argument," and Gottfried Benn thus concludes that one characteristic of modern poetry is the absence of the simile, because an explicit comparison would disrupt the unity of the poetic "vision."[43] Benn's opposition to the destruction of wholeness suggests another corollary of the emphasis on intuition over logic: the desire to create a timeless moment of revealed truth rather than a structure of consecutive thoughts or events. Symbolist and post-Symbolist poets, therefore, in addition to employing a difficult syntax which impedes forward movement, also prefer the copula and juxtaposition, both of which leave temporal or causal relationships undefined, and frequently leave ambiguities and oppositions unresolved, relying on a principle of equivalence rather than logical sequence. Moreover, their poems are often noun-heavy, to create an overall effect of simultaneity. Closely related to these practices is their preference for more condensed lyrics, for, as Mikel Dufrenne has suggested, the shortness of modern poetry may be an attempt to escape the temporality of reading.[44] The development of brevity as an aesthetic standard is a reflection of the nineteenth century's renewed interest in Longinus, whose essay "On the Sublime" had emphasized fleeting flashes of sublimity and a concentrated text that would "leave in the mind more food for reflection than the words seem to convey."[45] Longinian theories were particularly influential on Poe, who held that a poem should be short—no more than one hundred lines—in order to evoke the essential and effect this "transport" in the reader;[46] Poe in turn, of course, proved a fruitful source of ideas for the French Symbolists.

Like the Chinese metaphysical theorists, the European poets, while emphasizing an intuitive apprehension of reality, did not advocate a spontaneous, effortless poetry, but were extremely concerned with the necessity of patience, calculation, and choice. Thus Rilke, speaking of his eight-year hiatus in writing, likens the patience he has learned to that of a tree, "the secret slowness that prepares, that distills every work of art."[47] He compares himself to Valéry, who experienced a similar silence of years, evoked in his poem "Palme," and who also repeatedly emphasizes the crucial role of labor and choice. In *Problems of Poetry* Benn also stresses the importance of preparation and work:

> The poet can never know enough, he can never work enough; he must be in touch with everything, must orient himself as to how the world

stands today and what hour it is on earth this noon. You have to struggle up close to the bull, the great matadors say, then perhaps victory will come. There must be nothing accidental in a poem. (p. 38)

The Symbolists' reliance on the image or symbol to convey meaning impersonally, rather than direct description or personal expression, suggests a third affinity between their poetics and those of the Chinese metaphysical critics. We must be careful, however, about how we interpret this doctrine of impersonality. The Chinese can speak of the fusion of emotion and scene and the self-transcendence of subjective consciousness in merging with the Tao and leave it at that, for the language itself can carry the rest of the burden. Both poetry and prose in classical Chinese, after all, can partake of a certain degree of universality allowed by absence of gender, number, tense, articles, and usual omission of subject, although writers will exploit these possibilities to varying degrees. At the same time, of course, the hidden subjectivity of even the most apparently impersonal poem should be obvious. In the West, however, the discussion becomes quite complicated and often contradictory.

Mallarmé provides perhaps the most famous formulation of a type of impersonality in "Crisis of Poetry":

> The pure work implies the elocutory disappearance of the poet, who yields the initiative to words, mobilized by the clash of their inequality; they illuminate each other with reciprocal reflections like a virtual trail of fires on precious gems, replacing the respiration perceptible in the ancient lyric breath or the personal and enthusiastic direction of the sentence. (p. 366)

Here he suggests that in a "pure" poetry we no longer sense the poet speaking directly in his own voice of his personal emotions, because our attention is drawn rather to the interactions or "reciprocal reflections" of the words themselves. In "The Situation of Baudelaire" ("Situation de Baudelaire") Valéry combines these notions of purity and the absence of an empirical speaker with his conception of poetry as a qualitatively different language from prose: "The poet therefore consecrates and consumes himself in defining and constructing a language within language; and his operation . . . tends to constitute the discourse of a being more pure, more powerful, and more profound in his thoughts, more intense in his life, more elegant and more happy in his words, than any real person" (I, 611). Poems, he writes in "Poetry and Abstract Thought," are "strange discourses that seem to have been made by a person *other* than he who says them and to be addressed to someone *other* than he who listens" (I, 1324).

Rimbaud echoes this sense of otherness—that the speaker in a poem is somehow no longer the person of the poet himself—when he mentions in his well-known *voyant* letter that "Someone thinks me" and "*I* is an other."[48] And Eliot speaks in "Tradition and the Individual Talent" of a "depersonalization" in which the artist is merely a "catalyst" or "medium" for emotions. Poetry, in its concentration of experiences and impressions, is an "escape from personality."[49] All of these statements imply that impersonality, and thus a kind of "purity," result when the poet no longer speaks for or of himself in the poem.

Yet we can find an equal number of arguments to the contrary in other post-Symbolist writings. Rilke, for example, in a letter to Lisa Heise of 2 August 1919, posits that the work of art is autonomous and unconcerned with man, like the self-contained fountain that appears as a frequent image in his own poetry. Yet he goes on to assert that it is made "of the human, out of the extremes of suffering and joy" (II, 136), and he regards this quality as the source of the work's inexhaustible powers of solace. Eliot himself agrees that "All poetry may be said to start from the emotions experienced by human beings in their relations to themselves, to each other, to divine beings and to the world about them." He therefore concludes that a pure, autonomous poetry with reference to nothing outside its verbal interactions is an impossible goal, because "poetry is only poetry so long as it preserves some 'impurity' in this sense: that is to say, so long as the subject matter is valued for its own sake."[50] In *Problems of Poetry* Benn concurs with Eliot's belief in the necessity of some degree of "impurity," and he asserts, in fact, that the "impure" subject matter of poetry is the poet himself (pp. 22–23). And Stevens agrees that "The subjects of one's poems are the symbols of one's self or of one's selves" (OP, p. 164).

These various formulations are actually not so much contradictory as complementary. On the one hand, the Symbolists oppose a directly expressive lyrical sentimentality, hence their statements that the empirical poet, and particularly the self-centered, rhetorical, romantic ego, must disappear from the stage, "yielding the initiative to words" and things to evoke his meaning. This notion is obviously closely related to their preference for imagistic presentation over discursive description. On the other hand, they also affirm that poetry is concerned not only with the human but, more specifically, with the emotions, thoughts, and actions of the poet himself. What is important, however, is that these appear indirectly, externalized as objects and symbols, in what Stevens describes in "The Figure of the Youth as Virile Poet" as an essential "indirect egotism" (NA, pp. 45–46).

The Symbolist and post-Symbolist writers thus agree that poetry is personal, in that it embodies a relationship between the poet and the world. Although not revealed directly, this may be what Wang Shizhen termed the "spiritual resonance" or *shenyun* recognizable in the work of each individual. At the same time, however, because it is an embodiment rather than a statement, the ideal poetry is impersonal; the poet can apparently transcend his personal concerns by objectifying them, discovering the external equivalents for his internal states of mind, fusing emotion and scene. In other words, the less we hear of subjective ruminations, the greater our sense of impersonality, which nevertheless does not negate the force of the poetry's human concerns. Classical Chinese offers the poet means unavailable to the Westerner to avoid reference to a particular speaker, and Wang Wei exploits these opportunities more than most. In addition, because of his unusual emotional restraint and the dispersal of his consciousness in the scene—if he draws attention to himself at all, it is generally as one thing among many others—his work represents the clearest example of the impersonality defined here.

In *The Birth of Tragedy* Nietzsche also subscribes to this ideal; he denounces the "subjective artist" as a "bad artist" and demands a "deliverance from the self, the silencing of every personal will and desire" in "objectivity and disinterested contemplation." The poet should be "Dionysiac," identify with the underlying oneness of the universe, and become images which reverberate as "objectified versions of himself." In this way, his "I [dwells] in the ground of being."[51]

This last notion, taken up by the Symbolists and post-Symbolists, brings us to the fourth major similarity between their theories and those of the Chinese metaphysical critics. Both traditions regard poetry as the manifestation of a unitary principle and the poet's intuitive or mystical union with it. A crucial difference, of course, rests in the fact that for the Chinese the Way already exists as a given, to be revealed, whereas Western poets must create their unifying myth. Nevertheless, they both conceive of an essential unity between man and the universe that allows the poet to transcend the subject–object duality, link the external and internal by means of the symbol, and thus become "impersonal."

In his *Chinese Theories of Literature* Liu compares Baudelaire's adaptation of Swedenborg's notion of correspondences to the Chinese belief in an analogy between earthly and heavenly "patterns" (*wen*) (p. 54). This analogical mode of thinking establishes the principle and possibility of relationship between the self and the world and underlies the Western poets' theory of the symbol as the fusion of inner and outer realms; hence their aversion to similes, which imply a separation or possible dissimilarity. Thus Baudelaire writes in "Philosophical Art": "What is pure art, according to modern conceptions? It is creating a suggestive magic containing object and subject at the same time, the world external to the artist and the artist himself."[52] Similarly, Mallarmé asserts in his comments to Huret that "things exist, we don't have to create them; we only have to seize the connections between them, and it is the threads of these connections that form verses and orchestras" (p. 871).

The Symbolists' conception of the fusion of subject and object also expresses itself in mystical terms, where the submergence of self in the universe may lead to the boundary of silence. As Zhuangzi expresses it, language necessarily destroys the mystical union:

> We have already become one, so how can I say anything? But I have just *said* that we are one, so how can I not be saying something? The one and what I said about it make two, and two and the original one make three. If we go on this way, then even the cleverest mathematician can't tell where we'll end, much less an ordinary man. If by moving from nonbeing to being we get to three, how far will we get if we move from being to being? Better not to move, but to let things be. ("Discussion on Making All Things Equal," 5/2/53; trans. Watson, p. 43)

But Zhuangzi himself did not "let things be" and instead used differentiating words to describe a state of nondifferentiation. Similarly, the Symbolists, though they realize the implications of pure selflessness and write a distilled poetry where the unspoken spaces, represented by such typographical devices as the colon and dash, are as important as the spoken, do not succumb to the silence that Hugo von Hofmannsthal implies at the end of his Lord Chandos letter must be a necessary consequence of mystic loss of self. Rather, they may claim, as does Rimbaud in *A Season in Hell* (*Une saison en enfer*), to have invented a poetic language accessible to all the senses and thus capable of expressing the inexpressible. Or they may simply describe the attempts of words to reach a stillness of stasis, permanence, and silence, as does Eliot in "Burnt Norton." Or finally, they may realize, with Rilke in his ninth Duino elegy, where the bounds of the unsayable lie and go on to affirm what can be said.

Like the Chinese metaphysical critics, the Symbolist and post-Symbolist poets know that no poetry could arise from a truly mystical selfless union with the universe. Thus they affirm, ultimately, the mutual implication of subject and object; though the duality can be transcended, neither element extinguishes itself. Stevens, therefore, can write, from the point of view of the world, that because poetry is a revelation of nature, "the world arranges itself into a poem" (OP, p. 165). Yet in "Effects of Analogy" he can also regard, from the subjective pole, "*the poet's sense of the world as the source of poetry.*" And because he affirms the existence of the world, this "sense" can be communicated: "The corporeal world exists as the common denominator of the incorporeal worlds of its inhabitants. . . . The corporeal world, the familiar world of the commonplace, in short, our world, is one sense of the analogy that develops between our world and the world of the poet. The poet's sense of the world is the other sense" (NA, p. 118). This affirmation provides the philosophical foundation for phenomenological criticism and our access into Wang Wei's world.

III.

Before discussing the assumptions underlying my approach to Wang Wei's poetry, I should stress that my primary focus in this volume is on that work itself, and not on the methodology. I certainly do not intend to provide an exhaustive analysis of the philosophical underpinnings of phenomenological criticism, nor of the differing practices which various writers have engaged in, all under the rubric of phenomenology. This body of criticism is hardly monolithic, and it would lie beyond the scope—and the point—of this brief discussion to break it down. Rather, just as I presented, in the first two sections of this introduction, a summary of Chinese metaphysical and Western Symbolist and post-Symbolist literary theories mainly because they provide a useful framework for dealing with Wang Wei, so I have drawn only on those ideas and practices of phenomenological criticism which I consider most apt and illuminating in understanding his poetry. Here my aim is simply to summarize them briefly.

Phenomenological criticism bases itself on two fundamental epistemological positions, both involving a rejection of Descartes' notion that thought is self-enclosed, knows only itself, and hence participates in no mutual interaction with the world. On the one hand, opposing an idealism which posits consciousness as actively projecting objectivity and ultimately denies the existence of an external reality as a source of knowledge, phenomenologists affirm the givenness or "facticity" of the world, prior to any experience or analysis of it. As Merleau-Ponty phrases it, "the world is always 'already there' before reflection begins—as an inalienable presence; and all its efforts are concentrated upon re-achieving a direct and primitive contact with the world. . . ."[53] And, on the other hand, rejecting the empiricist view of the passivity of thought, they maintain that consciousness is an intentional act, not a faculty for knowing but rather a consciousness *of* something. "Consciousness is an act wherein the subject intending and the object intended are reciprocally implicated (and wherein the subject is real and the object is real, i.e., truly emanating from the outside)."[54]

Thus phenomenological literary critics view the work of art not as a discrete, autonomous object but as an act of consciousness which is inextricably bound up with the intentionalities of both its creator and its interpreter. As David Halliburton explains it in an elucidating introduction to his own phenomenological study of Poe, the opposing view of a pure text-in-itself stems from other critics' efforts to claim the "objectivity" of science (which "objectivity," of course, has since been quite devastatingly undermined). The phenomenologist, however, describes writing as

> an act in which a subjectivity passes into an objectivity without surrendering its own identity. . . . The author has created something apart from himself, an entity at once concrete, accessible to others, and reproducible. Yet this new thing preserves the intentional acts through which it came into being. The final product of the creative act is, then, a fusion in which both elements, the subjective and the objective, merge.[55]

Moreover, just as writing involves a number of intentional acts that fuse subject and object, so the literary work itself embodies the author's network of relations with the world in which, similarly, subject and object are mutually implicated. This network of relationships is made accessible through language to the reader, who, if he stands open to the work, can participate in the author's consciousness of the world and eliminate the distinction between himself as subject and the work/author as object.

When phenomenologists speak of intentionality, then, they refer to three fundamental self-world relations: first, the author's consciousness of and relationship to the world, expressed in the work; second, the author's intentional acts which occur while actually composing the work; and third, the critic's reading of the work, which attempts to relive the first relationship. As Halliburton rightly explains, the interpreter does not concern himself with the second type, "simply because it is nowhere to be found." During the process of writing many of the author's intentions may disappear in place of others, and only "the totality of surviving intentions is the literary work" (p. 26). One can only discuss, therefore, the interactions between author and world and between reader and work.

Agreeing with Stevens that poetry involves the "relation between a man and the world" (OP, p. 172), or, as cited above, "the poet's sense of the world," phenomenological critics maintain that the literary work expresses this relationship, transformed into a universe embodied in language. Magliola observes that "The next phase of the phenomenologist's description, however, takes us a crucial step further. It states that precisely because language is gestural, is expressive, the literary work bears within itself the unique imprint of the author's consciousness" (p. 83). This "imprint" reveals itself in the points of view or perspectives in which objects of the world appear, in experiential patterns of, for example, perception, space, and time, which may express themselves in clusters of imagery, syntax, and diction—in short, in the author's very "style." As Dufrenne defines it, this is more than mere doctrine or technique: it is "the locus in which the artist appears, . . . a certain vision of the world, a vision which makes an adventure and a confession out of creation." He later states that this "style" of an author never really changes from work to work, for it is

> his immutable posture, present in all the adventures which he pursues. . . . One can say that our incapacity to recognize the same author, and thus the same style, because of different techniques, is due to our being accustomed to identifying the work with exterior signs and not with its more profound significations.[56]

The author's "style," then, is a singular mode of being which expresses itself in all his works and in fact may only be recognized when seen within the larger context. Implicitly agreeing with Heidegger that "Every great poet writes only from a single poem,"[57] the phenomenological critic, therefore, concerns himself with the author's entire corpus.

When phenomenological critics speak of the author's mode of being manifested in this style, of course, they are referring not to the empirical person but to the consciousness accessible in his works alone. Furthermore, because they conceive of the subject–object relationship as one of solidarity or reciprocal implication, they may maintain that the work reveals as much about the world as it does about the self. In *The Poetic*, for example, Dufrenne combines these two notions when he writes that the poet, even if he happens to speak of himself in a poem, is only one element of the world expressed by the work, not distinct from it but "coextensive" with it and owing any reality that we know to it. And, paradoxically, "the poet never expresses himself better than when he does not worry about expressing himself, when he renounces speaking of himself to say a world, or when he has forgotten himself enough to figure no longer in person except as an element of this world" (p. 91). Dufrenne rephrases this idea in *Language and Philosophy*, where he writes:

> The less expressive his [the artist's] language—that is to say, the more reticent, more discreet, more impersonal—the better he expresses himself. The less he speaks of himself, the more he reveals of himself. Of what does he speak then? He speaks of the world; and we learn to know him in terms of the world which he talks about and which is one possible type of world among others.[58]

Although Dufrenne here emphasizes the uniqueness of each author's particular world and also defines the world in *The Poetic* as "the real arranged according to the singular life of a perceiving consciousness" (p. 139), later in the same work he shifts his focus to the world pole of the self–world relationship and states that the work of art, in fact, reveals Nature or Being. This follows naturally from the inseparability of man and Nature. "Man realizes his nature in integrating himself with Nature or rather in realizing that he is integrated with her" (p. 161). Because of this preexisting unity, Nature is the actual source of the poet's images, which in turn reveal that unity. But Dufrenne goes on to say that Nature actually has the upper hand over man and uses him to appear to consciousness: "Nature becomes a world through man, as time becomes history, but she has the initiative in this metamorphosis in that she inspires him in order to accomplish herself through him" (p. 164). The sum of all possible poetic worlds, then, is Nature, which makes up the basic content of each individual world:

> World of the poet, of course, and world for the complicitous reader: there is no question of challenging the intentional correlation. But the for-itself does not mask the in-itself, the singular world arranged according to a singular conception is one possibility of the world. And the world as the seat of worlds is, like the universe from another perspective, man's idea of Nature. (p. 170)

Similarly, in *The Phenomenology of Aesthetic Experience* Dufrenne writes that the poet does not invent meaning but bespeaks it, that meaning is Being "which precedes both the object in which it is manifested and the subject to whom it is manifested and which appeals to the solidarity of subject and object in order to be actualized" (p. 547). And as he depicted Nature in *The Poetic* as creating man in order to realize itself, here he states that this Being expects its meaning to be spoken by the artist: "Since art's mission is to express this meaning . . . we must say that the real or nature wills art" (p. 549).

In his *Chinese Theories of Literature* Liu suggests that this notion of art's speaking Being is analogous to the Chinese metaphysical critics' concept of literature as the manifestation of the Tao, and he goes on to examine some other similarities, which may arise from an underlying affinity between phenomenology and Taoism (pp. 58–59). At least one fundamental difference is equally crucial: Dufrenne's notion in *The Phenomenology of Aesthetic Experience* of Nature's needing art, and thus man, to complete and reveal herself ("the real calls on the artist in an effort to express itself in the work. . . . The result is that art becomes something essential to nature" [p. 551]) finds no counterpart in the Chinese theories. Dufrenne does not, to be sure, express himself as strongly as does Heidegger, who writes: "Poetry is the establishing of being by means of the word." But he would agree with the latter's statement that "poetry is the inaugural naming of being and of the essence of all things—not just any speech, but that particular kind which for the first time brings into the open all that which we then discuss and deal with in everyday language."[59]

The Chinese theories impute no such vital role to man or art, nor do they conceive of man as creating himself while fulfilling this mission, as does Dufrenne in *The Phenomenology*: "Through art, man gains his being, while at the same time nature acquires its meaning" (p. 552). Although both philosophies posit the solidarity of subject and object, phenomenology focuses on the activities of subjective consciousness, an implicit primacy that Taoism does not recognize.

Nevertheless, many assumptions of phenomenological criticism are similar to those of the Chinese metaphysical critics and thus perhaps a congenial method of approaching Wang Wei. I find Dufrenne's formulation that the poet expresses himself best when he does not seek to do so and instead forgets himself enough to become a mere element, among others, in his world a suggestive, if inadvertent, insight into Wang Wei's poetry. While it stresses the value of an apparent impersonality, it nevertheless recognizes that this very impersonality is simultaneously a means of expression—that although the subject–object duality is transcended, neither element is eliminated. And, when compared with Chinese metaphysical theories in general, the Western critics' emphasis on the unity of self and world recalls the fusion of emotion and scene. Furthermore, the phenomenologists' manner of approaching the work implies a definition of poetry as evocative, open-ended, with a "meaning beyond flavor."

Dufrenne, in fact, deliberately echoes Valéry when he links the intentionality of the author and the world to that of the reader and the work in *The Poetic*: "It is always a question of a certain relationship with the world by means of language; the poet invents this language in order to arouse the poetic state when the reader finds the poem in front of him" (p. 136). When he speaks of a poetic state evoked by the poet in the reader, he posits the same possibility of the latter's participation in the work implicit in the Symbolists' and the metaphysical theorists' conception of a suggestive poetry. The shared notion that a poem is not a self-enclosed object but an open, indeterminate schema waiting to be concretized by the reader, yet never fully exhausted in any one reading, grounds most of phenomenological critical practice. These critics maintain that language itself as a mediator guarantees this access to the work, as Dufrenne explains it in *The Phenomenology*:

> language is both endowed with meaning—that is, the instrument of objectification or the depository of objectivity—and an instrument for communication through which individuals recognize one another as counterparts. Thus language constitutes an intersubjectivity for which the objectivity of the thing or idea has merely mediatory value. (p. 130)

By recognizing the author as his "counterpart," by collaborating with him in reliving and actualizing the work, the critic can parallel the process experienced by the author. Just as the work is the expression of a subject's consciousness of and eventual fusion with his world, so the act of reading dissolves the boundaries between the critic's consciousness and that of the poet. Georges Poulet describes this relationship in a 1966 lecture:

> In short, since everything has become part of my mind thanks to the intervention of language, the opposition between the subject and its objects has been considerably attenuated. And thus the greatest advantage of literature is that I am persuaded by it that I am free from my usual sense of incompatibility between my consciousness and its objects.[60]

In this notion of intersubjectivity, phenomenological critics recognize the action of their own subjectivities in entering the poem. Thus Jean-Pierre Richard writes that

> all understanding is necessarily subjective and that a text, in order to be assimilated, must always be read from within. The most "objective" criticism does not avoid this necessity. The mind will not possess one work, one page, even one word, except on the condition that it reproduce within itself (and it never succeeds absolutely) the act of consciousness of which those constitute the echo.[61]

But at the same time they remain aware of their own intervention and emphasize that the aim of this involvement, as Halliburton explains it, "is not to extend my subjectivity but to reach the subjectivity of the character in the work. To render the situation of another is to stand outside of myself, and to draw the subjectivity of the other to a kind of objectivity" (p. 28).

The author's subject–object relationships leave their imprint in the work in, for example, spatial and temporal perspectives, patterns of imagery, syntax, and diction, considered against the background of the work as a whole. Although interactions among experiential patterns may vary from work to work, the essential "style" remains the same. Phenomenological critics may frequently, though not necessarily, discover an inner dialectic within this total *oeuvre* that does not conform to the actual chronology of authorship. Poulet employs the metaphor of a spider in a web to depict the work's network of self–world relations in this description of Jean Rousset's criticism:

> There is not in his eyes any system of the work without a principle of systematization which operates in correlation with that work and which is even included in it. In short, there is no spider-web without a center which is the spider. On the other hand, it is not a question of going from the work to the psychology of the author, but of going back, within the sphere of the work, from the objective elements systemati-

cally arranged, to a certain power of organization, inherent in the work itself, as if this latter showed itself to be an intentional consciousness determining its arrangements and solving its problems. So it would scarcely be an abuse of terms to say that it speaks, by means of its structural elements, an authentic language, thanks to which it discloses itself and means nothing but itself. Such then is the critical enterprise of Jean Rousset. It sets itself to use the objective elements of the work in order to attain, beyond them, a reality not formal, nor objective, written down however in forms and expressing itself by means of them. (pp. 70–71)

In his emphasis on systematic organization, Poulet suggests the one criterion for judgment which many phenomenological critics admit may guide them in their reading: coherence. In his own *Studies in Human Time* (*Etudes sur le temps humain* [Paris: Plon, 1956]), for example, Poulet himself seeks in the works of postmedieval writers for an ideal coincidence between existence and duration enjoyed during the Middle Ages. And Richard, in the introduction to his study of Mallarmé, defines the two essential qualities of a *chef d'oeuvre* as coherence and simplicity. This assumption is the "hypothesis" underlying his phenomenological reading:

Our effort has been to understand Mallarmé globally, to join again in him the spirit and the letter, the "substance" and the "form," and to reunite in a single cluster all of the exhalations provoked by this incomparable work. At all levels where the same consciousness pursues the same project of being, it has wished to discover again the identical lines of development, the parallel principles of organization. Criticism, we believe, can be at the same time a hermeneutic and a combinatory art. Thus it deciphers while reuniting. In so doing, it does not act by prejudice but always by hypothesis; far from placing an unmovable grill on the work, it lets itself go very freely into the object it claims to understand, confident that the latter will know well by itself, and through the happiness of its presentation alone, to indicate the virtual outline of its coherence. (pp. 14–15)

These are the precepts which have influenced my selection, translation, and interpretation of the one hundred fifty poems by Wang Wei presented here. In reading his total *oeuvre* I have been guided, like Richard, by a hypothesis of coherence and have sought "identical lines of development, parallel principles of organization." These manifest themselves in what Richard calls "themes," such as recurring objects, movements, and schemata, which tend to combine themselves according to the law of isomorphism and the search for the best possible state of equilibrium, i.e., into antithetical couplets or complementary systems. Moreover, as he phrases it, "what is important, then, is to perceive how these oppositions resolve themselves, how their tension is relieved by new synthetic notions or indeed in concrete forms where satisfactory equilibria are realized" (p. 26). I have focused primarily on the spatial, temporal, and perceptual aspects of the self–world relationships manifested in Wang Wei's poetry, for I find this perspective to be both the most concrete and also the most "global" way of identifying the complementary themes and the unifying principles of his work.

Critics have often noted his remarkable laxity in observing the traditional, finely drawn distinctions between two major types of Chinese poetry—"ancient-style verse" (*guti shi*) and "recent-style verse" (*jinti shi*)[62]—and I suggest that we may attribute that to the unusually strong unity of his "style" or harmonious world view. Thus I have not arranged the poems along these quasi-generic lines, although that is how the standard edition of his works presents them, but have organized them instead into four sections. The next chapter, "Juvenilia and Other Literary Exercises," includes his earliest poems— among the few that can be dated accurately at all—and other works employing conventional themes and forms. The third chapter, "Court Poems," presents several works Wang Wei wrote as a government official and other poems treating an important issue in his life— political service versus eremitic retreat. These are some of his less well known compositions, since very few of them present the contemplative depictions of natural scenes for which he is justly famous, yet they embody many of the same principles which underlie the more frequently translated poems. In chapter four, "Buddhist Poems," I have translated a number of works dealing explicitly and implicitly with Buddhist themes; the fifth chapter, "Nature Poems," is of course the largest. In the interests of comprehensiveness, I have included many of the finest as well as some of the less interesting poems in his collection: that is the only way to get a sense of his poetic universe as a whole.

Although the introductions to each chapter provide my own fairly extensive exegeses of the poems, the translations themselves are accompanied only by notes and commentary supplying background information on literary and historical allusions, biographical and geographical references, etc., so that the texts may speak for themselves. Wang Wei's poems are deceptively simple yet extremely subtle and complex. They move with an ease that I cannot capture in my translations, an ease which prevents their profundity from imposing an unbearable weight on the reader. The ideal interpretation, therefore, would recognize and seek to harmonize with that lightness. Richard discovers the same quality in Mallarmé's poetry and provides a warning to be echoed here:

> The greatest danger here lies in heaviness, that is to say, the forced imposition of a dogmatic edifice on a work that is all lightness and

instinct. If that should happen, if the critical tapestry comes to press itself too heavily on texts above which it should, on the contrary, suspend itself, or behind which it should inscribe itself as a filigree, the author can only recognize it frankly and apologize in advance. (p. 37)

Notes to Chapter One

1. James J. Y. Liu, *Chinese Theories of Literature* (Chicago: University of Chicago Press, 1975), p. 5. I am indebted to Liu's work for the following discussion of the metaphysical critics.

2. This point has been argued most convincingly by Joseph Needham and Wang Ling in *Science and Civilisation in China*, Vol. II: *History of Scientific Thought* (Cambridge: Cambridge University Press, 1951), pp. 279–344, and again by Frederick R. Mote in *Intellectual Foundations of China* (New York: Alfred A. Knopf, 1971) and "The Cosmological Gulf Between China and the West," in *Transition and Permanence: Chinese History and Culture*, ed. David Buxbaum and Fritz Mote (Hong Kong: Cathay Press, 1972), pp. 3–21.

3. For a brief discussion of Aristotle's modification of Plato's view, see Walter Jackson Bate, ed., *Criticism: The Major Texts*, enlarged ed. (New York: Harcourt Brace Jovanovich Inc., 1970), pp. 2, 14–15.

4. For an illuminating discussion of the relevance of this idea to Western theories of representation, see Erich Auerbach, *Mimesis: The Representation of Reality in Western Literature*, trans. Willard R. Trask (Princeton: Princeton University Press, 1963), pp. 174–202.

5. This comparison was first made in English by Sir Philip Sidney in "An Apology for Poetry":

> Only the poet, . . . lifted up with the vigour of his own invention, doth grow in effect another nature, in making things either better than Nature bringeth forth, or, quite anew, forms such as never were in Nature . . . : so as he goeth hand in hand with Nature, not enclosed within the zodiac of his own wit. . . . Neither let it be deemed too saucy a comparison to balance the highest point of man's wit with the efficacy of Nature; but rather give right honour to the heavenly Maker of that maker, who, having made man to His own likeness, set him beyond and over all the works of that second nature: which in nothing he showeth so much as in Poetry, when with the force of divine breath he bringeth things forth far surpassing her doings. . . .

From Bate, pp. 85–86.

6. For a discussion of this relationship see M. H. Abrams, *The Mirror and the Lamp: Romantic Theory and the Critical Tradition* (New York: Oxford University Press, 1953), pp. 239ff.

7. Included in the *Anthology of Literature* (*Wen xuan*) edited by Xiao Tong, Prince Zhaoming of Liang (501–31) (Rpt. Taipei: Wenhua, 1969), 45/636. Unless otherwise noted, all translations are my own.

8. Included in the *Wei Jin Nan Bei Chao wenxueshi cankao ziliao* (Rpt. Hong Kong: Hongzhi, n.d.), p. 254.

9. Archibald MacLeish, *Poetry and Experience* (Baltimore: Penguin, 1960), p. 15.

10. Fan Wenlan, ed., *Wenxin diaolong zhu* (Rpt. Taipei: Daming, 1965), 2/65.

11. From "Discussion on Making All Things Equal" (*Qi wu lun*); *Zhuangzi yinde*, Harvard-Yenching Institute Sinological Index Series Supplement 20 (Cambridge, Mass: Harvard University Press, 1956), 5/2/52 (references to this index will be given with all further citations from the work). Trans. by Burton Watson, in *The Complete Works of Chuang Tzu* (New York: Columbia University Press, 1970), p. 43. All subsequent translations of chapter titles and passages from the *Zhuangzi* are Watson's.

12. From the "Appended Judgments" (*Xi ci*) to the *Classic of Changes*; *Zhou yi yinde*, Harvard-Yenching Institute Sinological Index Series Supplement 10 (Rpt. Taipei: Chengwen, 1966), 44/Xi–A/12. Quoted in Achilles Fang, trans., "Rhymeprose on Literature," *Harvard Journal of Asiatic Studies*, Vol. 14 (1951), p. 554; rpt. in John L. Bishop, ed., *Studies in Chinese Literature* (Cambridge, Mass.: Harvard University Press, 1966), pp. 3–42.

13. In the preface to his *Shi pin* (*Classification of Poetry*), Zhong Hong (fl. 483–513) writes that "the text has ended but the meaning lingers on"; however, this is describing not an ideal literature in general, but rather the particular effect of the *xing*, a rhetorical trope of association or allusion first discussed with reference to the *Classic of Poetry*. See He Wenhuan, ed., *Lidai shihua* (1740 ed., rpt. Taipei: Yiwen, 1974), p. 7/2b.

14. Henzō Kinkō (i.e., Kūkai [774–835]), ed., *Bunkyō hifuron*; ed. Zhou Weide (Peking: Renmin, 1975), p. 139. For a discussion and partial translation of this work, see Richard W. Bodman, "Poetics and Prosody in Early Mediaeval China: A Study and Translation of Kūkai's *Bunkyō Hifuron*" (Diss., Cornell University, 1978).

15. Included in *Lidai shihua*, p. 21/8a.

16. Included in *Bunkyō hifuron*, p. 147. Cf. trans. by Bodman, p. 419.

17. Zu Baoquan, ed., *Sikong Tu shi pin zhushi ji yiwen* (Hong Kong: Shangwu, 1966), p. 40.

18. As Fung Yu-lan explains it:

> [T]he man who sees things from the point of view of the *Tao* stands, as it were, at the center of the circle [of endless changes]. He understands all that is going on in the movements of the circle, but does not himself take part in these movements . . . because he has transcended the finite and sees things from a higher point of view.

From *A Short History of Chinese Philosophy*, trans. Derk Bodde (New York: The Free Press, 1948), p. 112.

19. "Letter to Jipu" (*Yu Jipu shu*), in Zu Baoquan, p. 77. Jipu was Wang Ji's *zi* or cognomen. Dai Shulun was an official during the Tang dynasty who also left a collection of poems. Lantian was an area in Shaanxi province which produced jade.

20. As Roman Ingarden phrases it, "aspects that are imposed on the reader in the reading can never be actualized as genuine perceptual aspects but can be actualized only within an imaginational modification, even though in the work itself they are commonly determined as being perceptual." From *The Literary Work of Art*, trans. George C. Grabowicz (Evanston: Northwestern University Press, 1973), p. 269.

21. *Zhongguo wenxue piping shi* (Rpt. Hong Kong: Hongzhi, n.d.), p. 129.

22. From his *Liuyi shihua*, included in *Lidai shihua*, p. 158/5b–6a. This passage has also been translated by Jonathan Chaves, in *Mei Yao-ch'en and the Development of Early Sung Poetry* (New York: Columbia University Press, 1976), p. 110.

23. From his *Chengzhai ji*, 77; quoted in Guo Shaoyu, p. 216.

24. *White-stone Taoist's Discourse on Poetry* (*Baishi daoren shishuo*), included in *Lidai shihua*, p. 440/3a.

25. Guo Shaoyu, ed., *Canglang shihua jiaoshi* (Peking: Renmin, 1961), p. 10.

26. *Tan yi lu* (Shanghai: Kaiming, 1948), p. 49.

27. Guo Shaoyu cites two occurrences of this antelope simile in the speeches, recorded in *The Transmission of the Lamp* (*Jingde chuan deng lu* [*Taishō shinshū daizōkyō* (Rpt. Tokyo: The Taisho Shinshu Daizokyo Kanko Kai, 1973), Vol. 51, No. 2076, 16/328b and 17/335b]), of late Tang dynasty Chan masters, who used it to describe and advocate a nonverbal, nonrational means of communication; *Canglang*, p. 25.

28. Yan Yu is alluding to a passage in *Mencius* V.B.6, where Confucius is described as someone who gathered together all that was good of such earlier sages as Bo Yi, Yi Yin, and Liuxia Hui. Cited in Günther Debon, trans., *Ts'ang-lang's Gespräche über die Dichtung* (Wiesbaden: Otto Harrassowitz, 1962), p. 184, n. 484.

29. A similar point has been made by Richard John Lynn in "Orthodoxy and Enlightenment: Wang Shih-chen's Theory of Poetry and Its Antecedents," in William Theodore deBary, ed., *The Unfolding of Neo-Confucianism* (New York: Columbia University Press, 1975), p. 224.

30. From his *Siming shihua*, *Congshu jicheng*, vol. 2581 (Shanghai: Shangwu, 1935), 3/41. Cf. trans. by Liu, *Chinese Theories of Literature*, pp. 40–41.

31. From his *Yiyuan zhiyan*, 5/2b, in *Yanzhou shanren si bu gao* (Rpt. Taipei: Weiwen, 1976; 15 vols.), XIII, 6754.

32. *Daijingtang shihua* (Rpt. Taipei: Qingliu, 1976; 2 vols.), II, 3/2b.

33. From the poem "Harmonizing with the Poem of Cui Fuda," *Wang Youcheng ji zhu*, ed. Zhao Diancheng (1736 ed., rpt. Taipei: Zhonghua, 1966), 6/9a.

34. This was not, however, the only anthology Wang Shizhen compiled: in another of his collections of Tang poetry, Li Bo and Du Fu are both quite well represented. The reason for the rather one-sided selection here can be found in the meaning of the term *samādhi*, which has been defined as "putting together, composing the mind, intent contemplation, perfect absorption, union of the meditator with the object of meditation" (W. E. Soothill and L. Hodous, *A Dictionary of Chinese Buddhist Terms* [Taipei: Chengwen, 1972], pp. 66–67). It is the highest of three levels of meditation, the aim being to concentrate the mind, still active thought, and liberate the spirit. Because of its characteristically impassive, self-oblivious contemplation of scene, the work of Wang Wei and his school would have seemed the obvious poetic equivalent of this meditative state.

35. *Hiding the Universe: Poems by Wang Wei* (New York: Grossman, 1972), pp. vii–ix.

36. Burton Watson, *Chinese Lyricism: Shih Poetry from the Second to the Twelfth Century* (New York: Columbia University Press, 1971), p. 172.

37. "Three Meanings of Symbolism," *Yale French Studies*, No. 9 (1952), p. 12. Frye's comment points out a significant distinction between Symbolist and Chinese theories: the former posit a Platonic dichotomy between the two realms of matter and spirit, whereas the latter do not. However, the emphasis on evocation is of primary importance, and that is a shared one.

38. "Réponses à des enquêtes sur l'évolution littéraire," *Oeuvres complètes*, ed. H. Mondor and G. Jean-Aubry (Paris: Gallimard, 1945), pp. 868–69.

39. *Oeuvres*, ed. Jean Hytier (Tours: Gallimard, 1959; 2 vols.), I, 1320–21.

40. For a discussion of this notion, see Ingarden, pp. 246–54.

41. *Die Struktur der modernen Lyrik* (Hamburg: Rowohlt, 1956), p. 120.

42. "The Figure of the Youth as Virile Poet," *The Necessary Angel* (henceforth abbreviated as NA) (New York: Vintage, 1951), p. 58. Stevens also writes that "Poetry has to be something more than a conception of the mind. It has to be a *revelation* of nature. Conceptions are artificial. Perceptions are essential." From "Adagia," *Opus Posthumous* (abbreviated henceforth as OP) (New York: Alfred A. Knopf, 1957), p. 164.

43. *Probleme der Lyrik* (*Problems of Poetry*) (Wiesbaden: Limes Verlag, 1951), p. 16.

44. *Le Poétique* (*The Poetic*) (Paris: Presses universitaires de France, 1963), p. 66.

45. Included in Bate, p. 65.

46. See his "The Philosophy of Composition," in *The Complete Works of Edgar Allan Poe,* ed. James A. Harrison (New York: AMS Press, 1965; 17 vols.), XIV, 193–265, and "The Poetic Principle," XIV, 266–96.

47. Letter "A une amie," 3 February 1923, in *Briefe,* ed. Ruth Sieber-Rilke and Karl Altheim (Wiesbaden: Insel-Verlag, 1950; 2 vols.), II, 388.

48. Letter to Georges Izambard, 13 May 1871, in *Oeuvres,* ed. Suzanne Bernard (Paris: Garnier, 1960), p. 344.

49. Included in *The Sacred Wood* (Rpt. London: Methuen and Co., 1972), pp. 53–58.

50. "From Poe to Valéry," in *To Criticize the Critic* (New York: Farrar, Straus and Giroux, 1968), pp. 38–39.

51. *The Birth of Tragedy and the Genealogy of Morals,* trans. Francis Golffing (Garden City: Doubleday, 1956), pp. 37–39.

52. "L'Art philosophique," in *Oeuvres complètes,* ed. Y.-G. Le Dantec (Tours: Gallimard, 1958), p. 926.

53. From his preface to *Phenomenology of Perception,* trans. Colin Smith (London: Routledge and Kegan Paul, 1962), p. vii. Reprinted in *European Literary Theory and Practice: From Existential Phenomenology to Structuralism,* ed. Vernon L. Gras (New York: Dell Publishing Co., 1973), p. 69.

54. Robert Magliola, "The Phenomenological Approach to Literature: Its Theory and Methodology," *Language and Style,* Vol. V, No. 2 (Spring 1972), p. 80.

55. *Edgar Allan Poe: A Phenomenological Study* (Princeton: Princeton University Press, 1974), p. 22.

56. *The Phenomenology of Aesthetic Experience,* trans. Edward S. Casey et al. (Evanston: Northwestern University Press, 1973), pp. 105, 505.

57. "Georg Trakl: Eine Erörterung seines Gedichtes," in *Unterwegs zur Sprache* (Pfullingen: Verlag Günther Neske, 1959), p. 37. First published in *Merkur,* 7 (1953), pp. 226–58.

58. Trans. H. B. Veatch (Bloomington: Indiana University Press, 1963), p. 97. Quoted in Liu, *Chinese Theories of Literature,* p. 60.

59. "Hölderlin and the Essence of Poetry," in *Existence and Being,* trans. D. Scott (Chicago: H. Regnery and Co., 1949). Reprinted in *European Literary Theory and Practice,* pp. 34, 36. Dufrenne, for example, writes in *The Phenomenology* that "Man is a moment in being, the moment in which meaning gathers itself together" and goes on to provide an anthropocentric view of art's relation to reality:

> Art is, properly speaking, that element "without which things would be only what they are." Neither science nor praxis recognizes human qualities in things. Only art does, and art does so even when it expresses the inhuman. . . . The aesthetic object is an object which does

justice to and thus authenticates the human dimension of the real. (pp. 550–51)

60. "Criticism and the Experience of Interiority," in *The Structuralist Controversy: The Languages of Criticism and the Sciences of Man*, ed. R. Macksey and E. Donato (Baltimore: Johns Hopkins University Press, 1970), p. 58.

61. *L'Univers imaginaire de Mallarmé* (Paris: Editions du Seuil, 1961), p. 36.

62. These were the two basic forms within which Tang dynasty poets worked. Ancient-style verse dated from the Han dynasty (206 B.C.–A.D. 220). These poems could be indefinite in length, but there were generally five or seven syllables per line; rhymes, which could be changed within a poem, usually occurred at the end of the even-numbered lines. The "Music Bureau Songs" (*yuefu*), which Tang poets wrote in imitation of folk songs collected by the government Music Bureau during the reign of the Han emperor Wu (140–86 B.C.), can be regarded formally as similar to ancient-style verse. They were, however, originally set to music and maintained set titles and a limited variety of themes, such as the neglected wife or the hardships of frontier duty.

Recent-style verse was not fully developed until the Tang dynasty. One major subdivision was "regulated verse" (*lüshi*), and, as the name implies, this form was much more rigidly defined than ancient-style verse. A standard poem consisted of eight lines, all either five or seven syllables long, and with only one rhyme. Moreover, the middle four lines had to form two parallel or antithetical couplets, and a complex pattern of tonal variation had to be maintained throughout (for purposes of versification, the four tones of classical Chinese were divided into two large categories, termed "level" [*ping*] and "oblique" [*ze*]). Two other subgroups of recent-style verse were "quatrains" (*jueju*), autonomous units but metrically half of an eight-line poem in regulated verse, and "regulated couplets" (*pailü*), which consisted of the first and last couplets of a *lüshi*, with more than two antithetical couplets in between. For a fuller discussion of various Chinese verse forms see James J. Y. Liu, *The Art of Chinese Poetry* (Chicago: University of Chicago Press, 1962), pp. 22–34, and Hans H. Frankel, *The Flowering Plum and the Palace Lady: Interpretations of Chinese Poetry* (New Haven: Yale University Press, 1976), pp. 212–17.

The forms and line lengths of Wang Wei's poems in the original can be determined by looking at the *juan* ("fascicle") number of the *Sibu beiyao* edition given with each translation (the first Arabic numeral before the slash). The first fascicle contains ancient-style verse of irregular line lengths; fascicles 2–5 contain pentasyllabic ancient-style verse; and fascicle 6 contains heptasyllabic ancient-style verse. The rest are all recent-style poems: pentasyllabic regulated verse in fascicles 7–9; heptasyllabic regulated verse in fascicle 10; pentasyllabic regulated couplets in fascicles 11–12; pentasyllabic quatrains in fascicle 13; and heptasyllabic quatrains in fascicle 14.

TWO

Juvenilia and Other Literary Exercises

SINCE the fifty poems translated and discussed in this chapter and the next are generally linked more closely to specific events and issues in Wang Wei's life than will be the case later, some background biographical information is crucial to their understanding. Unfortunately, although biographies of the poet do appear in the standard histories of the Tang dynasty (618–907), details concerning his life are few and often spurious or contradictory. The account in the *Old Tang History* (*Jiu Tang shu*) was written by Liu Xu (887–946) and that in the *New Tang History* (*Xin Tang shu*) by Song Qi (998–1061), and while their information overlaps to a considerable degree, some disagreements do occur; moreover, despite the former's closer proximity in time, it is not necessarily more reliable.

Controversy begins with the years given for Wang Wei's birth and death. Neither dynastic history provides an explicit birthdate, and whereas the *Old Tang History* says he died during the second year of the Qianyuan reign period (759), the later account places his death during the first year of the Shangyuan reign period (760), at the age of sixty-one Chinese years (*sui*).[1] In fact, however, at least three of his works have been ascribed to a period as late as the fifth month of 761. These include two poems or poem series: "Five Coffin-puller's Songs for Prince Gongyi" (9/10a; I, 168–71), known to have died during the sixth month of the first year of Shangyuan (760), and a "Farewell to Xing of Guizhou" (8/9a; I, 147 [poem 92 below]), who was appointed to office in Guizhou in the second year of the same reign period (761). Furthermore, Wang Wei's essay thanking the emperor for transferring his brother to a post near him in the capital, "A Memorial in Gratitude for My Younger Brother Jin's Having Newly Received [the Post of] Grand Counselor on the Left to the Emperor"

(18/3b; II, 326), is dated the second year of Shangyuan (761), fifth month, fourth day. Modern Chinese biographers, therefore, have tended to accept the figure of sixty years and settle on 701–61.

Wang Wei was born in the district (*xian*) of Qi, in present-day Shanxi province, to a family which had held provincial government posts for at least three generations; his father Chulian, for example, attained the position of Superior Administrator of Fenzhou (*Fenzhou sima*) in Shanxi. The poet had at least four younger brothers—any sisters have remained unrecorded—of whom the eldest, Jin (d. 781?), is the most famous. Both boys were well known for their precocious poetic, musical, and artistic talents, as well as for their close friendship and filial piety. Because of his abilities Wang Wei was already welcomed during his teens at the homes of various aristocratic patrons of the arts who lived in the capitals of Chang'an and Luoyang. He passed the most literary of the three main types of imperial civil service examination at an early age, probably in 721, received the *jinshi* ("presented scholar") degree, and was appointed to the post of Associate Secretary of Music (*da yuecheng*) at the court in Chang'an. Sometime thereafter, however, he committed some minor infraction[2] and was demoted to the post of Administrator of Granaries (*sicang canjun*) in Jizhou (Shandong province), far enough removed from the capital to be considered in exile.

The dynastic histories provide no information about events in Wang Wei's life until his nomination to another post in Chang'an in 734. At some point he married, but his wife died around 730 and he remained celibate thereafter, which, as has been pointed out, was unusual for the times and provides an index of his devotion to Buddhist principles.[3] It was in fact during this time that he began the serious study of Buddhism under the Chan master Daoguang, for in the "Pagoda Inscription at Dajianfu Monastery for the Chan Master of Great Virtue, Daoguang" (25/10a; II, 459–60), carved after the monk's death in 739, Wang Wei notes: "For ten years I sat at his feet and obediently received the teachings."

When the poet's friend Zhang Jiuling (673–740), to whom he had been introduced by Pei Yaoqing (681–743), the prefect of Jizhou, was named President of the Grand Imperial Secretariat (*zhongshu ling*, a post roughly equivalent to that of prime minister), he reappointed Wang Wei to a court position in 734, this time as Advisor on the Right (*you shiyi*), charged with reproving the emperor for oversights. Although popular belief has long held him to have been but a reluctant bureaucrat, this was not quite the case, for he had, in fact, actively petitioned Zhang Jiuling for office. His poem "Presented to the Duke of Shixing" (5/11a; I, 85–86), written in 734), for example, praises Zhang and concludes:

Humbly I kneel down in petition:
May I serve under you or not?
Grateful for a principled decision;
Selfish advantage is not what I seek.

Henceforth, until 755, Wang Wei's career consisted of a slow but steady rise through government ranks—though he never exerted any major influence—and travels through various provinces in official capacities. Three years later, in the fall of 737, he was promoted to the office of Inspector Censor (*jiancha yushi*) of Hexi and dispatched to the border province of Liangzhou, in present-day Gansu. There he assisted the Grand Imperial Commissioner of the border region (*jiedu dashi*), Cui Xiyi, a general who had waged several campaigns against the non-Chinese "barbarian" tribes on the northwest frontier. Wang Wei remained in Liangzhou until sometime after his superior's death in the fifth month of 738.

During this absence from the capital, Zhang Jiuling had been replaced in 736 as the most influential person in the government by Li Linfu (d. 752), and although the poet's biographers have agreed with the traditional casting of Zhang and Li as hero and villain, respectively, in the drama of Tang politics and placed Wang Wei squarely on the side of virtue,[4] he was not above flattering the new minister (see poem 27 below) and continued to be named to office. After serving as Court Censor (*dianzhong shiyushi*), he traveled south in 740 as Supervisor of the Southern Provincial Examinations (*zhi nanxuan*). He received another court censorate position in 742—Admonitor on the Left (*zuo buque*)—and was promoted in the same year to the post of Secretary of Military Stores (*kubu langzhong*), which he held for nine years. After observing a period of mourning for his mother's death, which probably occurred in the spring of 750, Wang Wei was named Secretary of the Ministry of Civil Office (*libu langzhong*) in 752.[5] Around two years later, in 754, he rose to the post of Policy Reviewer (*jishizhong*).

Sometime during this period Wang Wei acquired the country estate at Lantian on the Wang River (about thirty miles south of Chang'an) which had belonged to an earlier poet, Song Zhiwen (656–712). Again, scholars have disagreed on when Wang Wei might have purchased the property and, more generally, when and where he may have left office for retreats to other places. Because much of his poetry dealing with Wang River scenery seems relatively quietistic and removed from official concerns, some biographers maintain that he did not actually retire there until the last years of his life. Chen Yixin, however, has shown that Wang Wei bought the Wang River villa before his mother's death, thus sometime before 750. He suggests, furthermore, that Wang Wei had enjoyed an earlier period

of retreat in the Zhongnan Mountains, also south of Chang'an, per-
haps around 740.[6] Other biographers maintain that the poet actually
began to withdraw periodically from political life at an even younger
age.[7]

What we should keep in mind amid these controversies over
dates, however, is that Wang Wei never interrupted his career to cut
himself off completely from official duties. Certainly, all the places
suggested as possible retreats were quite close to the post he occu-
pied at the time, and rather than living as a total hermit, he seems to
have found ways to divide his time between the court and the coun-
try, as did many other literati of the era. However committed he may
have felt to a Taoist-Buddhist withdrawal from worldly affairs or to
his deposed friend Zhang Jiuling, it is clear that he was willing to
compromise these allegiances and remain in office.

One such "compromise" for which biographers must always
find excuses was his behavior during the rebellion of An Lushan,
which began in 755. When this general of Sogdian ancestry moved
from his power center on the northeast frontier to capture both
Chang'an and Luoyang in 756, Emperor Xuanzong (r. 713–55) and
his entourage fled to the mountainous western province of Shu (pres-
ent-day Sichuan). According to his biography in the *Old Tang History*,
Wang Wei attempted to join the imperial retinue but failed to catch
up with it and so was captured by the rebels; he is said to have taken
drugs in an effort to induce intestinal illness and to have pretended
to be mute. Although he was imprisoned for a time in a monastery,
he did nevertheless later serve the illegitimate government, main-
taining his previous imperial office of Policy Reviewer. While incar-
cerated, however, he dictated two poems to his friend Pei Di (see
poems 34–35) which effectively conveyed his anguish over the recent
political events and which were somehow preserved and circulated.
They are said to have moved the new emperor Suzong (Xuanzong's
son), after his defeat of the rebels and return to Chang'an, to pardon
Wang Wei for his collaboration.

A more likely explanation, however, can be found in the suc-
cessful intercession of Wang Wei's brother Jin, who had in the mean-
time risen to the relatively high office of Vice-President of the Minis-
try of Justice (*xingbu shilang*) and had also served valorously in battles
against An Lushan's forces. Wang Jin petitioned the emperor to re-
duce his own office, if necessary, and spare his brother from his due
punishment. In 758 Suzong generously acceded and nominated
Wang Wei to two consecutive posts serving the crown prince (*taizi
zhongyun* and *taizi zhongshuzi*). The same year the poet was promoted
to the office of Grand Secretary of the Grand Imperial Secretariat
(*zhongshu sheren*) and then to his original position before the rebel-
lion, as Policy Reviewer. Sometime in 759 he attained his highest

rank, that of Under-Secretary of State (*shangshu youcheng*), a post "nominally of high rank but in fact a sinecure,"[8] and is thus frequently referred to as Wang Youcheng.

Little is known of Wang Wei's activities during these last years. Some biographers maintain that the poet did not retreat to his Wang River estate until after the rebellion, and thus could not have written the numerous poems situated there until that time. On the other hand, Chen Yixin writes: "after such political upheavals, Wang Wei was disheartened and he became increasingly inactive. He seldom went to his villa in Wangchuan and stopped writing songs about nature, staying for the most part in the capital, reading Buddhist sutras at home every day after work and doing good deeds [he provided meals daily for several monks]."[9] And yet his corpus does contain at least one work which indicates that he was still involved in court activities in 758 (see poem 24 below).

According to the *Old Tang History* biography, when Wang Wei was about to die, he asked for a brush and wrote letters of farewell to his brother and to a number of old friends. "He exhorted his friends several times to receive the Buddha's teachings of mind-cultivation, put down his brush, and died." He was buried next to his mother, to the west of the Qingyuan Monastery he had established on his Lantian estate.

Some four hundred poems have been collected in the standard Qing dynasty edition of Wang Wei's complete works, but of this number one modern researcher has argued that only 371 can be attributed definitely to Wang Wei, since the remaining poems also appear in the collected works of various other Tang dynasty poets.[10] The *Old Tang History* biography suggests that these poems may in fact represent only a fraction of his original poetic production. According to this account, when Wang Jin was serving Daizong (r. 763–80) as prime minister, the emperor asked him how many of his older brother's works had been preserved and requested that they be presented to him.

> Jin said: "During Kaiyuan (713–42) my older brother's poems [numbered] in the hundreds and thousands, [but] after events of Tianbao (742–55) only one out of ten remained. Recently, from among paternal and maternal relatives and his old friends I have collected them, acquiring over four hundred pieces in all." The next day he presented them, and the emperor generously proclaimed his praise and appreciation.

The truth of the anecdote, unfortunately, cannot be confirmed.

Of the approximately four hundred poems that have survived, those for which Wang Wei is best known to Western readers focus

primarily on limpid depictions of natural scenery. These works de-
serve their popularity, but they present only one side of his achieve-
ment. In this chapter and the next, therefore, I have translated a
number of poems that reveal other aspects of his poetic universe
while displaying the fundamental patterns of thought and perception
that structure his entire *oeuvre*. Poems 1–9 represent Wang Wei's ear-
liest datable works (a tenth, "Lamenting Zu Zixu the Sixth" [12/13a;
I, 236–37], is both extremely long and undistinguished), all written
by the age of twenty-one *sui* and arranged in chronological order.
Many of these juvenilia introduce themes or methods that reappear
in the thirteen other poems presented in this chapter.

The first three works are brief and immediate responses to
events in the poet's life but are worth discussing at some length.
Poem 1, "An Inscription for a Friend's Mica Screen," focuses on an
effortless integration of man and nature: a human artifact, represen-
tative of cultured elegance, is placed in uncultivated surroundings
yet engenders no sense of conflict or ludicrous inappropriateness.
Rather, the two realms of art and artlessness merge; the screen re-
flects nature "naturally," both because the real mountains and
streams cannot be distinguished from those produced by artificial
paints and also because no question arises as to the possibility of such
an immediate intermingling. This is an assurance characteristic of
Wang Wei's work as a whole. Also typical here is the negative phras-
ing of the last line: by stating what is not the case, the poet can refrain
from making an affirmative declaration and instead allow the reader
to draw conclusions. At the same time, he provides a sense of bal-
ance to his world by suggesting the opposite yet equally possible
state of affairs; in other poems, rhetorical questions create a similar
open-ended effect.

This method of indirection and denial also structures poem 2,
"Visiting the Qin Emperor's Grave." As we might expect, the visit to
a gravesite occasions thoughts on time, but Wang Wei's attitude is
typically complex and equivocal. On the one hand, for example, he
suggests the human vulnerability to the vicissitudes of time: the em-
peror's grand mausoleum has become but a grassy ridge, and his
attempts to reproduce the universe in it have been unsuccessful.
There may be an ocean, but men cannot travel on it because it is
artificial, and so, in effect, there is no ocean. And even if there were
an ocean, men could not cross it to reach the fairy isles the ruler had
searched for, for they, along with their promise of pills and elixirs
granting immortality, do not exist. Yet, on the other hand, Wang Wei
also implies that the emperor has transcended time through artifice,
for a replica of his palace *does* still exist. And though the mausoleum
may lack a spring when artificial birds could "fly" home from winter
retreats, in one sense those birds are paradoxically superior to their

natural counterparts because they in fact do not need to return; like the golden bird in Yeats's "Sailing to Byzantium," they are always there, unmoving and unaffected by seasonal cycles. Wang Wei hedges in the last couplet, for though he writes that he "still" hears the piercing sound whistling through a tree, he cannot be sure that it is in fact the same pine that the emperor is playfully supposed to have appointed to office. This final element of the perceiver's uncertainty appropriately concludes a poem structured on ambiguous conceptions of time. From a more traditional work written on visiting a gravesite, we might expect a straightforward lament on human transience, to be contrasted with the cyclical permanence of nature. "Visiting the Qin Emperor's Grave," however, is remarkably free of emotion; Wang Wei refuses to make a choice between change and changelessness, allowing the two possibilities to exist simultaneously.[11]

Similarly, poem 3, "On the Ninth Day of the Ninth Month, Remembering My Brothers East of the Mountains," avoids elaborate outbursts despite its emotion-charged situation. Although the quatrain opens with a direct depiction of loneliness and homesickness, the final couplet subtly reveals a possible transcendence of those feelings. In an imaginative act that spans the space between them, Wang Wei is able to visualize his brothers' activities. The phrase "from afar I know" recurs in several later poems and suggests an immediacy, interpenetration, and obliteration of distances similar to that embodied in William Carlos Williams' poetic world:

> no difficulty in knowing other people, no uncertain approach to external objects by the subjective mind. . . . [Williams] establishes a self beyond personality, a self coextensive with the universe. Words, things, people and God vanish as separate entities, and everything becomes a unit.[12]

And while these last two lines intensify the speaker's feelings through a contrast between the emotional reticence and the power of those emotions, at the same time, that very reticence suggests a movement beyond them. Instead of commenting on his feelings, Wang Wei objectifies them in a natural image. Although the profusion of dogwoods implicitly heightens the poignancy of his absence and isolation, by revealing the ability to span distances through imagination and conclude with an objective description, he evokes a sense of unity which ultimately overcomes the pain of separation.

While these three poems are specifically personal and occasional in nature, most of the other works translated in this chapter can be characterized as "literary exercises," in that they draw heavily on traditional forms, conventions, and allusions rather than on the poet's own experience. Poem 5, "On the Theme, 'Pure as the Ice in the Jade Vase,'" in a sense bridges both situations: it is highly allusive and was at the same time written as part of Wang Wei's civil service examination. Similarly, poem 8, "Lady Xi," refers simultaneously to an event early in Wang Wei's career and to a classical text. Poems 11 and 12, "Sacrificial Songs to the Goddess of Fish Mountain," employ the literary devices and themes of an ancient southern anthology of poetry. And poems 7, "Song of Li Ling," and 9, "Song of Mt. Yanzhi," center around a number of well-known military figures and events from the Han dynasty.

Although in these few works Wang Wei stays fairly close to the stories or conventions he is employing, in most instances here he departs from them in significant ways. Poem 6, "Song of Peach Blossom Spring," for example, is based on an account by Tao Qian (365–427) of a fisherman's accidental discovery of a political utopia, but unlike the earlier poet, Wang Wei is more interested in the nature of the search itself than in the characteristics of its destination. Only because he embarks on a journey whose distance, route, and outcome he does not know does this fisherman arrive at the Peach Blossom Spring in the first place. He proceeds without conscious intentions and in total harmony with nature, passively trusting the water until he reaches its end, then traveling on foot along a hidden, winding path. Each new element of the scene appears as a sudden surprise to him. And this ignorance is absolutely essential: precisely because it consists in a freedom from mental calculation and a spontaneous appreciation of and reliance on nature, it leads him to a true moment of intuitive recognition, a vision of purity.

But this positive ignorance of an unconscious journey becomes the negative ignorance of the failure to understand the meaning of his arrival. Having achieved a kind of enlightenment, the fisherman abandons it for rational modes of thought and the purposeful plan to repeat his travels in a more orderly fashion, but he thereby only demonstrates the uselessness of intellectual cognition in such an endeavor. Wang Wei reflects this turn of events in the last ten lines of the poem through the use of negatives, limiting adverbs, and rhetorical questions suggesting the inevitable futility of the second journey. The final line—"Not distinguishing the faery spring, where can he seek?"—is particularly telling. There is, in fact, no place where the fisherman can "seek" the Peach Blossom Spring, for enlightenment cannot be actively or willfully pursued. Nor can it be "distinguished," for the true intuition is not divisive but unifying. Remaining limited by his attachment to rational cognition, he will never be able to repeat his original spontaneous experience, which has been altered in many ways from that described in Tao Qian's narrative.

Many of these juvenilia and literary exercises are literary *yuefu*, "Music Bureau Songs," imitations of folk songs collected several centuries earlier, with established titles, forms, themes, and methods of presentation.[13] Thus poem 4, "Song of the Girl from Luoyang," centers around a figure appearing in several anonymous ballads and surrounded by stock appurtenances such as piebald horses, minced carp, seven-fragrance carriages, and nine-flowered canopies—all of which traditionally evoked the world of the wealthy—yet its numerous allusions mark it as the work of a literatus. Other elements which Hans Frankel has singled out as characteristic of Tang dynasty imitations include the apparently abrupt shifts in focus and a diction somewhat more relaxed than that of ancient-style or regulated verse. Yet the absence of three other distinguishing features—oscillation between narrative and lyric poles, directness of presentation, and the impersonality of a persona—reveal Wang Wei's significant deviations from convention.

The poem is not structured on a narrative sequence, for it contains no chronological listing of events typical of other long *yuefu*, describing instead simultaneously existing situations. Although Wang Wei must present them in succession, he is concerned with creating a generalized conception of the girl's predicament, a static image frozen in time. Nor does the lyric mode play a significant role; from the very beginning we know that the speaker is a third-person observer, and the poem contains no emotional buildup or explicit comment on the girl's attitudes and feelings. Rather than having her speak directly, Wang Wei evokes her plight in a more subtle manner. He suggests ennui, for example, by several monotonous, almost tonally perfect parallelisms, unusual in a *yuefu*, and from the dying sunlight and the flickering, flying pieces of the lamp we sense the melancholy and boredom which contrast poignantly to the subject's youth. And it is this evocation of internal states in such an indirect way that makes the poem impersonal, not a more traditional assumption of a persona. Wang Wei never "steps outside himself" to speak as the girl. Perhaps he feels no need to, for she, along with the other characters and objects in his poetry, exists in a universe of mutual interpenetrability; to purposely assume a persona would thus create a hitherto unrecognized distinction. The poet does enter at the end, but in a typically indirect and open-ended manner, posing an allusive rhetorical question which leaves us to derive its relevance and conclude the poem for ourselves: the humble washgirl is not to be pitied at all, for she, albeit idealized, possesses a simple freedom which the rich wife from Luoyang can never enjoy.

This girl washing silk becomes the subject of poem 10, "Song of Xi Shi," where Wang Wei's individual style again thwarts certain generic expectations. Remarkably absent in both poems are physical descriptions of the women themselves: we see their actions and surroundings to some extent, but no flesh-and-blood entities. The·level of abstraction in the second poem becomes particularly clear when it is compared, for example, with one by Li Bo entitled "Xi Shi,"[14] which works in a strictly chronological fashion, providing specific details about the woman's background and her role in the struggle between the ancient rulers of Wu and Yue. Wang Wei, on the contrary, is again not interested in the historical narrative so much as in the generalized portrait and conclusion to be drawn from it. Selecting arrogance as the dominant character trait of the famous beauty, he constructs the entire poem on the oppositions which make it possible—the contrasts between her present and past situations, between herself and erstwhile companions, between herself and the legendary, pathetic Dong Shi. The concluding rhetorical question is a typically double-edged critique: other girls are advised not to imitate Xi Shi's mannerisms not only because of the hopelessness of a mere gesture, but also, by implication, because the price for success is too high, if Xi Shi's personality can serve as an index.

The remaining poems in this chapter focus on official and military life in the northwest frontier, and most were probably written during Wang Wei's period of service in Liangzhou from 737 to 738. Poems 13, "Song of Yulin Commandery," and 14, "Song of Mt. Long," are both structured on a contrast between the independent knight-errant and the government official, though from opposite points of view. In the first, Wang Wei evokes the plight of the former, who is afraid that he will not be recognized by the new imperial messenger, an official member of the government bureaucracy. His isolation has already been suggested by the course of the poem itself, which develops the traditional opposition of natural continuity to human mutability. Although Wang Wei provides no explicit reasons for the traveler's grief, the image of the river flowing eastward is a familiar one in Chinese poetry, connoting both the inexorable movement of time and, simultaneously, the eternal changelessness of nature. Thus the sound of the stream's flow, like that of the Yellow River, may be a painful reminder that time as flux means permanence for nature but transience and discontinuity for man.

Poem 14 testifies to the equally futile life of a government official. In contrast to the youthful knights-errant, who are hopeful enough to seek some astrological indication of their future and care-free enough to play enemy melodies, the lone aging general knows that despite extensive battle experience, he has received no rewards, unlike some more fortunate subordinates who have already been enfeoffed with vast holdings. The closing allusion to Su Wu emphasizes the precarious nature of government service: the Han figure's tasseled staff wore out in vain because he could use it only to tend sheep as a prisoner of the frontier tribes, and not to exercise official duties.

Similarly, in the first of the four "Songs of Youth" (poems

15–18), Wang Wei shows the high-spirited young knights-errant en-joying their fellowship, good wine, and probably women (willows were often planted near houses of pleasure). Then in the second qua-train he brings in the opposite fate of government soldiers, who must fight difficult battles on the frontier and, presumably, die bloody deaths with no compensation of pleasure or glory. As in "Song of Yulin Commandery" and "Song of Mt. Long," time is thus seen here as moving in but one direction, and life as an inexorable progression toward its end. In the third and fourth "Songs of Youth," however, the picture shifts, and Wang Wei shows soldiers performing valor-ously in battle and receiving appropriate rewards from the emperor. Though all four poems are quatrains in regulated verse, "Songs of Youth" is also an official *yuefu* title, and the subject of earlier poems with that title had usually been the failure of soldiers to avenge their country and their subsequent needless deaths. Perhaps Wang Wei felt obliged here to conform to accepted conventions before altering them; the same may be true of the other military poems discussed above, for it was certainly the tradition of *yuefu* on such topics to include lament and criticism. Wang Wei, in fact, moves quickly from a focus on transience to quite a different conception of time: from the limited dimensions of these poems, his world expands to grant man the timelessness of nature.

We can see this movement in the confident turn at the conclu-sion of poem 19, "Marching Song." *Yuefu* with this title customarily were concerned with the laments of soldiers over endless travels, and Wang Wei certainly begins in this vein. Verbal repetition suggests the exhausting monotony of their routine, while specific images of noise and confusion depict their fierce struggle. Yet he definitely reverses the traditional thrust of the *yuefu* with the final sure pledge that the soldiers will in fact have no difficulty capturing enemy chieftains. Here the future promises not certain death but victorious return, and this escape from the conventional obsession with evanescence and futility is characteristic of Wang Wei's attitude toward time.

Finally, poems 20–22 use historical allusions to create this sense of time as space, a vast entity in which movement does not occur in one direction only. Although "Farewell to Overseer Ping Danran" (poem 20) begins with a journey outward into unfamiliar territory, Wang Wei notes that his friend is merely repeating history, so that he can be certain of success in his mission. Poem 22 describes the poet's own observations "On Going out from the Border" and opens by establishing a similar sense of connectedness; space is an immense expanse in which individual elements are physically linked, located in relation to each other or, like the grass and sky, merging impercep-tibly. In the first half of the poem, each line involves a juxtaposition of timeless scene and human activity occurring over an unspecified period of time. The second half then moves exclusively into the human realm, with specific allusions to military personages and exploits of the Han dynasty. Typically, we find Wang Wei moving effortlessly through the centuries, drawing freely from the Han to refer to the Tang without explicit comparison or contrast—as if there were no distinction between them.

Poem 21, "Mission to the Frontier," relies almost exclusively on visual images of inhuman or inanimate objects to convey human activities and emotions indirectly. We see first not the traveler himself but a synecdoche, his carriage, journeying alone through foreign territory to the limits of the familiar, accompanied by or identical to a tumbleweed passing from the known to the unknown. Yet Wang Wei immediately counters this impression of one-directional movement outward. Although the wild geese may be flying in a line parallel to the carriage, toward barbarian territory, they are seen here as "returning"; for them the skies they are entering are familiar, as if the poet has been able to observe the scene from another point of view, the other side of the border. And the following famous couplet does indeed present a desert scene not tied to any particular perspective. In contrast to the movement depicted in the first four lines, here each line graphically freezes an action, filling space in all directions: we see the vast sands and river extending infinitely along the horizontal plane, with the lone column of smoke and the setting sun coming toward each other from earth and sky to define the vertical dimension. Although Wang Wei's Qing dynasty annotator explains with positivistic authority that the smoke from a fire burning on wolf manure would stay straight even in the strong desert wind, I feel that the meaning of this image lies rather in its evocation of an unusual, eerie absence of wind which emphasizes the stark isolation of this fire and smoke, the absolute silence and solitude in which the traveler finds himself. This sense of quiet stasis is reinforced by the image of the sun, whose downward motion has been frozen, so that we see just the round still ball hanging above or reflected in the river.

In these first six lines, then, Wang Wei moves from the limited perspective of a Chinese emissary journeying out into unfamiliar spaces to another point of view from within barbarian territory, and finally to a static, timeless image which encompasses and evokes a universal desert experience. This fusion of emotion and scene is in fact characteristic of most of his depictions of nature, for the concrete objects in his poems speak not just for themselves, but for the human presence behind them as well. And "Mission to the Frontier" does conclude with a specific allusion from history, the realm of men. Because the Han and Tang dynasties were seen to be linked by their peace, prosperity, and successful imperialistic conquests, Wang Wei can refer to one to suggest the power and stability enjoyed during the other, and end the poem on a reassuring note: events in time and space are simultaneous and interconnected, not discontinuous. In this respect he again differs distinctly from the practice of his contemporaries, for although he frequently employs historical allusions, he does not place them in the context of the *huai gu* ("cherishing antiquity") subgenre of poems popular with other Tang poets, in which convention would demand laments over the passage of time and incommensurability of the present with the past.

POEM

1

(13/10b; I, 253)

An Inscription for a Friend's Mica Screen

> *The mica screen belonging to your family*
> *Is carried out to the rustic yard and opened.*
> *Naturally there are mountains and streams that enter,*
> *Not produced by brightly colored paints.*

NOTE

This poem was written at the age of fifteen.

POEM

2

(9/5b; I, 160)

Visiting the Qin Emperor's Grave

> *The ancient grave is now a verdant ridge;*
> *The secluded palace resembles the Purple Pavilion.*
> *Among the stars, the Seven Glories separate;*
> *From Yellow and Han Rivers, nine streams open out.*
> *There is an ocean: how can men cross it?*
> *Without a spring, wild geese do not return.*
> *Still I hear the piercing pine harmony:*
> *Perhaps it is the Minister's lament.*

NOTES

Title: The burial site of the iron-handed Qin dynasty ruler who styled him-self the First Emperor (r. 221–209 B.C.) is located to the north of Mt. Li near the Tang capital of Chang'an (present-day Xian) in Shaanxi province. The grave was actually a huge mausoleum over a mile and a half in circumference and almost six hundred feet high. Inside, the emperor is supposed to have ordered the construction of an extravagant topographical representation of his palace ("the Purple Pavilion") and the empire, with celestial bodies de-picted on the ceiling with jewels. Below there were said to be rivers and seas of mercury, bronze buildings, buried treasures, and lamps which burned on human fat. A detailed account of the contents of the grave is included in the *History of the Former Han* (*Han shu* [Peking: Zhonghua, 1975], 36/1954).

This poem was written at either fifteen or twenty.

Line 3:   The "Seven Glories" are the sun, moon, and five planets.

Line 5:   This alludes to the emperor's belief in popular Taoist superstitions, which were still common during the Tang dynasty. During his reign he made attempts to procure herbs of immortality said to grow on the three mythical islands in the eastern sea: Penglai, Fangzhang, and Yingzhou (*History of the Former Han*, 25A/1204).

Line 8:   According to Sima Qian's (145–90 B.C.?) *Records of the Historian* (*Shi ji* [Peking: Zhonghua, 1972], 6/242), after performing sacrifices on the eastern sacred peak, Mt. Tai in Shandong, the First Emperor was caught in a fierce, windy rainstorm on his descent from the mountain. He found shelter under a pine tree, which he then named in jest his "Fifth Minister" (*wu daifu*).

POEM

3
                                                      (14/3a; I, 260)

On the Ninth Day of the Ninth Month, Remembering My Brothers East of the Mountains

Alone in a foreign province as a foreign guest,
Each time I come to a holiday, doubled my thoughts of home.
From afar I know my brothers have climbed on high:
Putting dogwoods everywhere but missing one person.

NOTES

Title: On the ninth day of the ninth lunar month, known as the Double Ninth Festival, people traditionally climbed mountains, drank wine, com-posed poems, admired chrysanthemums, observed rites for the dead, and plucked sprigs of dogwood to wear as protection against evil spirits. For a translation of the traditional account of the origin of this festival and a discussion of the use of this theme in Chinese poetry, see A. R. Davis, "The Double Ninth Festival in Chinese Poetry: A Study of Variations upon a Theme," in *Wen-lin: Studies in the Chinese Humanities*, ed. Chow Tse-tsung (Madison: University of Wisconsin Press, 1968), pp. 45–64.

This poem was written at seventeen.

POEM

4

(6/7b; I, 99)

Song of the Girl from Luoyang

The young girl from Luoyang lives across the way;
From her appearance, she could be just about fifteen.
Her husband has a jade bridle and rides a piebald horse.
4   *Attendants serve minced carp upon golden plates.*
Painted chambers and crimson pavilions face one another;
Red peach trees and green willows droop against the eaves.
In a gauze curtain she is ushered up to a seven-fragrance carriage;
8   *Precious fans greet her return to the nine-flowered canopy.*
Her dashing husband is rich and honored, in the prime of youth;
In high spirits he spends with pride, exceeding even Jilun.
Of course he loves his Biyu and teaches her dances himself;
12   *He does not regret the coral given to other people.*
By the spring window as sunlight dies, a nine-subtleties lamp:
The nine subtleties piece by piece fly like flowers of jade.
When amusements are over, she never has time to practice her melodies;
16   *Her makeup completed, all she does is sit amid fragrant clouds.*
Within the city the people he meets are all rich and wild,
Day and night he goes to visit the Zhaos and the Lis.
Who pities the maiden of Yue, her face like jade,
20   *Humble and poor at the river's source, simply washing silk?*

NOTES

This poem was composed at either sixteen or eighteen.

Line 10: Jilun was the cognomen (*zi*) of Shi Chong (249–300), who was renowned for his riches and extravagance. He and another wealthy man, Wang Kai, were said to have engaged in a constant battle to outdo each other's lavish expenditures, with Shi Chong consistently emerging on top. He delivered his *coup de grâce* after the emperor sympathized with Wang and bestowed on him a two-foot-high coral tree. When Shi saw it, he promptly smashed it to pieces, then acquired six or seven taller coral trees and gave them to Wang, who subsequently abandoned the competition. The story is in the *Jin History* (*Jin shu* [Peking: Zhonghua, 1974], 33/1007).

Line 11:   Biyu was the beloved concubine of the King of Runan, who lived during the Liu Song dynasty (420–79). The "Song of Biyu," supposed to have been written by the king, appears as a *yuefu* title in the twelfth-century *Collection of Music Bureau Songs* (*Yuefu shi ji*), ed. Guo Maoqian (Rpt. Shanghai: Zhonghua, 1930), 45/8a.

Line 13:   Commentators are unsure about the precise nature of the "nine-subtleties lamp."

Line 18:   "The Zhaos and the Lis" were two famous families of the Han dynasty who were related to the empress and enjoyed both wealth and power; they appear frequently in *yuefu* to suggest such a milieu. They may also, however, be used to recall two Han imperial concubines, Zhao Feiyan and Li Ping, thus suggesting some adulterous affairs.

Line 19:   The "maiden of Yue" refers to Xi Shi, the renowned fifth-century-B.C. beauty who was the daughter of a woodseller in the kingdom of Yue (see poem 10).

POEM

5   (12/10b; I, 232)

On the Theme, "Pure as the Ice in the Jade Vase"

Ice stored within a jade vase:
Frozen water like a dewy mirror.
Before being melted by the fiery sun,
4   Both shine together by the latticed window.
Embracing brilliance, it hides nothing within.
Holding purity, it seems a void from without.
Its breath is like frost gathered in the courtyard,
8   Its gleam, lingering moonlight on stone steps.
At dawn more icy than a flying magpie-mirror,
At night it shines on books like gathered glowworms.
But when I turn to you in comparison:
12   Its pure heart is still no match for yours.

NOTES

Title: This poem was written as an examination piece when Wang Wei was nineteen. The theme in the title is the second line of a poem by Bao Zhao (421–65), entitled "Song of White Hair" (*Baitou yin*; *Anthology of Literature*, 28/ 395), which in turn alludes to a poem written by Zhuo Wenjun, the wife of the Han dynasty writer Sima Xiangru (179–117 B.C.). Having heard that her husband was about to take a concubine, she wrote a poem which ended: "I would like to have a single-hearted man / Who though white-haired would never leave"; this is included in the *Fountain of Ancient Poetry* (*Gu shi yuan jianzhu*), ed. Shen Deqian (1673–1769) (Rpt. Taipei: Guting, 1970), 1/22a. Bao Zhao's poem similarly celebrates faithfulness and attacks fickleness, using the ice in a jade vase as an emblem of purity.

Line 2: A *fangzhu* was a large mirrorlike basin used to collect pure dew at night.

Line 9: The *Record of Spirits and Marvels* (*Shen yi zhuan*) includes the story of a couple who had to separate and broke a mirror, each taking half as a pledge of fidelity. When the wife proved unfaithful, her half of the mirror turned into a magpie and flew to the husband, alerting him.

Line 10: This is an allusion to a passage in the *Jin History*, 83/2177, about an extremely diligent scholar named Ju Yin; his family was too poor to afford oil for lamps, so he captured fireflies and kept them in a thin paper sack to read by.

POEM

6

(6/6b; I, 98–99)

Song of Peach Blossom Spring

The fisherman's boat follows the water; he loves spring in the
    mountains.
On both banks peach blossoms enclose the ancient ford.
Sitting he looks at the rosy trees, unaware of distance.
4   Traveling to the green creek's end he does not see any men.
At the mountain valley a hidden path begins to twist and turn.
From the mountain a broad view opens out: suddenly, flat land.
Afar he looks at a whole expanse of gathered clouds and trees;
8   He nears and enters—a thousand homes, scattered flowers and
    bamboo.
Woodcutters have just passed on the names of the Han,
And residents have not yet altered Qin dynasty clothes.
The residents lived together at Wuling Spring,

12   *And yet from beyond this world started fields and gardens.*
     The moon shines beneath the pines on houses and windows at
         peace.
     The sun rises within the clouds as cocks and dogs clamor.
     Startled to hear of the worldly guest, they rush and gather to-
         gether,
16   *Vying to bring him home with them to ask about their districts.*
     At dawn on the village lanes, they sweep the flowers away,
     Toward evening woodsmen and fishermen enter along the water.
     At first to escape from disaster, they left the midst of men.
20   *Then, it's heard, they became immortal and so did not return.*
     Amid these gorges who knows that human affairs exist?
     Within the world one gazes afar at empty clouded mountains.
     Not suspecting that ethereal realms are hard to hear of and see,
24   *His dusty heart has not yet ceased to long for his native home.*
     He goes out of the grotto, not thinking of the mountains and
         water between,
     Then leaves his family, planning at last a long, leisurely journey.
     Telling himself that what he passed through before cannot be lost,
28   *How can he know that valleys and peaks when he comes today*
         have changed?
     Of that time all he remembers is entering mountains deep.
     How many times does the green creek arrive at a cloudy forest?
     When spring comes, everywhere are peach-blossomed waters:
32   *Not distinguishing the faery spring, where can he seek?*

NOTES

This poem was written at the age of nineteen.

Line 2:   I have selected the variant "ancient" (*gu*) for "leaving" (*qu*).

COMMENTARY

This poem is based on the short narrative and poem of a similar title by Tao
Qian (365–427),[15] which describes the accidental discovery by a Wuling fish-
erman of a community of political refugees who had been isolated from
events and changes in the outside world for hundreds of years. When the
fisherman in that story leaves to return home, they ask him not to tell others
of their existence; instead, however, he reports his journey to local officials,
who then attempt, unsuccessfully, to retrace his route. The differences be-
tween the two accounts, however, are more significant than any superficial
thematic similarities. In his prose piece the earlier poet reports the story in a
matter-of-fact manner; he states that the journey occurred sometime during
his own youth (the Taiyuan reign period of the Jin dynasty [376–97]), and it

may, in fact, as James Hightower notes in his discussion of the story, "have been inspired by the report of a contemporary discovery of such an enclave" (p. 256). The accompanying 32-line poem provides more specific details of the daily activities of the recluse farmers and clarifies the suggestion in the prose narrative that the residents of the Peach Blossom Spring had purposefully withdrawn from society in protest against a corrupt government. Tao's poem concludes in a didactic, sermonizing fashion; the poet claims that "the pure and the shallow" are two absolutely distinct realms, and he rather contemptuously inquires of his readers: "Let me ask you who are convention-bound, /Can you fathom those outside the dirt and noise?" In the final couplet he implies, not without a certain degree of self-righteousness, that he alone possesses this understanding: "I want to tread upon the thin thin air / And rise up high to find my own kind" (trans. ibid.).

In both his prose narrative and poem, then, Tao Qian presents the Peach Blossom Spring as a political utopia whose inhabitants have correctly retreated on principle from the dusty world. To heighten the journalistic realism of his story, he locates the fisherman's discovery during an actual time and place, mentions a local official by name, and provides much information about the routine events in and social organization of the farmers' lives. Moreover, he suggests that the fisherman's main weakness and explanation for his inability to find the spring again consisted in his failure to honor the residents' request to keep their existence a secret.

Except for mentioning the Han people, Qin dynasty, and Wuling (in present-day Hunan province) in lines 9–11, however, Wang Wei's poem provides no such "realistic," concretizing details. In contrast to Tao Qian's account, the Peach Blossom Spring appears here as a distinctly philosophical or religious, rather than political, utopia. The fisherman discovers not merely some morally pure alternative society, but rather an ethereal realm of the spirit whose inhabitants are explicitly described as being more than human: "At first to escape from disaster they left the midst of men. / Then, it's heard, they became immortal and so did not return" (11. 19–20). Wang Wei does retain both the prototypical Taoist ideal figures of the fisherman and wood-cutter, as well as the terminology potentially descriptive of a this-worldly retreat ("worldly guest" [1. 15] and "dusty heart" [1. 24], for example). And furthermore, the distinction he establishes in lines 21–22 between the realms of "human affairs" and "clouded mountains" frequently appears in later poems about the pure life of Buddhist monks. Yet it is equally clear that he is not merely concerned here with contrasting two ways of life.

The Peach Blossom Spring proved to be one of the more fruitful motifs in Wang Wei's poetic world. This is his earliest, most famous, and most extensive exploration of the implications of the story, but the allusion recurs in several later works. See, for example, poems 35, 63, 90, 105, and 121 below.

POEM

7

(5/8a; I, 80)

Song of Li Ling

In the house of Han the general Li Ling
Followed father and grandfather as a general.
Before knotting his hair he had marvelous strategies;
4   In youth he became a valiant warrior.
Far away he drove the enemy on the border,
Entering deep within the chanyu's walls.
Banners and flags lined up facing each other;
8   Pipes and drums were mournful beyond description.
The sun dusked on the edge of the desert;
Battles sounded within the smoke and dust.
About to cause the proud barbarians' demise,
12   How could he only demand their king as hostage?
But then he lost another general's aid
And encountered the shame of Mongolian yurts.
When young he had been graced by imperial favor:
16   Now how could he bear to think of this?
Deep in his heart he wished to repay his ruler—
He offered his life but was not able to die.
Craning his neck, he looked for Ziqing:
20   "If not you, who will care for me?"

NOTES

This was written at the age of nineteen.

Title: Grandson of the famous general Li Guang, Li Ling (d. 74 B.C.) was
both a general and a *cause célèbre* under the Han emperor Wu. In 99 B.C.
emperor Wu sent Li Ling and another general, Li Guangli, to attack the
Xiongnu, non-Chinese tribes on the northern border. The two generals went
in two different directions, intending to divide and conquer their enemy. Li
Ling, however, penetrating deep into Xiongnu territory north of Juyan (in
present-day Inner Mongolia), found himself and his five thousand men sur-
rounded by eighty thousand enemy troops. He managed to keep fighting for
eight days, with heavy losses on both sides, until his supplies ran out and
his path of retreat was cut off. When Li Guangli and his forces failed to ar-
rive, Li Ling was forced to surrender and remain in enemy hands. Angered
by the news of this defeat, and erroneously informed that Li Ling was in-
structing the Xiongnu in Chinese military arts, the emperor executed Li

Ling's entire family; Li Ling eventually married a Xiongnu princess. For defending Li Ling and urging more lenient treatment, the historian Sima Qian (145–90 B.C.?) was punished by castration. The account is included in the *History of the Former Han*, 54/2454–57.

Line 3: Children knotted their hair upon reaching adulthood.

Line 6: *Chanyu* was the title of the Xiongnu chieftain.

Line 19. Ziqing was the cognomen of Su Wu (fl. 81 B.C.), who was sent by emperor Wu as Han emissary to the Xiongnu. Instead, they forced him to serve as a shepherd in what is now Siberia, holding him captive in the desert. Nineteen years later he was finally released, returned to the Han court, and granted another office (*History of the Former Han*, 7/223). When Su Wu left the Xiongnu in 81 B.C., Li Ling bade farewell to him, complaining that the emperor had not given him a chance to redeem himself.

POEM

8 (13/9b; I, 252)

Lady Xi

Let not affections of the present day
Allow loves of the past to be forgotten.
Seeing the flower filled her eyes with tears,
And she did not speak to the king of Chu.

NOTES

This poem was written at the age of twenty.

COMMENTARY

This quatrain both alludes to a classical text and also subtly (in line 3) refers to an event in Wang Wei's youth which was the occasion for composition. One of the poet's patrons, Li Xian, the prince of Ning and half-brother of the emperor Xuanzong, had been attracted by the wife of a cake-seller and had acquired her with gifts. After a year had passed he asked her if she still thought of her husband, but she did not answer. The prince then summoned the man, and when his wife saw him, her eyes filled with tears. There were ten or so people present at the time, among them Wang Wei, and the prince commanded them to write a poem on the subject. "Lady Xi" was completed first, and everyone else agreed that none better could be written. The prince then returned the cake-seller's wife to her husband.[16]

The textual allusion is to a story in the *Zuo zhuan*, a commentary on the annals of the Spring and Autumn period (722–481 B.C.), one of the thirteen Confucian classics. According to the records for the fourteenth year of Duke

Zhuang's reign (680 B.C.), the king of Chu defeated the ruler of Xi and took
the latter's wife as his own. Although she bore him children, she never spoke
to him. When finally queried why, she is said to have responded: "It has
been my lot to serve two husbands. Though I have not been able to die, how
should I venture to speak?" Trans. James Legge, *The Chinese Classics*, Vol. 5:
The Ch'un Ts'ew with the Tso Chuen (Rpt. Taipei: Wenxing, 1966), p. 93.

POEM

9

(6/5a; I, 95–96)

Song of Mt. Yanzhi

In the house of Han the imperial general is talented and brave.
When he comes to Chang'an he bows to the ruler at Mingguang
    Palace.
The emperor himself pushes his chariot beneath the twin turrets;
4   A thousand officials emerge to fête his departure east of Wuling.
He vows to refuse a fine dwelling inside the Golden Gate
And to serve himself as a Great Wall within the Jade Pass.
Wei and Huo could only serve as his cavalry generals,
8   And the court would discount the achievements of Ershi.
There are many vigorous warriors in Zhao, Wei, Yan, and Han;
West of the Pass knights are young—how fierce and bold they
    are!
Revenge is only a matter of having tasted gall,
12   And drinking wine he never prevents the scraping of the bone.
Painted halberds and carved spears chill in the white sun;
Successive banners and great colored pennons vanish in yellow
    dust.
Repeated drumrolls in the distance rouse the desert's waves;
16   Flutes crying in confusion move the moon over Heavenly Moun-
    tain.
A brocade girdle embroidered with unicorns, a belt with hooks
    from Wu,
Prancing and snorting blue-black steeds and dancing roans.
He grasps a sword and has already severed the arm of "Heaven's
    favorite."
20   Back in his saddle, he shares a drink from a Yuezhi skull.
When a Han soldier shouts aloud, one could face a hundred;
Barbarian horsemen look at him, tearful and in grief.

> *Commanding in battle he must lead men through boiling water*
> *and fire,*
24 *But they know in the end the best general will devise his plans in*
> *advance.*

NOTES

This poem was written at twenty-one.

Title: Mt. Yanzhi, in Gansu province, was originally a Xiongnu fortress but was the scene of a great Chinese victory under the Han general Huo Qubing (d. 117 B.C.).

Line 2:   Mingguang Palace was located to the west of the Han emperors' Weiyang Palace.

Line 3:   Rulers traditionally pushed the chariots of generals in bidding farewell, as a gesture of encouragement.

Line 5:   This is an allusion to general Huo Qubing, who was offered a first-class dwelling by the Han emperor Wu but refused, saying that he would not accept it while the Xiongnu were still alive (*History of the Former Han*, 55/2488).

Line 6:   The Jade Pass is in Dunhuang district, Gansu province.

Line 8:   Wei Qing, Huo Qubing, and Li Guangli were all famous Han generals. Li Guangli was known as General Ershi because he conquered a western territory of that name; he was eventually captured and killed by the Xiongnu (*History of the Former Han*, 97A/3775–81).

Line 11:   This is an allusion to Gou Jian, king of Yue during the fifth century B.C. After being humiliated in battle by the king of Wu, Fu Chai, Gou Jian hung a gall bladder above his seat and constantly drank its liquid to strengthen his will for revenge (*Records of the Historian*, 41/1742ff.).

Line 12:   This refers to Guan Yu, a general of Shu during the Three Kingdoms era (221–65). Wounded by a poisoned arrow which pierced his left arm, he allowed a doctor to operate and scrape the poison from the bone, while he continued to drink and talk with fellow generals (*Chronicle of the Three Kingdoms* [*Sanguo zhi*] [Peking: Zhonghua, 1973], *Shu*, 6/941).

Line 16:   Heavenly Mountain is in present-day Xinjiang.

Line 17:   "Hooks from Wu" alludes to a story recorded in the *Spring and Autumn Annals of Wu and Yue* (*Wu Yue chunqiu*), compiled by Zhāo Ye of the Latter Han dynasty. The king of Wu ordered his people to make some hooks, with the producer of the best to be rewarded with a hundred gold pieces. There were many good makers of hooks in the country, but one man who particularly coveted the prize killed his two sons and consecrated his two hooks with their blood. When he arrived at the palace to seek the reward, the king asked him for proof of his hooks' special nature; the man called out the names of his dead sons, and the hooks flew to him. Astounded, the king gave him the gold.

Line 19:   In the *History of the Former Han*, 94A/3780, the non-Chinese "barbarians" (*hu*) refer to themselves as "the proud favorites of Heaven."

Line 20:   The Yuezhi, or Tocharians, were an Indo-European people who lived in the Gansu area during early Han times. They were defeated by the Xiongnu, who, during the Jianyuan reign period (140–134 B.C.), killed their king and made a drinking cup from his skull (*Records of the Historian*, 123/3157).

POEM

10
(5/7b; I, 80)

Song of Xi Shi

> *Beauty is what the world deems of value:*
> *How could Xi Shi long remain unknown?*
> *In the morning she was a girl by a stream in Yue,*
> 4 *In the evening served as royal consort of Wu.*
> *During humble days how different from the crowd?*
> *When status came, then they realized how rare.*
> *She asks others to apply her rouge and powders:*
> 8 *Not by herself does she don her gauze silk clothes.*
> *Her lord's affections increase her proud demeanor:*
> *In his love, she can do no wrong.*
> *Of her washing-silk companions of the past,*
> 12 *None has a chance to return with her in her coach.*
> *Restrain and discourage the neighbor family's daughter:*
> *How can a mere frown hope to imitate her?*

NOTES

Title: Xi Shi was a famous fifth-century-B.C. beauty who was the daughter of a woodcutter in Yue (present-day Zhejiang) and washed silk by a stream. She was sent by king Gou Jian to distract king Fu Chai of Wu and enable the former to avenge an earlier humiliating defeat (see also poem 9, line 11n.).

Line 14:   Xi Shi was said to suffer from a heart ailment which caused her to draw her eyebrows together in a frown, thereby enhancing her beauty. An envious neighbor girl known in legend as Dong Shi (*xi* = west, *dong* = east) attempted to imitate this look, yet only succeeded in making herself even more ugly. The anecdote is included in the *Zhuangzi*, "The Turning of Heaven" (*Tian yun*, 38/14/42).

POEMS
11–12   (1/4b; I, 6–7)

Sacrificial Songs to the Goddess of Fish Mountain

11. Welcoming the Goddess
Kan kan *strike the drum*
At the base of Fish Mountain.
Blow bamboo flutes,
Gaze to the farthest reach.
The shamaness approaches
With one dance after another.
She spreads a precious mat
And pours clear wine.
The wind blows chill   in the night rain.
Will the goddess come   or not?
It makes my heart   suffer again and again.

12. Sending off the Goddess
Many come to worship   in front of the hall.
She gazes fondly   at the jeweled mat.
Coming she did not speak,   her wishes untransmitted.
She made the evening rain   and grieved the empty mountain.
Lamenting quickens the pipes,
Longing tightens the strings:
The divine chariot   seems about to depart.
Suddenly clouds gather   and the rain ceases;
On the verdant mountain   water flows like tears.

NOTE

Title: Fish Mountain is located in Shandong province. According to a story
in the *Narratives of Journeys* (*Shu zheng ji*), during the Jiaping reign period of
Wei (249–53), a goddess named Zhiqiong descended from Fish Mountain and
met a man named Shi Xuanchao. When his neighbors suspected that he was
involved with a strange being, he told them about her, whereupon she dis-
appeared. Five years later he was passing by the mountain and saw a woman
in a carriage who looked like her. They went off together and lived happily
ever after.

COMMENTARY

These two *yuefu*, probably written during Wang Wei's exile in Shandong (ca. 725), illustrate a literary tradition which proved extremely fruitful for him—poems very likely derivative of shamanistic performances and best exemplified by the *Nine Songs* (*Jiu ge*) of the ancient southern anthology, the *Songs of Chu* (*Chu ci*).[17] Although Wang Wei's "sacrificial songs" are of course addressed to a mountain spirit geographically remote from those of the southern songs, the basic elements are the same: the elaborate preparation in anticipation of the goddess' arrival, the erotic overtones, the all-too-brief visit, and the predominantly melancholy mood. The frequent use of a trisyllabic line produces an appropriately incantatory effect. Moreover, the entire second poem, as well as the last three lines of the first, employ a meaningless particle (pronounced *xi* in modern Chinese and indicated by a space within the line), some sort of breathing interval or carrier sound whose usage is most strongly associated with the *Songs of Chu*.

POEM

13
(6/8b; I, 101)

Song of Yulin Commandery

On top of the mountain, pine and cypress forests;
Beneath the mountain the sound of a stream wounds the traveler's heart.
For a thousand miles, a myriad miles, the color of spring grass;
The Yellow River eastward flows, flowing without rest.
At Yellow Dragon Fortress the young knight-errant
Fears that on meeting the Han envoy, he will not be recognized.

NOTE

Title: Yulin Commandery was located in present-day Inner Mongolia.

POEM

14
(6/3a; I, 92)

Song of Mt. Long

On the Great Wall the young knights-errant
At night ascend the ramparts to look at the evening star.

Above Mt. Long the bright moon overlooks the pass from afar.
4 *At Long Mountain marching men play barbarian flutes at night.*
West of the pass the aged general is overcome with grief;
As he stops his horse to listen, two streams of tears flow.
He has gone through, large and small, a hundred battles or more;
8 *Men he once commanded are now lords of ten thousand homes.*
But Su Wu was only given the rule of a tributary state,
Wearing out in vain his tasseled staff west of the desert sea.

NOTES

Title: Mt. Long overlooks a pass between the provinces of Shaanxi and Gansu.

Line 9: For Su Wu, see poem 7, line 19n.

Line 10: A tasseled staff (here actually one with an animal tail attached) was always given an official away from court as a sign of his imperial mission.

POEMS
15–18   (14/2a-b; I, 258–59)

Songs of Youth

15.

At Xinfeng, fine wine—a gallon for ten thousand cash.
In Xianyang the knights-errant are mostly young in years.
Meeting together in high spirits they offer each other toasts,
And tie their horses at the tall tower next to the weeping willows.

NOTES

Line 1: Xinfeng ("New Feng") was a town built by the first Han emperor (r. 206–194 B.C.) northeast of Chang'an for his father, who was homesick for his native town of Feng, further to the east.

Line 2: Xianyang was the capital of the Qin dynasty (221–207 B.C.), near Chang'an in Shaanxi province.

16.

They began their careers serving the Han as imperial body-
*   guards,*
And followed the cavalry general to their first battle at Yuyang.

Who would know that those not facing the frontier's miseries
Even after death would leave behind "fragrant chivalrous
bones"?

NOTES

Line-2:   Translated here as "cavalry general," the title of *piaoji* general was
first created for Huo Qubing, who was named to this position in 121 B.C. by
the Han emperor Wu. He was given command of ten thousand cavalrymen
and distinguished himself in battle against the Xiongnu west of the pass at
Mt. Long. See the *Records of the Historian*, 22/1138.
Yuyang, in present-day Hebei, was the scene of a Han dynasty battle against
the Xiongnu.

Line 4:   The phrase "fragrant chivalrous bones" is from the second of two
poems entitled "Two Songs of Knights-Errant from the Palace of the King of
Boling" (*Boling wang gong xia qu er shou*) by Zhang Hua (232–300) and in-
cluded in *The Complete Poems of the Han, Three Kingdoms, Jin, Northern, and
Southern Dynasties* (*Quan Han Sanguo Jin Nan Bei Chao shi*), ed. Ding Fubao
(Rpt. Taipei: Yiwen, n.d.; 6 vols.), II, 375. They have been translated by
James J. Y. Liu in *The Chinese Knight-Errant* (Chicago: University of Chicago
Press, 1967), p. 59.

17.

A single soldier is able to draw two carved wooden bows:
Barbarian horsemen, a thousand or more, seem like nothing.
Sitting sideways on a golden saddle he adjusts his white-plumed
arrows:
Amid the flurry he shoots and kills the five chanyu.

NOTE

Line 4:   During the reign of the Han emperor Xuan (r. 73–49 B.C.), after the
Xiongnu *chanyu* (chieftain) Xulüquanqu died, there was a struggle for power,
after which five princes claimed the title of *chanyu* (*History of the Former Han*,
8/266).

18.

In the house of Han after lords and officials have feasted,
In lofty discussion at Cloud Pavilion they talk of great victories.
The emperor comes in person to bestow a marquis' seal,
Which the general wears at his girdle on emerging from Ming-
guang Palace.

NOTE

Line 2:   Cloud Pavilion was located in the Han imperial palace (Mingguang). Emperor Ming (r. 57–75) placed twenty-eight portraits of famous generals there.

POEM

19
(2/2a; I, 11)

Marching Song

Blowing horns rouse the marching men.
In a clamor, the marching men ready to leave.
Pipes are mournful, horses' neighs confused,
As they struggle to cross the Golden River's waters.
The sun dusks on the desert's edge;
Battle sounds amid the smoke and dust.
We'll all bind a famous prince's neck
To return and present to our ruler.

NOTE

Line 4:   Now called the Black River, the Golden River is located in Inner Mongolia.

POEM

20
(8/5a; I, 140)

Farewell to Overseer Ping Danran

You are a stranger on the road to Yang Pass,
A new follower of the "Marquis Settling Distant Lands":
There yellow clouds sever the colors of spring
And painted horns arouse a frontier grief.
On the Gobi Desert you will spend the year
Where the Forked River flows out from the pass.
Be sure to teach envoys to foreign states
How to drink from Yuezhi skulls.

NOTES

Line 1:   Yang Pass is one of the two main passes through the mountains in Dunhuang, Gansu province; Jade Pass is to the north of it.

Line 2:   Ban Chao (71–102) was a famous general who pacified the western border tribes and was thus enfeoffed as *Dingyuan hou*, or the "Marquis Who Settled [Pacified] Distant [Lands]." See the *History of the Latter Han* (*Hou Han shu* [Peking: Zhonghua, 1973]), 47/1582.

Line 8:   For "Yuezhi skulls," see poem 9, line 20n.

POEM

21

(9/2b; I, 156)

Mission to the Frontier

A single carriage heads out for the border,
In tributary states, passing through Juyan.
A traveling tumbleweed leaves the Han frontier;
Returning wild geese enter barbarian skies.
On the great desert, a lone straight column of smoke;
Above the long river, the setting sun is round.
At Xiao Pass I meet a mounted patrol:
The governor-general is at Yanran Mountain.

NOTES

Line 2:   Juyan in Inner Mongolia was a city in the center of Xiongnu territory which was conquered by Han dynasty armies under generals Huo Qubing and Gongsun Ao (*History of the Former Han*, 6/176).

Line 7:   Xiao Pass is located in Gansu province.

Line 8:   Mt. Yanran was near the scene of another great victory over the Xiongnu at Mt. Jilu during the Latter Han dynasty, under generals Dou Xian and Dou Hong. Dou Xian (d. A.D. 92) carved a record of the victory on Mt. Yanran. See the *History of the Latter Han*, 4/168.

POEM

22

(10/13a; I, 192)

On Going out from the Border

Beyond the Juyan citywall, he hunts for "Heaven's favorites."
White grasses join the sky, wilderness fires burn.
Dusk clouds, empty dunes: at times he presses his horse.
An autumn day on the level plain is fine for shooting vultures.
The Commandant-Guarding-the-Qiang climbs the barricades in
 the morning;
The General-Destroying-Barbarians "crosses the river Liao" at
 night.
Jade reins, composite bows, a pearl-bridled horse—
The house of Han will bestow on its valiant general Huo.

NOTES

Line 1: For "Heaven's favorites," see poem 19, line 19n.

Line 5: The Qiang were one of the northern border tribes; the two military posts mentioned in this line and the next were established by the Han emperor Wu.

Line 6: The Liao River, in present-day Liaoning (northeastern China) was in foreign territory, and because of the Han general Fan Mingyou's successful venture across it, "crossing the Liao" came to mean attacking barbarians. Fan Mingyou was appointed to his command on the Liao in the summer of 78 B.C (*History of the Former Han*, 7/229 and 19B/796).

Line 7: A composite bow was made from a combination of horn, wood, and sinew.

Line 8: Huo Qubing was renowned for his exploits against border tribes on the northwest frontier. His biography is in the *Records of the Historian*, 111/ 2928ff. and the *History of the Former Han*, 55/2478ff.

Notes to Chapter Two

1. Traditionally a person was considered one year old at birth, so ages in Chinese years (*sui*) are always one digit greater than by Western reckoning. All ages given here will be in *sui*.
  Biographies of Wang Wei can be found in the *Jiu Tang shu* (Peking: Zhonghua, 1975), 190C/5051–53, and in the *Xin Tang shu* (Peking: Zhonghua, 1975), 202/5764–66.
2. No one is quite sure what it was. In a short biographical article, how-

ever, Chen Yixin explains that Wang Wei was banished because "the artistes under him gave a private performance of the *Yellow Lion Dance*, reserved exclusively for the court." See his "Wang Wei, the Nature Poet," *Chinese Literature*, No. 7 (July 1962), p. 15.

3. See Kenneth K. S. Ch'en, *The Chinese Transformation of Buddhism* (Princeton: Princeton University Press, 1973), p. 182.

4. In the "Postface" to his selection of Wang Wei's poems, for example, Chen Yixin cites an anecdote from Sima Guang's (1019–86) history, the *Zizhi tongjian*, which claims that Zhang refused to win people's favor by awarding them empty offices, and he goes on to contrast Zhang's general uprightness, fairness, and sympathy for the peasants with Li's alleged unprincipled ambitions and intrigues, toadying to the aristocracy in the capital, prejudices against officials coming in from the provinces, and refusal to accept criticism (*Wang Wei shixuan* [Peking: Renmin, 1959], pp. 141–45).

Chen defends Zhang and attacks Li in two other essays on Wang Wei's poetry and politics: "Lun Wang Wei di shi," *Wenxue yichan cengkan*, No. 3 (1956), pp. 79–95, and "Wang Wei di zhengzhi shenghuo he ta di sixiang," in *Tang shi yanjiu lunwenji*, No. 2, Pt. I (Peking: Zhongguo yuwenxue shebian, 1969), pp. 12–20. Other modern critics, including Liu Weichong, *Wang Wei pingzhuan* (Taipei: Zhengzhong, 1972), pp. 33–34, and the Wang Wei Study Group (*Wang Wei xiaozu*), "Lun Wang Wei shige di pingjia," in *Wenxue yanjiu yu pipan zhuankan*, No. 1 (Peking: Renmin, 1958), pp. 59–75, generally agree with this assessment.

5. The name of this office was changed to *wenbu langzhong* in the third month of the eleventh year of Tianbao (752), so biographers have concluded that Wang Wei must have been appointed before this time. Some disagreement exists concerning the date of his mother's death. Because the biographies in the standard histories both note that the poet observed a three-year period of mourning, Chen Yixin counts backward from the 752 appointment as *libu langzhong* and places Wang Wei's mother's death during 748 or 749 ("Postface," pp. 149–50, n. 1, and "Wang Wei shengping shiji chutan," *Wenxue yichan cengkan*, No. 6 [1958], p. 141). Lu Huaixuan in "Wang Wei di yinju yu chushi," *Wenxue yichan cengkan*, No. 13 (1963), agrees with the 749 date (p. 166). Lewis C. and Dorothy B. Walmsley suggest 751, in *Wang Wei the Painter-Poet* (Rutland, Vt.: Charles Tuttle, 1968), p. 69.

In an article dealing exclusively with establishing these dates, however, Jin Ding convincingly demonstrates that Wang Wei could not have been in mourning in 748 or 749. Jin points out that Wang Wei wrote five poems and three memorials to the throne for specific occasions during this period, as late as the second month of 750, and therefore could not yet have withdrawn from office. Furthermore, Jin provides evidence from various books of rites which indicate that "three years of mourning" was merely a standard formula used by historians and that, in fact, the actual period only lasted twenty-five months. Now figuring backward from the spring of 752, when Wang Wei returned to office, Jin concludes that his mother died in the spring of 750. See "Wang Wei dingyou shijian zhiyi," *Wenxue yichan cengkan*, No. 13 (1963), pp. 172–76.

6. Chen cites a petition Wang Wei wrote to the emperor in 758, "A Memorial Requesting [Permission] to Convert My Estate into a Monastery" (17/13b; II, 320–31), in which the poet states that he had bought the Wang River villa so that his mother could enjoy peace and solitude in her old age ("Postface," p. 149, n. 1). Wang Yunxi, in his introduction to the recent Peking reprinting of the Qing dynasty collection of works, agrees that Wang Wei probably lived there during the mid-740s. See "Wang Wei he ta di shi"

(I, 3). Cao Jiping and Lu Huaixuan, however, suggest an earlier date, sometime between 737 and 740 (see Lu, pp. 166–67).

Regarding the temporal precedence of a Zhongnan retreat, Chen cites a poem written by Wang Wei's friend Pei Di at the Wang River estate which refers to an earlier period at Zhongnan ("Postface," p. 147 and p. 149, n. 1 [see poem 75 below]).

7. In his article on Wang Wei's periods of reclusion and government service, Lu Huaixuan suggests a series of probable places and dates of withdrawal: Mt. Song (726–28); Mt. Zhongnan and Wang River (738–40); Qi River (744–46) (*passim.*). With the exception of Wang River and some slight differences in specific dates, Zhuang Shen agrees with Lu's basic chronology in *Wang Wei yanjiu*, Vol. I (Hong Kong: Wanyou, 1971), pp. 2–12.

8. E. G. Pulleyblank, *The Background of the Rebellion of An Lu-shan* (Oxford: Oxford University Press, 1966), p. 58.

9. Chen Yixin, "Wang Wei the Nature Poet," p. 215.

10. Han Weijun, "Wang Wei xiancun shige zhiyi," *Wenxue yichan cengkan*, No. 13 (1963), pp. 177–84.

11. For a discussion of the "topoi" frequently associated with evocation of the past in the works of Wang Wei's contemporaries, see Hans Frankel, "The Contemplation of the Past in T'ang Poetry," in *Perspectives on the T'ang*, ed. Denis Twitchett and Arthur F. Wright (New Haven: Yale University Press, 1973), pp. 345–65.

12. J. Hillis Miller, *Poets of Reality* (New York: Atheneum, 1969), pp. 328, 291.

13. For an examination of the types and conventions of the *yuefu*, see Hans Frankel, "*Yüeh-fu* Poetry," in *Studies in Chinese Literary Genres*, ed. Cyril Birch (Berkeley: University of California Press, 1974), pp. 69–107.

14. *Li Taibo ji* (Rpt. Taipei: Heluo, 1975), 22/498.

15. "Record of Peach Blossom Spring" (*Tao hua yuan ji*), included in Ding Fubao, ed., *Quan Han Sanguo Jin Nan Bei Chao shi* (Rpt. Taipei: Yiwen, n.d.; 6 vols.), II, 639–40. Both the narrative and the poem have been translated by James Robert Hightower in *The Poetry of T'ao Ch'ien* (Oxford: Clarendon Press, 1970), pp. 254–56; citations from these texts are taken from his translation.

16. This event is recorded in Meng Qi's *Ben shi shi*, a collection of anecdotes surrounding the composition of poems, whose preface is dated the twelfth month of 886. Included in *Lidai shihua xubian*, ed. Ding Fubao (Rpt. Taipei: Yiwen, n.d.; 5 vols.), I, 1/1b.

17. *Chu ci buzhu*, ed. Hong Xingzu (Rpt. Taipei: Yiwen, 1973), pp. 97–144. For translations and a discussion of the shamanistic origins of these songs, see David Hawkes, *Ch'u Tz'u: The Songs of the South* (Oxford: Clarendon Press, 1959), pp. 35–44, and Arthur Waley, *The Nine Songs: A Study of Shamanism in Ancient China* (San Francisco: City Lights Books, 1973).

THREE

Court Poems

THIS chapter presents a number of works which have frequently been neglected by other translators of Wang Wei's poetry: poems written during or about his life as a government official. As was the case with his contemporaries, Wang Wei's political career and poetic production were integrally related; indeed, throughout Chinese history the instances when the two activities were not combined in the same person tend to be the exception rather than the rule, particularly since the ability to write poetry was tested at times on the imperial examinations. As I mentioned in the biographical account in chapter two, from the mid-730s onward Wang Wei occupied successive government posts either at the capital or in the provinces, interrupted only by an obligatory period of mourning for his mother's death; much to his partisans' dismay, he even held office under the rebel An Lushan. His career was not an especially meteoric one, but neither was it unsuccessful, and the number of poems in his collection reflecting a positive attitude toward political involvement suggests that it was also not unimportant to him, a point which many biographers have chosen to ignore.

Poems 23 through 33 all deal directly with Wang Wei's experiences as a government official, the first two presenting a general view of activities surrounding the morning audience of the emperor at the capital. Poem 23, "Morning Audience," is actually set just before the levée begins, focusing on one of the poet's favorite times of day—the dawn—a moment of transition which belongs neither to night nor day. Wang Wei juxtaposes qualities and events of both periods and contrasting temporal adverbs (such as "not yet" and "already") to suggest that the dawn can be defined as neither darkness nor light because it embraces both. The stars are still gleaming and the night mists heavy, yet the sky is also lighting up in the distance. Appropri-

ately, sound—the sense most crucial during the night—is empha-
sized as much as sight. Only in the final line does the poet, in his
typically open-ended manner, firmly commence with the activities of
the day. Poem 24, "Harmonizing with Secretary Jia Zhi's Poem,
'Morning Audience at Daming Palace,'" deals more directly with the
bustling scene inside the palace and also demonstrates the highly
social nature of poetry-writing during Wang Wei's time. Works such
as this which were written to "harmonize" (*he*) with the topics,
forms, and rhymes of the poem of another poet, with several others
often chiming in, can be found in abundance in the collections of
most Tang figures, Wang Wei included. Given the date of its compo-
sition, this poem is also interesting because of its neutral, if not posi-
tive, attitude toward activities at court. Most of Wang Wei's biogra-
phers have claimed that he spent his last years in reclusion at his
Lantian estate, disillusioned by and therefore rejecting the whole
business of government. This poem, on the contrary, indicates that
he was still maintaining contact with other bureaucrats and palace
life as late as 758.

The following nine poems—arranged in roughly chronological
order—were written on specific official occasions, often at imperial
command. Many of them are composed in heptasyllabic regulated
verse, although Wang Wei generally preferred the pentasyllabic line
and rarely takes advantage of the extra two syllables to develop the
complex syntax for which Du Fu, for example, is renowned. The
longer line was, however, commonly used for such official composi-
tions, its more stately cadence and opportunity for greater accumu-
lation of detail proving particularly appropriate for such ceremonial
subject matter. Wang Wei also frequently employs regulated couplets
(*pailü*) for these court poems, perhaps because the opportunity to
string together an indefinite succession of parallel or antithetical
statements was so well suited to evoking the all-embracing nature of
imperial power.

Poem 25, "Written at the Prince's Command on the Emperor's
Having Lent the Jiucheng Palace to the Prince of Qi as a Retreat from
Summer Heat," was composed early in Wang Wei's career, most likely
while he held his first position at court as Associate Secretary of Mu-
sic and enjoyed the patronage of emperor Xuanzong's younger
brother. In his description of the summer retreat, the poet empha-
sizes the interpenetration of human and natural realms, an emphasis
which is also typical of his nonofficial works: when the people are
outside, they seem to be the very source of the surrounding clouds
and mist, while even indoors reflections of mountains and streams
enter from afar. Similarly, the next couplet juxtaposes sensations
from nature to evidences of human presences and activities. Wang
Wei keeps the obligatory praise to a minimum, preferring instead the

obliqueness of a concluding allusion that, again characteristically, asserts the equivalence of the present moment with past, or even supernatural, events.

Although poem 26, "Sacred Mt. Hua," is not strictly a court composition, since Wang Wei had not yet returned from virtual exile to office in the capital, it was written as a direct entreaty to and critique of the emperor for refusing to perform the imperial sacrifices on the mountain. The following poem, "Harmonizing with the Poem of the Duke of Jin, Vice-President of the Department of State, 'Following the Imperial Retinue to the Warm Springs,'" was written approximately ten years later. Wang Wei was most actively involved in court life during the 740s and the next few poems very likely date from this period as well. The chief interest of poem 27 lies in the evidence it provides—most biographers to the contrary—that Wang Wei was not one to let his allegiance to the deposed chief minister Zhang Jiuling prevent him from ingratiating himself with Zhang's successor. Almost the entire poem is a panegyric to Li Linfu: the allusions in lines 7–8 link him with past sage rulers, the descriptive statements in the next six lines attribute the present prosperity, peace, and triumph of Confucian orthodoxy to his noncoercive leadership, and the next couplet further praises his political and literary skills. Since Wang Wei was serving as Admonitor on the Left at this time, he can conclude by claiming that he has found nothing for which to reprove Li, for the wisdom and concern of his superior equal those of the revered ancients.

The next four poems were all written at imperial command as responses to various holidays or events, harmonizing with poems already composed by emperor Xuanzong. Although the diction and imagery of these works may strike us as somewhat formulaic, they should not be overlooked: one Qing dynasty literary critic in fact observed that "in writing poems at imperial command, [Wang] Youcheng was superior to everyone else."[1] Furthermore, they demonstrate the same notions of time, space, and the relationship of man to nature that underlie his work as a whole. In poem 28, "Written at Imperial Command to Harmonize with His Majesty's Spring-Detaining Poem, 'Spring View in the Rain,' on the Arcade from Penglai Hall to Xingqing Palace," for example, the first parallel couplet juxtaposes characteristic images of enclosure which apply to both temporal and spatial realms. As is typical of court poems in general, a sense of history is introduced through allusions to earlier dynasties. Yet, as we have seen before, Wang Wei establishes no distinction between the present and the past; Qin, Han, and Tang seem to exist in the same eternal moment. Space is equally enclosed, as natural phenomena and human artifacts naturally intertwine: the river winds about the man-made frontier just as mountains surround the Han palace and, by extension, Xuanzong's own dwellings. The last word in each line reinforces this sense of encirclement by referring back to the meaning of the main verb, thus literally enclosing the line itself.

The second and third couplets are equally replete with parallel images. Lines 3 and 4 embody the same circularity found in each of the first two lines. Though the emperor moves out onto the arcade, he then reverses his direction to look back upon what he has left, and his movement thus seems to contain the entire ground he has covered. Wang Wei also links human and natural realms by depicting the carriage as emerging from the willows about the palace gates and the emperor as gazing at the flowers in his garden, a man-made construct. The third couplet continues to stress this sense of unity and containment—of man within nature and of the whole scene itself as a self-enclosed static harmony. We see the Imperial City (where government offices were located) "amid the clouds" and the spring forests "in the rain." Wang Wei employs no verbs in these two lines and simply delineates the vast unmoving tableau of state, people, and natural scene, which the emperor can encompass within his gaze and, by implication, control.

The fourth couplet is also parallel, yet the hint of enjambment and almost prosaic diction (in line 7 the copula is used—rare in regulated verse) appropriately loosen the potential density of parallelism as Wang Wei comments on the scene in propositional language. He presents both an official explanation for this imperial excursion and, in the negative, an alternative possibility which might have been expected because of the preceding lavish description of the natural scene. The poet might thereby be praising the emperor's commitment to his duties by showing how he can rise above mere selfish appreciation of beauty for the benefit of the greater good. By placing the second alternative as the conclusion to the poem, however, Wang Wei may be indulging in some veiled criticism, suggesting that it is, in fact, the primary reason for the outing. In any case, this final couplet draws a distinction between the exercise of human power and the enjoyment of nature and thus seems to disrupt the unity evoked by the first six lines. Yet, considered again, an appreciation of natural beauty would imply another distinction between the observer and the observed. Wang Wei suggests here instead that the emperor's power derives not from some frivolous pleasure-seeking but rather from an underlying congruence between human and natural realms.

Similarly, poem 29, "Written at Imperial Command to Harmonize with His Majesty's Poem, 'At the End of Spring, Bidding Farewell to the Assembled Court Emissaries on Their Return to Their Commanderies,'" is concerned with revealing the bonds between political and cosmic realms. Almost every antithetical couplet here encompasses the totality of the empire, with a movement in from the provinces balanced each time by the subsequent return outward. The concluding four lines justify this imperial power in two ways. In the first place, the ruler has organized his government along natural principles: he is the fundamental brilliance, the Milky Way, while his officials in the provinces, like constellations, share his burden. And secondly, the heavens sanction his rule, illuminating his entire domain with the light of the stars. Poem 30, "Written at Imperial Command to Harmonize with His Majesty's Poem, 'With the Crown Prince and Other Lords on the Third Day of the Third Month at Dragon Pond for the Spring Lustration Festival,'" concludes with almost identical images.

Poem 31, "Written at Imperial Command to Harmonize with His Majesty's Poem, 'On the Double Ninth Festival the Ministers and Assembled Officials Offer Their Wishes for Longevity,'" also celebrates imperial power, opening with a statement about the general peace and abundant harvest that implicitly sanction the reign. This implication of naturally conferred legitimacy is made explicit in the following poem, "At Datong Hall a Jade Iris Grew, and There Were Auspicious Clouds by Dragon Pond; the Hundred Officials Observed [These Phenomena] Together; Imperial Kindness Bestowed a Banquet with Music, so I Dared to Write on This Occasion." The auspicious omens provide indisputable evidence that "heaven's will accords with the will of men" and that the emperor is clearly entitled to rule. Such unusual occurrences also explain Wang Wei's treatment of history in this poem: no longer is the present age merely equal to great reigns of the past, for its glory and good fortune far exceed those of even the most joyous occasions during the Zhou and Han dynasties. Only mythological sage rulers like Yao and Shun can be used as comparisons to the present, with its demonstrated achievement of a total harmony between man and nature.

This same congruence is emphasized in poem 33, "Having Received Pardon for My Offense and Been Returned to Office, Humbly Moved by Imperial Kindness I Write My Lowly Thoughts and Present Them to My Superiors." As the title indicates, this work was composed not at a state occasion, but after the new emperor Suzong had pardoned Wang Wei for his collaboration with the An Lushan rebels. In this encomium the poet appropriately stresses the notion of *return*, the return of a government post to him as well as the return of officials from all over the empire to the capital. Though a new era has begun, it marks a return to the prerevolutionary order, and such an emphasis calls naturally for historical allusion. Wang Wei not only grounds the restoration in the legitimacy of the Han, he again grants it quasi-mythical status by equating the emperor with the founder of the Shang or Yin dynasty, and the following couplet continues this extreme praise by stating that imperial longevity and brilliance may equal or even exceed that of the heavens. In any case, the universe responds affirmatively to the new political situation—flowers blossom and birds sing—underscoring the integrality between human and natural realms.

Mikel Dufrenne has written in *The Poetic* that the European court poet is concerned only with the former domain: "Rather than the cosmic order, it is now the glory of the prince that he must speak of and maintain, and the social order that this prince defends and incarnates within himself" (p. 95). Wang Wei, however, emphasizes the integrality of man and nature, and the attitude is by no means unique to him: any Tang dynasty poet steeped in the Confucian tradition would see the universe itself as inherently moral, with an indivisible, organic connection existing between the cosmic and social orders. The ruler was felt to possess an implicit "mandate from heaven," a notion expanded by Han dynasty Confucians into a complex correlation of natural phenomena with governmental legitimacy. This "philosophy of organism," which, as I mentioned earlier, Joseph Needham and Wang Ling have described as fundamental to Chinese thought, no doubt underlies Wang Wei's emphasis on human and cosmic harmony and interpenetration in these poems, as does the encomiastic tone required by the context of composition. The basic structures he employs are also characteristic of court poems written by other poets before and during this period.[2] What is significant, however, is the consistency with which such balanced and integrated perceptions and thought patterns recur throughout his work.

This becomes particularly clear in the second large group of poems translated in this chapter (34–50), all of which focus on the relative attractions of public service and eremitic retreat. Poems 34–35, written one after another, typify Wang Wei's ability to identify with both the committed official and the escapist recluse. Like the ceremonial works above, "While I Was Imprisoned in Puti Monastery . . . " was written on the occasion of a specific government festivity—a concert for the rebel leader An Lushan—but it neither celebrates nor praises. Significantly, though, Wang Wei retains the vocabulary characteristic of those poems, as if to intensify the cruel twist of events. The "ten thousand homes," previously used to indicate a massive imperial power and popularity, are united now only in their lament and widespread destruction. Similarly, "the hundred officials," once members of an impressive and responsible bureaucracy, now call attention to themselves because of their absence. There are natural and human counterparts of the desolate scene: leaves fall like the fortunes of the ruling dynasty, and the palace, though perhaps filled with enemy soldiers, is "empty" because its rightful occupants have fled.

In these first three lines Wang Wei provides no explanation for

the scene and its emotional charge. We are left to find it in the final
line, where the poet alludes but indirectly to the concert. Only from
the juxtaposition of the joyous festivities implied here to the lament
of the rest of the quatrain and the resulting conflict of moods, and
not from any explicit statement, can we derive the meaning of the
poem and the protest against the rebellion. Subtle though this op-
position may be, it nevertheless implies an awareness of and concern
about the present and future political situations on Wang Wei's part,
as well as a nostalgia for the former rule and his own role in it. This
attitude thus contrasts with the desire to withdraw from such affairs
expressed in the long extended question of the following poem, "Re-
cited and Again Presented to Pei Di."

Poem 36, "Given to My Paternal Cousin, Military Supply Offi-
cial Qiu," continues in this vein, expressing the wish to escape from
politics that most readers have come to expect from Wang Wei's po-
etry. And the next three works, "Playfully Presented to Zhang Yin
the Fifth Brother," also celebrate the peace and purity of life in retreat,
revealing a subtle change in attitude as Wang Wei grows more confi-
dent of his commitment to reclusion and playfully criticizes his re-
cluse friend's "lapses." Poem 37 describes Zhang Yin living in total
harmony with his mountain environment and following his natural
instincts in a carefree manner. Lines 13–16 provide the abstract philo-
sophical premises behind the concrete scenes just presented, the
Taoist conviction of a nonanthropocentric universe. And the conclud-
ing couplet suggests that Wang Wei has previously been uncertain of
his commitment to this view; now, however, he is able to eliminate
"fleeting thoughts" of worldly fame and success from his mind.

Poem 38 is thus written from the perspective of someone who
is in the process of shedding his ties to the official "world of men."
Once again Wang Wei presents a positive depiction of his friend, in-
troducing some more scholarly aspects of his life, linking him with
one of the best-known officials-turned-recluse, and turning finally to
himself and his response. Leaving the "world of men" obviously
does not mean going into total seclusion, but merely seeking the
company of other like minds away from court.

Finally, in the third and most playful poem of the group, Wang
Wei presents himself as now secure in his withdrawal from mundane
enticements and chides his friend for not living as austerely as he
should. What had just been praised as the habit of "an old rustic of
the wilds"—going fishing—now becomes an impure appeasement of
"mouth and belly." The selfless, tranquil existence at one with all
creatures that had previously been Zhang's has been appropriated by
the speaker himself, who now declares himself willing to live as a
total hermit. But the title, of course, has alerted us as to how to read
such hyperbolic depictions of the one's dissoluteness or the other's

freedom from corruption. Such a self-righteous self-portrait is rare in Wang Wei's poetry, and even the jesting context of composition does not totally allay a suspicion that he is protesting too much, that his own commitment to retreat is not quite hard and fast.

And indeed, poems 40–41 once again argue the two contrary points of view. They are both farewell poems written to the same person, Wang Wei's friend during his early years in office, Qiwu Qian. The first, "Farewell to Qiwu Qian on His Return Home after Failing the Examination," was written sometime before 726, and the second, "Farewell to Collator Qiwu Qian on His Leaving Office to Return East of the Yangzi," around 742. While the former advocates aspiring to officialdom, the latter rejects it and announces the poet's own intention of retiring from office. Granted, the differing contexts or a possible change in perspective from youth to middle age on Wang Wei's part might be responsible for this apparent contradiction in attitude, but it is too persistent in other works to be explained away by these two factors.

The next two poems, for example, both written from the point of view of the official, express contrasting wishes. In poem 42, "Written in Reply to He the Fourth's Gift of a Cloth Cap," Wang Wei presents the two inclinations of his life in an adjective-noun phrase ("reclusive official heart") which unifies them. But the possibly greater attraction of withdrawal becomes clear in the following couplet: the poet puts the cap, a symbol of the simplicity and purity of retreat, away while performing official duties, but the adverb "awhile" suggests that perhaps these daily commitments will also be but a temporary deviation from the desired life in the country. Only after cleansing himself symbolically from the taint of involvement does he don the cap; then, even though he is still at court and not totally free from its clamor, he can nevertheless distance himself from its influence. The word "sitting" calls to mind the Buddhist "sitting in meditation" or Chan, also associated with the private rather than public life of a bureaucrat. In the final line here Wang Wei suggests that he would like to resolve the issue of service versus retreat in favor of the latter, yet in poem 43, "In Response to Policy Reviewer Guo," although he closes with an announcement of his imminent retirement from office, he has by no means presented official life as an undesirable alternative. Throughout the poem his depictions of both the nocturnal peace and the diurnal bustle certainly suggest a positive attitude to activities at court, and in the final couplet Wang Wei writes that he would like to be equally involved in them: if he retires it will be caused by his physical condition and not any intellectual opposition to engagement. Again, as was the case with the Qiwu Qian poems, because of Guo's situation, any other statement would be impolite; the poet would undoubtedly find it imprudent to reveal a negative opinion of service to someone actively engaged in it. But again, this is not an anomalous instance.

The next "Six Casually Written Poems" (44–49) explore the implications of both courses of action. In the first poem of the group Wang Wei employs several allusions and rhetorical questions to indicate indirectly his opposition to an overly rigid espousal of any one particular doctrine or attitude. He focuses on the "madman of Chu" as someone who followed no school and neither questioned nor rejected his fate, accepting it instead in a carefree manner. Jieyu rejects the keystones of Confucian orthodoxy, which emphasized, of course, commitment to public service, as well as the self-righteous and ultimately suicidal withdrawal of Bo Yi and Shu Qi. He, of course, also refused to serve his government, but he accomplished this with an attitude of equanimity rather than inflexibility.

Poem 45 also questions the absolute authority of Confucian behavior in particular: even the highest minded of rulers, the Five Emperors and Three Kings, disagreed on the proper way to succeed one another. Since no other firm guidelines exist for proper political action, Wang Wei opts for the undemanding, carefree life of a rustic farmer, whose few wishes are easily satisfied. And poem 46 presents him caught in a net of worldly involvement, constantly tantalized by the prospect of withdrawal from service. Familial obligations (the reference to a younger sister is curious, since there is no record that he had any) are seen here as obstacles lying in the path toward his own personal happiness; the speaker concludes by declaring that his resolve to shed these responsibilities grows stronger each day.

The fourth poem (47), however, looks at the act of retreat from government service from the other point of view. Here Wang Wei focuses on Tao Qian, who after retiring early from his post wrote about the joys of untrammeled, if impoverished, country living. He and Wang Wei have, of course, traditionally been linked as eremitic poets; Wang Wei no doubt sensed certain affinities—phrases borrowed from Tao's works and references to the man himself are more numerous in his collection than is the case with any other poet—but he was equally aware of the differences between them. The earlier poet was renowned for his love of wine, and Wang Wei elaborates on that fondness and on anecdotes associated with it to make his point: such a carefree life may entail a less than admirable neglect of familial or social responsibilities.

In any case, poem 48 returns to life in the city, juxtaposing and implicitly contrasting two figures: an irresponsible, profligate rake devoted to the pursuit of material pleasure and a noble, impoverished scholar whose commitment to Confucian teachings has brought him nothing but hardship. Which mode of life among many to select is an issue that remains unresolved throughout this entire series, and in the sixth poem we see Wang Wei perhaps suspecting which decision would be correct but still remaining unconvinced. His reluctance to choose is reflected in the predominance of negative constructions here—he is now "too lazy" to write, has "mistakenly" been a poet, is "unable" to shed old habits, and still "does not know." The failure to provide an unambiguous direct object for "know" also suggests his preference for hedging throughout. What do we know? That he is old, that he thinks he might once—perhaps in an earlier reincarnation—have been a painter, and that he has become famous. What does his heart still not know? Presumably what has just been stated, i.e., that his "name and cognomen really are both correct." Since the two combine to form the Chinese name of Vimalakīrti, the lay Buddhist sage who lived at the time of Śākyamuni Buddha (ca. sixth century B.C.), Wang Wei is suggesting either that devotion to his teachings would be something that could be asserted as proper, or that he is in fact truly devoted to them, to the point perhaps of being an actual reincarnation of him. But the final line refuses to allow a comfortable certainty, either to us or to the speaker himself. His heart/mind remains unaware or unconvinced of what to do; the solution, then, would seem to be to continue as always in balancing alternatives, to accept with equanimity and enjoy both the responsibilities of service and the tranquility of retreat.

This is precisely what we find him doing in poem 50, "On Leaving Monk Wengu of the Mountains; also Shown to My Younger Brother Jin." The title links representatives of both courses of action: a Buddhist hermit and the poet's own brother, a highly successful official. While Wang Wei describes his reluctance to leave the former's peaceful mountain retreat, at the same time he affirms the correctness of commitment during a period of wise rule. Lines 13–14 again juxtapose the two possibilities as he sees them, and the final couplet presents his apparent solution to the dilemma—to devote his time as equally as possible to both modes of life.

What these and other poems suggest, then, is that the "contradiction" between service and retreat was not the problematic issue that Wang Wei's modern biographers have made it to be, nor was he so unequivocally opposed to the former as many people believe. In his "Essay in Praise of Buddhism" (20/1a–2a; II, 361–62), for example, he explains his ability to lead the double life of official and recluse common to many Chinese poet-bureaucrats: "My body remains amid the hundred officials; my heart leaps beyond the ten stages [of the development of a Mahāyāna Buddhist bodhisattva]." From this statement one might indeed be tempted to conclude, as has generally been done, that he regarded his obligations at court as but an onerous burden. But his corpus also contains a "Letter to Kulapati [Buddhist layman] Wei" (18/8a–11a; II, 332–34), which, on the contrary, argues against making such a judgment. Urging his friend to leave his mountain retreat and return to government office, Wang Wei presents a number of precedents to be rejected. Of the poet Xi Kang (223–62), for example, he writes:

> He abandoned the tassels [of office] and looked madly about; he longed for the tall forest in the distance and remembered the abundant grass. Abandoning tassels and looking madly about: how is that different from bending down to receive the bonds [of office]? The tall forest and abundant grass: how are they different from the officials' gate and railing?

Here Wang Wei suggests that in the larger view of things, perhaps, there is really no difference between court and country, service and retreat. Then he moves on to Tao Qian, who would not accede to the demands of his office and bow to an inspector on tour, "so he let his seal and bands [of office] go and left his position. Afterward he was poor, and his 'Begging for Food' poem says: 'I knocked on the door and clumsily spoke.'[3] This means that he begged repeatedly and was much ashamed." Tao had thus allowed a petty issue to create a much greater problem: "Not bearing to be ashamed just once: did this not cause him to be ashamed for his entire life? This is also allowing the difference between 'Others' and 'I' to invade one's mind, forgetting the large and harboring the small." One should not, therefore, maintain such rigid categories distinguishing between the possible and the impossible, permissible and undesirable modes of activity.

> Confucius said: "I, however, am different from these [high-minded recluses]. There is nothing permissible, there is nothing impermissible."[4] What is permissible is what suits [one's] will, what is impermissible is what does not suit [one's] will. The gentleman regards spreading benevolence and exhibiting righteousness, enlivening the state and saving men as suiting his will. Even if his Way is not put into practice [however], he still does not think of it as not suiting his will.

In other words, Wang Wei's advice is to be flexible, embrace all possibilities, and adapt to the situation at hand, whether or not it conforms to one's principles. Written when he was almost sixty and thus shortly before his death, this letter reveals his ability to integrate both sides of the issue, an equilibrium which typifies his work as a whole. And this was also, of course, the advice of Zhuangzi—to compromise and harmonize, rather than categorize:

> Where there is acceptability, there must be unacceptability; where there is unacceptability, there must be acceptability. Where there is recognition of right there must be recognition of wrong; where there is recognition of wrong there must be recognition of right. Therefore the sage

does not proceed in such a way, but illuminates all in the light of heaven. ("Discussion on Making All Things Equal," 4/2/28; trans. Watson, pp. 39–40)

POEM

23
(5/10a; I, 83)

Morning Audience

> White and pure, the bright stars are high.
> The distant sky dawns on a vast expanse.
> Darkness of sophora mist does not disperse;
> Cries of citywall crows gradually cease.
> Just now I hear the sounds from the tall pavilion
> But cannot yet distinguish the wardrobe room.
> Rows of silver candles have already formed:
> Through the Golden Gate chariots solemnly drive.

NOTE

Line 8:   The Golden Gate was part of the Han dynasty Weiyang Palace, actually called the Golden Horse Gate because of a bronze horse there.

POEM

24
(10/3b; I, 177)

Harmonizing with Secretary Jia Zhi's Poem, "Morning Audience at Daming Palace"

> The crimson-bonneted cock man sends out the dawn marker.
> The clothing master has just entered with kingfisher-cloud furs.
> The nine imperial portals open out onto palace halls;
> From ten thousand states officials pay respects to the jade-tasseled crown.
> As the sun's color just rises above the immortal hands, stirring,
> Fragrant smoke is about to waft next to the dragon robe.

Once the audience ends you must trim the five-colored edicts
And return with pendants tinkling toward the edge of Phoenix
Pond.

NOTES

Title: Daming was a huge palace whose construction was begun in A.D. 634
by the Tang emperor Taizong (r. 627–50) in the southeast corner of the Im-
perial Garden, outside the Chang'an city wall.

The full title of Jia Zhi's (718–72) poem is "Morning Audience at Daming
Palace, Shown to My Colleagues in the Two Ministries." In addition to Wang
Wei, the poets Du Fu and Cen Shen (715–70) composed poems in response
to it, and these other three works are all included in the standard edition of
Wang Wei's poetry. They were probably written in the spring of 758, when
Jia Zhi and Wang Wei were both serving as Secretary of the Grand Imperial
Secretariat, Du Fu was Advisor on the Right, and Cen Shen was Admonitor
on the Left. The "two ministries" were the Grand Imperial Secretariat (*zhong-
shu sheng*), where Jia Zhi and Wang Wei were located, and the Imperial Chan-
cellery (*menxia sheng*), where Du Fu's and Cen Shen's offices were situated.
The two divisions were also known as the Right and Left Ministries, respec-
tively.

Line 1:   An official wearing a crimson headdress went through the palace
after cockcrow to awaken others; he held a stick on which the time was
marked.

Line 2:   These furs were worn by the emperor, whose wardrobe was man-
aged by a "clothing master."

Line 5:   The "immortal hands" were on the bronze statues of Taoist immor-
tals erected by the Han emperor Wu to collect dew in pans, which was then
eaten with fragments of jade as a means of gaining immortality.

Line 7:   Imperial edicts were issued on paper of five colors: black, red, blue,
white, and yellow.

Line 8:   Phoenix Pond was another name for the Grand Imperial Secretariat.

POEM
25

Written at the Prince's Command on the Emperor's Having Lent the Jiucheng Palace to the Prince of Qi as a Retreat from Summer Heat

The emperor's son bids farewell to the distant Red Phoenix Tur-
ret:
An imperial edict has lent the faraway palace of blue-green mist.
Outside the window vaporous clouds cling to our clothes;
With curtains rolled, streams and mountains come into the mir-
ror.
Below the woods the water's noise resounds over talk and laugh-
ter;
Between the peaks colors of trees obscure houses and dwellings.
An immortal's home would not perforce be finer than this abode:
Need we play the pipes, looking toward the azure sky?

NOTES

Title: The Prince of Qi was the younger brother of emperor Xuanzong and
held the post of grand tutor to the crown prince in 721. He was a great patron
of men of letters, among them Wang Wei during his early years in Chang'an.
This poem must have been written before 726, when the prince died.

Line 1:   Red Phoenix Turret was on the central gate (of five) on the south
side of Daming Palace.

Line 2:   The phrase "blue-green mist" (*cui wei*) alludes to the palace's hillside
location, since mountain air was said to be tinged with that hue.

Line 8:   This is an allusion to Jin, crown prince of King Ling of Zhou (r.
571–545 B.C.), generally known as Wangzi (Prince) Qiao. According to the
Records of Immortals (Lie xian zhuan), he liked to play the bamboo pipes and
imitate phoenix cries; he was said to have eventually flown away (to immor-
tality) on a white crane.

POEM

26
(2/12b; I, 28)

Sacred Mt. Hua

The Western Peak emerges from floating clouds,
Greenness amassed in the vast and limpid air.
Joining the sky it seems the color of ink:
4   For a hundred miles a dim and distant void.
Because of it, the white sun turns chill,
And Huayin city is buried in its shade.
Of old, it's heard, when heaven and earth were one,
8   Creation produced the river god Juling.
With his right foot he stepped on the Square Mountain;
With his left hand he pushed forth the Pared Peak.
Heaven and earth then suddenly split asunder:
12   The great river flowed to the eastern main.
Then the western sacred peak was fashioned,
Strong and grand to guard the capital of Qin.
Our great ruler has reigned for several years:
16   His perfect virtue embraces all living things.
The god on high awaits his official decree;
The Gold Sky king longs to greet him with respect.
Spirits expect imperial favor to last:
20   Why sacrifice only on Mts. Yun and Ting?

NOTES

Title: This was the westernmost of the five sacred peaks, located in Shaanxi. The other four were Tai (east) in Shandong, Heng (south) in Hunan, Heng (north) in Hebei, and Song (central) in Henan.

Line 8:   According to legend, Mt. Hua and Mt. Shouyang facing it were once a single mountain until the god Juling stepped in its center to allow the Yellow River to continue its eastward flow.

Line 9:   I have selected the variant "mountain" (shan) in place of "to stop" (zhi).

Line 18:   The Gold Sky king was the resident spirit of Mt. Hua.

Line 20:   Yunyun and Tingting were two mountains on which ancient rulers had offered sacrifices. This poem was probably written in 730, when officials and residents from the Mt. Hua area petitioned emperor Xuanzong to perform the sacrificial rites to heaven and earth on that peak; he declined.

POEM
27

Harmonizing with the Poem of the Duke of Jin, Vice-President of the Department of State, "Following the Imperial Retinue to the Warm Springs"

> The emperor is favoring Xinfeng with a visit:
> Flags and banners fly east of the river Wei.
> Cold mountains enclosed by the palace guard,
4   A warm valley amid a city of screens.
> He offers jade at the Altar of Gathered Immortals
> And burns incense in the Taiyi Palace.
> Going out for a journey he meets a tender of horses;
8   After the hunt he has "something that is not a bear."
> The great minister transforms through inaction;
> Our brilliant era is just like ancient times.
> The auspicious fungus has three purple blossoms
12   And grains displayed in a myriad cartloads are red.
> Royal rituals honor Confucian teachings;
> Imperial soldiers scorn the glories of war.
> Strategies are in the hands of a wise man;
16   Poems are composed by a doyen of letters.
> This censorate official has nothing to correct
> And is still unskilled at presenting poems.
> I shall long sing Jifu's song of praise
20   And morning and evening admire his stately air.

NOTES

Title: Li Linfu, who replaced Zhang Jiuling as chief minister to the emperor in 736, was enfeoffed as duke of the state of Jin in the fifth month of 737. In the eighth month of 742, when this poem was written, he was named Vice-President on the Left of the Department of Affairs of State (*shangshu zuopuye*).

Line 7: This is an allusion to a passage in the *Zhuangzi* (*Xu Wugui*, 66/24/26): The Yellow Emperor (a mythical ruler) was on a journey with six other sages when they lost their way. They came upon a young boy tending horses and were amazed to hear that he knew the exact location of their destination. The Yellow Emperor then asked him if he also knew how to deal with the world, and the boy responded: "As for dealing with the world, how is it different from tending horses? It's just a matter of eliminating what harms the horses—that's all."

Line 8:   This comes from a story in Gan Bao's (ca. A.D.300) *Records of Enquiries into Spirits (Sou shen ji)* about King Wen, the founder of the Zhou dynasty (twelfth century B.C.), who before going hunting had been told by a diviner that he would catch a quarry that was neither dragon nor bear. He came upon a certain Lü Wang fishing north of the Wei River, realized that the old gentleman was his "catch," and took Lü back with him in his carriage.

Line 9:   "Inaction" (*wu wei*) is the Taoist principle of allowing things to take their natural course without acting upon them, thereby ensuring that nothing will be left undone.

Line 11:   The *lingzhi*, a kind of purplish fungus (*fomes japonicus*), was associated with nobility and immortality; its appearance was regarded as an auspicious omen.

Line 18:   "Presenting" or "displaying poems" (*chen shi*) refers to the ancient dictum that ministers should collect and set out the poems of the people in order to gauge their sentiments.

Line 20:   This is an allusion to the concluding lines from a "Greater Elegance" (*da ya*) in the *Classic of Poetry* (poem no. 260), written by Yin Jifu in praise of Zhong Shanfu, advisor to King Xuan of Zhou (r. 827–782 B.C.):

> Jifu has made this song,
> Stately like a clear air.
> Zhong Shanfu has long harbored cares:
> May this song console his heart.

POEM

28   (10/1a; I, 173)

Written at Imperial Command to Harmonize with His Majesty's Spring-Detaining Poem, "Spring View in the Rain," on the Arcade from Penglai Hall to Xingqing Palace

The Wei River follows its bent and winds by the Qin frontier;
The Yellow Mountains slope as of old around the Han palace.
The emperor's carriage emerges from distant Immortal Gate's willows.

On the covered walkway he turns to look at the Imperial Park's
    flowers.
Amid the clouds the sovereign city: twin phoenix turrets.
In the rain, spring trees: ten thousand people's homes.
Spring's glory suits the season for issuing wise decrees—
It is not a royal excursion that prizes the beauty of things.

NOTES

Title: A "spring-detaining" (*liu chun*) poem was written to celebrate the glories of spring and lament the passing of the season. The arcade mentioned was a covered walkway linking the three Penglai halls of Daming Palace, situated along the northern wall of Chang'an, to the Xingqing Palace on the eastern citywall. The former palace had been constructed during the early years of the Tang dynasty and the latter by emperor Xuanzong himself.

Line 2:   This Han palace was built by emperor Hui near the Yellow Mountains in Shaanxi in 193 B.C.

POEM
29
(11/4b; I, 200)

Written at Imperial Command to Harmonize with His Majesty's Poem, "At the End of Spring, Bidding Farewell to the Assembled Court Emissaries on Their Return to Their Commanderies"

Ten thousand states revere Zhou's honored capital;
Robes and caps bow to the jade-tasseled crown.
The jade carriage greets the lofty guests,
4   And with golden tallies bids farewell to the lords.
At the farewell feast, wine is poured by the three ministries;
Lifting their curtains they go toward the nine provinces.
Willow catkins fly above the road,
8   And the sheen of sophora trees shades the canal.
They came to taste the celestial happiness
And return to share the Han ruler's cares.
Imperial brilliance resembles the Milky Way,
12   And stars hanging down fill the central domain.

NOTES

Title: Officials with the rank of governor-general, prefect, and above re-
turned to the capital from their posts once a year on the twenty-fifth day of
the tenth lunar month to report to and receive orders from the emperor.

Line 1:   According to the Mao commentary on the *Classic of Poetry*, "honored
Zhou" (*zong Zhou*) is a term for Hao, the capital of Zhou, as in the eighth
stanza of poem no. 192, a "Lesser Elegance" (*xiao ya*):

> The majestic honored capital of Zhou:
> Si of Bao has destroyed it.

Line 2:   "Robes and caps" is a common synecdoche for officials, as are "jade-
tasseled crown" and the "jade carriage" (line 3) for the emperor.

Line 5:   The "three ministries" were the major organs of the central govern-
ment: the Department of Affairs of State (*shangshu sheng*), the Department of
the Imperial Chancellery (*menxia sheng*), and the Department of the Grand
Imperial Secretariat (*zhongshu sheng*). The translations of the names of these
bureaus are taken from Pulleyblank's "Glossary," in *The Background of the Re-
bellion of An Lu-shan*, pp. 222–26.

Line 6:   Both the "nine provinces" and the "Middle Provinces" (line 12) refer
to the domains of China.
The phrase "lifting their curtains" alludes to a story in the *History of the Latter
Han*, 31/1112, about an official named Jia Zong, who reprimanded his subor-
dinates for greeting him—according to an ancient ritual—in a carriage with
drawn curtains; only after raising them would they be able to survey the
situation accurately and govern accordingly.

POEM

30   (11/1b; I, 195)

Written at Imperial Command to Harmonize with His Majesty's Poem, "With the Crown Prince and Other Lords on the Third Day of the Third Month at Dragon Pond for the Spring Lustration Festival"

> Since ancient times we have practiced the spring ablution;
> From the new palace the pleasant excursion begins.
> Our brilliant ruler moves in a phoenix sedan;
> 4   The crown prince comes out of the dragon tower.
> His rhymeprose surpasses Prince Chen's achievement,

And cups of wine flow like the river Luo.
Golden men arrive presenting swords,
8 *And painted seabirds leave as boats return.*
Palace turrets float above the park's trees;
The imperial pond reflects the pearl-fringed crown.
The emperor's glory extends to the Milky Way,
12 *And stars hanging down fill the imperial domain.*

NOTES

Title: The Lustration Festival was held by water's edge on the third day of the third lunar month. Originally a ritual connected with purification, fertility, and renewal, by the Tang it had become principally an occasion for springtime outings and merrymaking. For a discussion of its origins, see Derk Bodde, *Festivals in Classical China* (Princeton: Princeton University Press, 1975), pp. 273–88.

Line 5:   According to the *Chronicle of the Three Kingdoms* (Wei, 19/557), upon the completion of the Bronze Sparrow Pavilion in Ye in A.D. 210, the ruler Cao Cao (155–220) asked all present to ascend it and write a *fu* ("rhyme-prose," "prose poem," "exposition") to commemorate the occasion. His son Cao Zhi (192–232), Prince of Chen, picked up a brush and composed one without stopping, thus amazing everyone there.

Line 7:   When King Zhao of Qin (r. 255–250 B.C.) was feasting by the river he saw a golden man emerging from the water with a sword; the latter handed over the weapon to the king, telling him that it would give him hegemony over China. The anecdote is recorded in the *Jin History*, 51/1433.

POEM
31
(11/7a; I, 203)

Written at Imperial Command to Harmonize with His Majesty's Poem, "On the Double Ninth Festival the Ministers and Assembled Officials Offer Their Wishes for Longevity"

Within the four seas there are no untoward affairs;
In autumn's third month the harvest has been abundant.
A hundred officials come together this day
4 *To wish their ruler a life of a myriad years.*

Peony infusions are mixed in golden cauldrons,
And dogwood blossoms inserted in tortoiseshell mats.
The jade hall opens onto the right chamber;
8 *Celestial music stirs the palace bells.*
Imperial willows scatter autumnal shadows,
And citywall crows shake off the dawn mists.
Forever at chrysanthemum festival time
12 *We shall offer Boliang compositions.*

NOTES

Title: For the Double Ninth Festival, see poem 3, title note.

Line 5:   Peony roots were supposed to blend well with the five flavors (sweet, sour, bitter, pungent, and salty), and to possess medicinal properties.

Line 12:   When the Han emperor Wu built the Boliang Tower in the spring of 115 B.C., he invented a new poetic meter of heptasyllabic rhymed lines, which became known as the Boliang style. He started off the composition by writing one verse of poetry, and his ministers were required to contribute verses, one after another, employing the original rhyme.

POEM

32

(10/1b; I, 174)

At Datong Hall a Jade Iris Grew, and There Were Auspicious Clouds by Dragon Pond; the Hundred Officials Observed [These Phenomena] Together; Imperial Kindness Bestowed a Banquet with Music, so I Dared to Write on This Occasion

We wish to laugh at King Wen's singing and feasting at Hao.
From afar we scorn Wu's song written while crossing the Fen.
How can they match the three beauties grown at the Jade Hall?
How could they have had five-colored clouds emerging from Bronze Pond?
Above the paths the Big Dipper pours into goblets of Yao;
In front of the tower Shun's music stirs the south wind's warmth.

We rejoice together that heaven's will accords with the will of men:
May a myriad years, a thousand autumns be granted our august lord.

NOTES

Title: In the third month of 748 a jade iris was said to have grown by the pillars of Datong Hall in Xingqing Palace (on the eastern edge of Chang'an), giving off an eerie glow. It reappeared in the sixth month of 749. Brightly colored clouds in the shapes of dragons, regarded as auspicious omens, were also said to rise frequently from the pond at the palace.

Line 1:   This is an allusion to a poem in the *Classic of Poetry* (no. 221), whose third and fourth lines read: "The king is there in Hao, / Drinking happily." Zhao Diancheng, the annotator of Wang Wei's collection, points out that the poet has erroneously read the lines as a description of King Wen of Zhou, instead of his son King Wu (r. 1122–1115 B.C.). But Zhao also notes that since another Tang poet, Song Zhiwen (656–712), made the same error, it might have been a general misunderstanding of the period.

Line 2:   This refers to a feast following the performance of sacrifices held by the Han emperor Wu while floating on the Fen River, which inspired him to write the poem "Song of the Autumn Wind" (*Qiu feng ci*, included in Shen Deqian, ed., *Fountain of Ancient Poetry*, 1/18b).

Line 4:   The Bronze Pond was located in the Han dynasty palace.

Lines 5–6:   Yao and Shun were both mythical kings. Shun is supposed to have composed a song whose first two lines went: "The warmth of the south wind / Can melt my people's anger" (*Fountain of Ancient Poetry* 1/2a).

POEM

33

(10/8b; I, 185)

Having Received Pardon for My Offense and Been Returned to Office, Humbly Moved by Imperial Kindness I Write My Lowly Thoughts and Present Them to My Superiors

When I suddenly bowed to the Han edict returning my cap of office,

I began to feel the Yin king's bounty in discarding traps and nets.
The sun, compared to the emperor's brilliance, is dimmer still.
If Heaven could equal the ruler's longevity, it were not enough.
Flowers greet the joyous spirit and all know how to smile.
Birds recognize happy hearts and understand how to sing.
I've heard it said that new badges of office from a hundred cities
Have returned to the twin turrets, pendants tinkling together.

NOTES

Title: This poem was written in 758 after Wang Wei was pardoned by the new emperor Suzong (r. 756–63) for having collaborated with the An Lushan rebels.

Line 2:   The legendary founder of the Yin or Shang dynasty, Tang (r. 1766–1753 B.C.), was said to have demonstrated that his benevolence extended even to animals and birds by ordering all traps and nets to be untied on his lands (*Records of the Historian*, 3/95).

POEM
34   (14/6b; I, 265)

While I Was Imprisoned in Puti Monastery, Pei Di Came to See Me. He Spoke of How the Rebels Ordered Music Played at Frozen Emerald Pond; after the Court Musicians Began to Play, Their Tears Fell. I Secretly Recited and Presented This to Pei Di

From ten thousand homes of grieving hearts arises wild smoke.
The hundred officials—when will they again attend court?
Autumn sophora leaves fall within the empty palace.
Next to Frozen Emerald Pond, music from pipes and strings.

NOTES

Title: According to the *Chronicle of Chang'an* (*Chang'an zhi*), Puti Monastery was built during the Sui dynasty (589–618) and was located in the Pingkang section of Chang'an, east of the south gate. The *Old Tang History* biography of Wang Wei gives the monastery name as Pushi.

Pei Di (b. 716), a fellow poet and minor official, was one of Wang Wei's closest friends. Wang Wei's corpus contains 34 poems written to or about his friend, or answered by Pei Di's own poems. The most famous among these are the twenty quatrains of the Wang River Collection (see below, poems 131–50), to which Pei wrote twenty of his own. Wang Wei's "Letter from the Mountains to Pei Di" (18/7b–8a; II, 332) is his most famous prose evocation of the pleasures of life in retreat.

COMMENTARY

This is probably Wang Wei's only poem of political protest, veiled though the criticism may be. It was written not while he was serving the court of the emperor Xuanzong but during his incarceration by the rebels under An Lu-shan in 756, and it may have been partially responsible for the pardon granted him after the suppression of the revolt. The preface which serves as a title provides a spare summary of the background behind its composition. According to the *Miscellaneous Records of Minghuang* [Xuanzong] (*Minghuang zalu*), after entering Chang'an, An Lushan and his soldiers captured the members of the imperial conservatory, the Pear Garden (*Li yuan*), and ordered them to play at a victory banquet for the rebels by Frozen Emerald Pond. The musicians only consented to perform after being threatened with knives, but they could not control their grief. According to the *Recorded Conversations of the Jia Clan* (*Jia shi tanlu*), Pei Di somehow managed to visit Wang Wei in his monastery prison and told him of this event. This work and poem 35 are said to have been recorded on the back of a sūtra by the head abbot, a follower of the Chan patriarch Hongdao named Zhiman, and later circulated to vindicate the poet of charges of voluntary collaboration.

POEM
35
(13/11a; I, 254)

Recited and Again Presented to Pei Di

How can we get to shed the dusty net,
Brush our clothes and leave the worldly din,
To leisurely ply a brambleweed staff
And return to the Peach Blossom Spring?

NOTES

Line 1:   This alludes to the first of a series of five poems by Tao Qian entitled "Returning to the Farm to Dwell' (*Gui yuantian qu*, in Ding Fubao, ed., *The Complete Poems of the Han, Three Kingdoms, Jin, Northern and Southern Dynasties*, II, 605), in which the earlier poet had written: "By mischance I fell into the dusty net / And was thirteen years away from home" (trans. Hightower, *The Poetry of T'ao Ch'ien*, p. 50).

Line 2: "Brushing one's clothes" is an expression denoting the retreat from government service.

Line 3: This alludes to a man named Yuan Xian, one of Confucius' disciples, who appears in the *Zhuangzi* ("Giving Away a Throne," 78/28/44). He used a crude walking stick and was known for his frugal living habits.

Line 4: For the Peach Blossom Spring, see poem 6.

POEM

36

Given to My Paternal Cousin,
Military Supply Official Qiu

> *In younger years I knew little of worldly affairs:*
> *I forced myself to learn to seek fame and power.*
> *But vainly I heard of the years of frisking horses*
> 4 *And suffered for lack of wisdom surpassing others.*
> *As for managing things, have I indulged in mere talk?*
> *In post after post it's not that I haven't been tested.*
> *Since there are few joys that satisfy my nature,*
> 8 *I fear being blamed for going against the times.*
> *In clear winter I see the distant mountains,*
> *The gathered snow, the frozen azure green.*
> *Brightness emerges from the eastern woods*
> 12 *And brings out my thoughts of escaping from the world.*
> *Huilian, you have always had pure tastes;*
> *We have talked in the past of affairs beyond the dust.*
> *I wish to delay the time of my departure:*
> 16 *Yet the flowing years—how they hasten on.*

NOTES

Line 3: This is an allusion to Cai Ze of the Warring States period (403–221 B.C.), a debater who traveled from state to state seeking employment as a political advisor. After meeting with no success, he asked the physiognomer Tang Ju to tell his fortune. When told that he would live for forty-three more years, Cai Ze said that that would give him ample time, among other things, to press his frisking horses forward more quickly, serve rulers, and eat and live well. The story is told in the *Records of the Historian*, 79/2418.

Line 13: Wang Wei addresses his cousin as Xie Huilian (397–433), the talented younger cousin and friend of the poet Xie Lingyun (385–433). His biography is included in the *Song History* (*Song shu* [Peking: Zhonghua, 1974]), 53/1524–25.

POEMS

37–39

(2/10a–11a; I, 24–25)

Playfully Presented to Zhang Yin the Fifth Brother

37.

When you, younger brother, lived on the eastern mountain,
Your heart was still detached indeed.
The sun rose high but you slept on as before;
4   When bells tolled—only then would you eat.
Your hair remained unkempt above the collar,
Books were left unrolled at the head of your bed.
By a clear stream your spirit wandered afar;
8   You would lie down and rest by the empty woods.
Green moss upon the rocks was clean;
Delicate grass beneath the pines was soft.
Outside your window, the sounds of birds at leisure;
12   Before your steps even tigers were good-willed.
Meaningless are the myriad phenomena,
Tranquil is the great and distant void.
Once you realized that all things are the same,
16   You saw the insignificance of being a man.
Looking at you I suddenly feel contented:
Fleeting thoughts are not worth sending along.

NOTE

Title: Zhang Yin was a fellow painter, poet, and calligrapher who held office in the Ministry of Justice.

38.

My brother Zhang has five cartloads of books
And reads them while still living in reclusion.
His brushwork surpasses that of the Grass-Script Sage;
4   Writing poems he makes the Zixu fu look simple.

Behind closed gates beneath the Two Chamber Mountains,
He has lived in retreat for ten years or more.
Just like an old rustic of the wilds,
8   He sometimes follows the fishermen to fish.
Autumn winds each day become more desolate;
The five willows are tall but spare.
Gazing at this I leave the world of men
12   And cross the water toward my thatched hut.
At year's end holding hands together,
There should only be you and I.

NOTES

Line 1:   This is an allusion to a passage in the *Zhuangzi* ("The World," 93/33/
69), which describes Zhuangzi's friend Hui Shi as many-talented and pos-
sessing five cartloads, i.e., a great number, of books.

Line 3:   The "Sage of the Grass-Script" was Zhang Zhi, a famous calligra-
pher of the Latter Han dynasty (A.D. 25–220).

Line 4:   This refers to a rhymeprose (*fu*) by the Han dynasty writer Sima
Xiangru (179–117 B.C.), a masterly work which was supposedly composed
with great difficulty and which brought him to the attention of Emperor Wu;
it is included in the sixth-century *Anthology of Literature*, 7/102–5.

Line 5:   These two mountains, the "Great Chamber" (*Da shi*) and "Little
Chamber" (*Xiao shi*), were located to the east and west, respectively, of the
central sacred peak, Mt. Song, in Henan.

Line 10:   The phrase "five willows" has been associated with a peaceful life
in retreat since Tao Qian called himself "Master of Five Willows" (*Wu liu
xiansheng*) after the trees growing by his country home; see the *Song History*,
93/2286.

39.

Setting traps in wait for hares and rabbits
Or dangling a hook to watch for passing fish
Are only meant to appease your mouth and belly
4   And do not come from a love of peaceful retreat.
In my life I have loved pure tranquility,
A meatless diet, removing passions and dust.
Now you have grown lax and profligate
8   And long to eat the food from nobles' cauldrons.
My house lies at the foot of Southern Mountain:
As movements still I just forget myself.
When among birds I cause them no disturbance,
12   Seeing animals, I treat them all as friends.

Rosy clouds become my companions,
The empty whiteness serves as my attire.
For what reason need you, sir,
16 *Invite me, a Zhen of Gukou?*

NOTE

Line 16: Zheng Pu, whose cognomen was Zizhen, (hence the reference to "Zhen"), was a famous recluse who lived in Gukou (Shaanxi province) during the reign of the Han emperor Cheng (r. 32–6 B.C.) and refused to be pressed into government service.

POEM

40
(4/4a; I, 54)

Farewell to Qiwu Qian on His Return Home after Failing the Examination

Under sage rule there are no recluses:
Brilliant talents all come to serve at court.
This caused you, who dwelled on the eastern mountain,
4 *To be unable to go and pick some ferns.*
Arriving, you found the ruler's gate was distant,
But who should say that "Our Way has failed"?
Yangzi and Huai you crossed at Cold Food time,
8 *In Chang'an and Luoyang you mended spring clothes.*
I will pour some wine at Changdao postillion:
You, my like-mind, are abandoning me.
Soon you will be floating with cassia oar,
12 *And in no time will knock on your brushwood gate.*
Distant trees will accompany the traveler;
A lone citywall faces the dusking glow.
"By chance my counsel has not been followed,"
16 *But do not say that close friends are few.*

NOTES

Title: Qiwu Qian (692–749), cognomen Xiaotong, was a friend and fellow poet who received his *jinshi* ("presented scholar") degree in 726, held several minor posts, and left office for retirement around 742. In some editions of Wang Wei's poetry the title of this poem is simply "Farewell" (*Songbie*).

Line 3:   This refers to Xie An of the Jin dynasty (265–419), who left govern-
ment service in the capital to retire to Mt. Linan in present-day Zhejiang, on
the east coast of China (*Jin History*, 79/2072–77).

Line 4:   This is an allusion to Bo Yi and Shu Qi, two men who were outraged
when the Zhou ruler overthrew the Yin or Shang dynasty during the twelfth
century B.C. Vowing to refuse to eat the grain of Zhou, they retired to Shou-
yang Mountain, subsisting on ferns until they died of starvation (*Records of
the Historian*, 61/2123).

Line 5:   This is a euphemistic reference to Qiwu's failure to pass the *jinshi*
examination.

Line 6:   Confucius is said to have once asked his discipline Zilu: "The *Classic
of Poetry* [poem no. 234] says: 'We are neither rhinoceros nor tiger / Yet we
live on the desert wilds.' Has our Way failed?" (*Records of the Historian*, 47/
1931).

Line 7:   The Cold Food Festival was a period from the 105th to the 107th day
after the winter solstice, during which no food was to be cooked.

Line 15:   This is a quotation from the *Zuo zhuan*, a commentary on the *Spring
and Autumn Annals* (*Chun qiu*), a chronicle for the state of Lu said to have
been written by Confucius. In the records of Duke Wen, thirteenth year, Rao
Chao of Qin bids farewell to Sui Hui, who is being successfully taken back to
serve the state of Jin: "[As he was going], Jaou Chaou (an officer of Ts'in)
presented to him a whip, saying, 'Do not say that there are no men in Ts'in.
[You get away] because my counsel has not at this time been followed.'"
Trans. James Legge, *The Chinese Classics*, Vol. 5: *The Ch'un Ts'ew with the Tso
Chuen*, p. 264.

Line 16:   "Close friends" literally reads "understanding the music" (*zhi yin*),
an allusion to the friendship between Yu Boya and Zhong Ziqi. Whenever
the former played his zither, the latter would immediately know what kinds
of images were being evoked. When Ziqi died, Boya broke his strings be-
cause he no longer had anyone who really understood his music. "One who
understands the music" thus means an intimate friend.

POEM

41   (3/11a; I, 46)

Farewell to Collator Qiwu Qian on His Leaving Office to Return East of the Yangzi

> For long without success in a brilliant reign,
> Released from service, I resemble you.
> What heaven ordains you face without repining:

4   *Your demeanor in life is as before.*
     I think of you, brushing your clothes to leave:
     Within the four seas where will your travels end?
     The autumn sky is clear for a myriad miles;
8   *At sunset, the limpid river is empty.*
     Long and endless is this clear night—
     You beat time on the gunwale beneath the bright moon.
     You will blend your light beside the fish and birds,
12   *Tranquil amid the clusters of rushes and reeds.*
     What use in sojourning during glorious times?
     Receding temples turn white as tumbleweeds.
     Stubborn and dull, I know nothing of human affairs,
16   *Isolated, remote from imperial wisdom.*
     Even if I were worthy of selection,
     Who could be impartial about it?
     I too shall leave right now and go,
20   *Return home to plow and be an old farmer.*

NOTES

Line 5:   "Brushing one's clothes" denotes retreat from government service.

Line 11:   This alludes to a passage in the fourth section (*zhang*) of the *Dao de jing*: "Harmonize with its light; share its dust."

Line 14:   I am reading "white" (*bai*) for "day" (*ri*).

POEM

42   (7/5a; I, 121)

Written in Reply to He
the Fourth's Gift of a Cloth Cap

A rustic cap conveys your generous kindness;
This gift is worth as much as finest gold.
Enjoying this object of secluded life,
I can calm my reclusive official heart.
During morning levée I hang it up for awhile,
After evening bathing come pin it on again.
Sitting I sense the distance of din and dust
And long for you to enter the woods with me.

NOTE

Line 2:   "Finest gold" (literally, "double gold" [*jian jin*]) was a superior grade
of gold worth twice as much as regular gold. The *locus classicus* for this phrase
is *Mencius* II.B.3.

POEM

43
(10/8a; I, 184–85)

In Response to Policy Reviewer Guo

By the twin gates' tall tower, clouds and lingering glow:
Peach and plum trees are dense and dark; willow catkins fly.
Inside the palace, a distant bell: in the offices it is late.
Within the ministry, calling birds: officials now are scarce.
Mornings, waving jade pendants, you rush to the golden hall;
Evenings, receiving imperial edicts, you call at the carved palace
*   doors.*
I would try to follow you, but there is no way not to age—
And soon because of illness I'll discard my court robes.

NOTE

Title: Guo Chenggu served as Policy Reviewer in the Imperial Chancellery,
a post Wang Wei also occupied from 754–55, although the poem's date of
composition is unknown.

POEMS

44–49
(5/2a–4a; I, 72–75)

Six Casually Written Poems

44.

In the state of Chu there was a crazy man,
Ignorant, without a thought in his mind.
With unkempt hair, wearing no cap or belt,
4   *He walked and sang on the southern path.*
Confucius once spoke with him,
But ren and yi he could never praise.

He never once agreed to question heaven,
8   And why should he need to hit the clogs?
He laughed again at those fern-picking men—
Why did they run so far away?

NOTES

Line 1:   The "crazy man" was Lu Tong, cognomen Jieyu, who lived in the southern state of Chu during the Spring and Autumn Period. He feigned madness to avoid serving under the government of King Zhao, of whom he disapproved, and thus wore no official's "cap or belt." The story of his refusing to speak to Confucius (lines 5–6) is given in the *Analects* (*Lun yu*), XVIII.5.

Line 6:   *Ren* and *yi*, often translated as "benevolence" and "righteousness," respectively, are two key Confucian concepts, used here primarily to represent the entire orthodox way of thought.

Line 7:   This is an allusion to the "Heavenly Questions" (*Tian wen*) of the *Songs of Chu*, 3/145–99, which appear to be a group of questions and riddles about, among other matters, the origins of the universe; they are traditionally attributed to the poet Qu Yuan (343?–278 B.C.) and have been translated by Hawkes, pp. 45–58.

Line 8:   This refers to a legend, recorded in the Jin dynasty *Records of Emperors* (*Diwang shiji*), that during the reign of the mythical sage king Yao, there was such happiness and peace that a group of old men played a game (*ji rang*) similar to horsehoes which involved tossing one clog-shaped piece of wood to hit another, and sang the following song:

> We work when the sun rises.
> And rest when the sun sets
> We dig a well in order to drink
> And plow the fields in order to eat.
> What force does our lord exert on us?

Line 9:   For "fern-picking men," see poem 40, line 4n.

45.

In a farmhouse lives an old man
With drooping white hair, in his humble retreat.
Sometimes when finished with chores in the fields,
4   He summons his neighbors with a jug of wine.
Noisily beneath the thatched eaves
They sit around and then stand up again.
Coarse woolen clothes are not too mean for him
8   And garden sunflower seeds delicacy enough indeed.
If he stirs, it's just to bring up sons and grandsons;
He has never once gone to the city market.
The Five Emperors and Three Kings

12   *Since ancient times have been called Sons of Heaven.*
    Compare using arms with polite abdication—
    Which way is right after all?
    If wishes gained make up happiness,
16   *How then can a rustic farm be scorned?*
    For now I'll set my mind at ease and go,
    And travel on 'til all my teeth are gone.

NOTE

Line 11: These refer to mythical sage rulers. There are various lists of the Five Emperors, but they invariably include Yao and Shun; the Three Kings were the founders of the Xia, Shang (Yin), and Zhou dynasties—Yu, Tang, and Wen. The following two lines of the poem allude to the two ways in which these sage rulers supposedly succeeded each other: the Five Emperors were said to have yielded the throne to one another peacefully, while the Three Kings used arms.

46.

Day and night I see the Taihang Mountains:
Though pondering, I have not yet departed.
Should you ask me why this is so—
4   *I am entangled in the worldly net.*
My younger sister grows older every day,
And my brothers have not yet chosen wives.
The family is poor, our income but a pittance,
8   *Nor are we used to putting things away.*
How many times have I longed to arise and fly,
Then hesitated, looking at them again.
Sun Deng at Long Whistle Tower
12   *Had his retreat amid bamboo and pine.*
How far does it lie from here?
But friends and family stand right in the road.
The taint of passions daily grows more weak;
16   *Stillness of mind grows firmer every day.*
Soon I shall suddenly depart—
Why wait until the evening of my years?

NOTES

Line 1: The Taihang range extends from Shanxi through Henan and Hebei provinces.

Line 11: Sun Deng was a third-century A.D. hermit who retired to Mt. Sumen in Henan. He and his friend Ruan Ji (210–63) were particularly adept at the whistle or *xiao*, a kind of Taoist breathing exercise. Sun was said to be able to emit a *xiao* which sounded like a phoenix call. See the *Jin History*, 49/1362.

Line 15: The terms in this line and the next both come from Buddhism; the aim is to extinguish the "taint" of desires and passions and to achieve stillness of mind through meditation.

47.

Tao Qian let free his true spirit:
By nature he was rather fond of wine.
But once he quit his government office
4   *His family was too poor for him to have it.*
On the ninth day of the ninth month
Chrysanthemum flowers filled his hands in vain.
Within his heart he secretly wondered
8   *If someone would send him some or not.*
A white-robed man carrying jug and goblet
Did give some after all to the old man.
For a time he delighted in pouring it out—
12   *How could he ask if they were pints or gallons?*
Shaking his clothes amid the wilds and fields,
"Today," he sighed, "there isn't any more!"
Confusedly losing his sense of direction,
16   *He could not keep his bamboo rainclothes on.*
Stumbling and falling, forcing himself to walk,
With drunken song he went back to Five Willows.
About life's affairs he never once inquired:
20   *Would he feel ashamed before his wife at home?*

NOTE

Line 1: The poet Tao Qian, who dubbed himself "Master of Five Willows" (see poem 38, line 10n), was well known for descriptions of his life in the country as a poor gentleman farmer and for his love of wine. Although he served for some time in government office, he refused to observe the proper formalities in the face of a visiting superior and left his post. He has three biographies in the dynastic histories: *Song History*, 93/2286ff; *History of the Southern Dynasties* (*Nan shi* [Peking: Zhonghua, 1975]), 75/1856ff; and *Jin History*, 94/2460ff.

48.

The girl from Zhao can pluck a many-stringed harp
And perform the dances of Handan.
Her husband is a frivolous fellow,

4   *Fighting cocks while serving the lord of Qi.*
       His gold buys courtesans' songs and smiles—
       He never bothers to count his cash any more.
       He comes and goes with the Xus and Shis,
8   *Their noble gates filled with four-horse carriages.*
       In the guest-house is a Confucian scholar,
       A lofty, dignified product of Zou and Lu.
       He has studied books for thirty years
12   *But at his waist still lacks the tassels of office.*
       He must wear the teachings of the sages:
       A whole life of poverty and pain.

NOTES

Line 1:   The *konghou* was a musical instrument with several strings, although the exact number (7 or 23 or 25) is in dispute.

Line 2:   Handan was the capital city of the ancient kingdom of Zhao (in present-day Hebei).

Line 4:   This is an allusion to a passage in the *Zhuangzi* ("Mastering Life" [*Da sheng*, 50/19/46]) about a king of Qi who raised cocks for fighting.

Line 7:   Xu Bo was the father of the Han emperor Xuan's (r. 73–48 B.C.) wife, and Shi Gao was also related to the emperor by marriage. Their names are used to denote powerful aristocratic families in general.

Line 10:   Zou and Lu were the native kingdoms of Mencius and Confucius, respectively, and are therefore associated with Confucian learning.

49.

Old age has come; too lazy to write poems,
I have old age as my sole companion.
In this age mistakenly a poet,
In an earlier life I must have been a painter.
Unable to discard lingering habits,
I am somehow known by people of this world.
My name and cognomen really are both correct:
But this heart still does not know.

NOTES

Line 3:   I am reading "this age" (*dang dai*) for "former world" (*su shi*).

Line 7:   Wang Wei is alluding to his given name (*ming*), Wei, and his cognomen (*zi*), Mojie, which together make up the Chinese transliteration of the name of the Indian Buddhist sage Vimalakīrti.

POEM
50   (4/7a; I, 58–59)

On Leaving Monk Wengu of the Mountains;
also Shown to My Younger Brother Jin

> Removing hempen clothes to ascend the celestial court,
> I leave my master to meet wise men of the age.
> Not only the man within the mountains—
> 4   I'm even betraying the moon above the pines.
> In the past we strolled and rested together,
> Arriving at the edge of rosy clouds.
> We would open a window above the Ying's north bank
> 8   And lie and watch the flying birds disappear.
> We liked to dine while leaning on a flat rock,
> And often stopped before cascading streams.
> In times of order one seldom goes into reclusion;
> 12   When the Way prevails how can one leave the world?
> My younger brother holds a lofty position;
> My elder kinsman has received the tonsure.
> Just sprinkle and sweep in front of your brushwood gate:
> 16   When I have free time, I'll pass by and knock.

Notes to Chapter Three

1. Wu Qiao (ca. 1660), *Weilu shihua, Congshu jicheng*, vol. 2609 (Shanghai: Shangwu, 1935), 3/74.

2. For a discussion of the conventions of Tang court poetry, see Stephen Owen, *The Poetry of the Early T'ang* (New Haven: Yale University Press, 1977), esp. pp. 3–13, 234–55, 425–28. Indeed, throughout his study Owen argues quite persuasively that those features which I have singled out as the hallmark of Wang Wei's style were in fact shared by all Tang poets working within the tradition of court poetry. Nevertheless, I remain convinced that the pervasiveness of, for example, the impulse toward balance and integration in Wang Wei's work as a whole is distinctive and derives from more deeply rooted philosophical and religious convictions.

3. The poem is included in Ding Fubao, ed., *Quan Han Sanguo Jin Nan Bei Chao shi*, II, 607.

4. The quotation from Confucius is included in the *Analects* (*Lun yu*), XVIII.8.

FOUR

Buddhist Poems

ZHUANGZI'S refusal to make distinctions, which underlies Wang Wei's resolution of the apparent conflict between retreat and engagement, is one key Taoist notion that found its counterpart in the Buddhist thought imported from India into China. Introduced sometime during the first century A.D., Buddhism offered other similarities in both doctrine and practice which undoubtedly facilitated its acceptance and eventual sinicization. Since Wang Wei was a devout Buddhist, an awareness of certain of the fundamental concepts of this religion should lead to a deeper understanding of much of his work and will also confirm our sense of the unitary nature of his poetic universe. In this introduction, therefore, I will be discussing those ideas which came to enjoy great currency in China by the Tang dynasty; some of the issues are rather abstruse, but they should nevertheless be examined because of their relevance to Wang Wei's poetry.

Before we look at the many similarities between Buddhism and Taoism, it should be noted that there were equally crucial differences between the two bodies of thought. Perhaps most importantly, Buddhism in India evolved as a systematic theology, with an elaborate cosmology, extensive pantheon of holy figures, and large body of scriptures or sūtras. A clear distinction existed between the secular and clerical realms, and monasteries were definite centers of religious activity. Although both Taoism and Buddhism recognized reality as an eternal flux, they developed opposing responses; the former encouraged an attitude of equanimity and acceptance, whereas the latter was characterized by an intense pessimism, asceticism, and general sense of renunciation. Taoism, as we saw in Zhuangzi's refusal to discriminate between right and wrong, was fundamentally amoral. In Buddhism, on the contrary, morality was central, and various sects sought to define the proper practices, such as meditation, chanting, prayer, copying of the sūtras, good works, or just plain faith, that would guarantee enlightenment and deliverance. Furthermore, the Mahāyāna ("Greater Vehicle") school which, rather than the Theravāda ("Elders") or Hīnayāna ("Lesser Vehicle"), was adopted by the Chinese, developed the ideal figure of the bodhisattva, who altruistically postponed his own individual salvation in order to save others. The main thrust of Buddhism, in sum, was otherworldly—a constant effort to escape from the phenomenal world of change and suffering—saṁsāra—into the freedom and changelessness of nirvāṇa.

Nevertheless, most of these differences emerge only when we compare Taoism to Theravāda Buddhism, rather than the Mahāyāna thought which overwhelmingly appealed to the Chinese. Heinrich Dumoulin speculates that Mahāyāna was inspired by a more optimistic and "naturalistic apprehension of the world," so that China actually offered it more congenial ground for development than India, where people were "inhibited by their agonizing struggle for salvation."[1] Mahāyāna Buddhism, of course, was far from a monolithic entity. By Wang Wei's time, certainly, in addition to Chan (or Zen), whose influence we have already seen in later literary theory, there were three other major sects or "traditions" (*zong*) which enjoyed varying degrees of popularity: Tiantai, Huayan, and Pure Land. Each of these four groups revered different sūtras and historical holy figures; held different notions of the Buddha, religious authority, and the nature of enlightenment; drew on varying social bases for support; and maintained often mutually contradictory attitudes to faith, doctrines, scholarship, language, intellectual activity, and the master-student relationship.

Yet considered in general, Mahāyāna Buddhism did advocate several practices in common with Taoism. In his *Buddhism in China* Kenneth K. S. Ch'en notes that some superficial similarities included: worship without sacrifices and a certain amount of emphasis on concentration; meditation; breath control; abstinence; suppression of the passions; purity of thought and actions; and the avoidance of luxury. Most of the Chinese who helped translate the sūtras from the Sanskrit were Taoists. Moreover, the Taoists formulated the doctrine of *hua hu* ("conversion of the barbarians" or "to a barbarian"), according to which Laozi, the Taoist sage to whom the authorship of the *Dao de jing* is traditionally attributed but whose historicity has been questioned, is said to have left China to go to India, where he converted the "barbarians" and became the Buddha. The Buddha, then, was but an incarnation of Laozi. All of these factors, according to Ch'en, contributed to the rapid spread of Buddhism throughout China, because it could be regarded as but a variant of the indigenous way of thought (pp. 48–50).

Although recognition of essential differences between the two gradually overcame this cultural appropriation, Taoism and Buddhism, in addition to these external similarities, shared several common beliefs. The following four doctrines were of particular importance: nondiscrimination; universal *śūnyatā* or emptiness; the simultaneous transcendence and immanence of the absolute; and the ultimate inadequacy of language. These notions are all, of course, interrelated and all ultimately focus on some crucial epistemological questions.

First of all, just as several passages in the *Zhuangzi* advocate the rejection of all distinctions, so a Buddhist parallel to this nondiscrimination can be found in the notion of *prajñā*, "wisdom," the highest of the six *pāramitās* or "perfections" (literally, "ways to reach the other shore," i.e., enlightenment). In various Mahāyāna texts *prajñā* is defined as a kind of nondual, intuitive cognition, where subject and object, the knower and the known, coincide. It transcends the narrow divisiveness of speculative reason. As T.R.V. Murti phrases it:

> Only when we look at things from a distance, through the mediation of concepts and viewpoints, is there the possibility of discrepancy between what exists and our apprehension of it. Reason works through differentiation and distinctions. . . . In the Intuition of the Absolute there is not the consciousness of realisation; for, that would militate against the purity and fullness of intuition. To be self-conscious of the thing known, we must stand aside and away from it, distinguish it from ourselves and even contrast our present knowledge with our previous state of non-knowing. This is only possible in a discursive form of apprehension.[2]

Prajñā was formulated as the culmination of a rigorous negative dialectic by the second-century-A.D. Indian Buddhist philosopher Nāgārjuna, whose treatise, *Mādhyamika-kārikās*, was brought to China two centuries later and influenced both the Tiantai and Chan traditions. Nāgārjuna posits that there are four possible views on any subject: being, nonbeing, affirmation, and denial. By means of a series of negations he reaches a point where neither existence nor nonexistence is affirmed or denied; instead, all conceptual thought processes and necessarily one-sided views are transcended. He and the Chinese monk Jizang (549–623) developed this into a theory of "double truth" (absolute and mundane), where negations occur in three stages. First, affirmation of being is countered by affirmation of nonbeing. Then, affirmation of either being or nonbeing is opposed by denial of both being and nonbeing. And finally, the dialectic ends when either affirmation or denial of both being and nonbeing leads to its opposite, neither affirmation nor denial of being and nonbeing. "Thus, in a manner curiously reminiscent of Hegelian dialectics, the highest level of truth is to be reached through a series of successive negations of negation, until nothing remains to be either affirmed or denied."[3]

The nondual knowledge of *prajñā* embraces all alternatives and sees things in their essential *śūnyatā*. This term is generally translated as "emptiness" or "the void," but it does not involve such concepts as nothingness, annihilation, unoccupied space, or absence, as we might expect. The root of the world is *śūnya*, which means "swollen" and thus, appropriately, paradoxically suggests both emptiness and fullness at the same time. Technically, *śūnyatā* refers to the Mahāyāna Buddhist doctrine that because all phenomena arise from various causes and conditions in accordance with the principle of dependent origination (*pratītya-samutpāda*), exist only in relation to each other, and are constantly changing, they have no permanent selfhood (*svabhāva*) and are therefore "empty." Even the self, for example, is but a temporary aggregate of five *skandhas* or "heaps": form, feelings, perceptions, impulses, and consciousness.[4]

This emptiness or *śūnyatā* is the absolute truth, the ultimate reality which transcends all reasoning and particular viewpoints and about which nothing can be posited. And logically, it must also deny itself any fixed existence or selfhood. Thus in the sūtra supposedly spoken by Vimalakīrti, the layman who was a friend of the Buddha Śākyamuni, we read that a sick bodhisattva can cure himself by avoiding all such dualities as subject and object or ego and nirvāṇa, through the practice of impartiality: "What is impartiality? It means equality (of all contraries e.g.) ego and nirvāṇa. Why is this so? Because both ego and nirvāṇa are void [*śūnya*]. Why are both void? Because they exist only by names which have no independent nature of their own." Vimalakīrti goes on to warn that any kind of reifying idea of emptiness must also be rejected: "When you achieve this equality you are free from all illnesses but there remains the conception of voidness [*śūnyatā*] which also is an illusion and should be wiped out as well."[5] As Garma C. C. Chang summarizes it:

> The Absolute Emptiness is a thorough negation of everything, includ-
> ing itself, for Śūnyatā itself must also be negated if it is a genuine Emp-
> tiness. . . . If we assert Emptiness, and regard it in any way as existent,
> we then repudiate our own stand and admit the absurdity of all we
> have said previously. . . . Even Emptiness itself is empty and without
> a selfhood. This is called the Emptiness of Emptiness (Śūnyatā Śūn-
> yatā).[6]

When Wang Wei employs the word "empty" (*kong*, the Chinese trans-
lation of *śūnyatā*), then, we should consider possible resonances of all
these ontological and epistemological concerns.

The Buddhist notion of *śūnyatā* found its counterpart during the fourth-century-A.D. neo-Taoist revival of interest in the *Dao de jing*, the *Zhuangzi*, and the *Classic of Changes*. The cultured elite of southern China who, because of the collapse of the Han empire, no longer could engage in government service, turned to the passivity of Taoism. Cultivating the art of "pure conversation" (*qing tan*), they indulged in much cosmological and metaphysical speculation, out of which arose the idea that nonbeing or *wu* was the basis of the universe. After coming into contact with the literature and sūtras on *prajñā* and *śūnyatā* then circulating, they immediately identified the Buddhist notion of *śūnyatā* with *wu*. E. Zürcher describes this affinity as "almost predestined":

> According to neo-Taoism, all phenomena, all change and diversity, in short all "Being," is manifested and sustained by a principle which is unlimited, unnameable, unmoving, one and undiversified, and which therefore is referred to as "Non-Being." The basic problem is the relation between this "fundamental Non-Being" and "final Being." They do not form a pair of mutually exclusive opposites. In the words of the *Tao te ching*, "they emerge together, but have different names," and the insight into this fundamental unity of the phenomenal world and "Non-Being" is, again according to the *Tao te ching*, "the Mystery of Mysteries, the gate of all wonders." It cannot be expressed in words, but is intuitively realized by the Sage in silent contemplation. It is easy to see that the Mahāyāna doctrine of "Universal Emptiness," once it was introduced into the inner circle of literati, was almost predestined to merge with this indigenous doctrine of "Emptiness and Non-Being."[7]

Zürcher's mention here of the neo-Taoists' insight into the "fundamental unity of the phenomenal world and 'Non-Being'" brings us to the third major doctrine shared by both Taoism and Buddhism, that of the absolute's simultaneous transcendence of, and immanence in, the particular. This notion, of course, is closely linked to the principles of nonduality and dialectical embracing of contradictions already discussed. In the *Zhuangzi*, for example, there are several descriptions of the Tao as formless, actionless, ungraspable, inexhaustible, independent, unnameable, and beyond all categories of space and time. The following passage is a typical example:

> The Way has its reality and its signs but is without action or form. You can hand it down but you cannot receive it; you can get it but you cannot see it. It is its own source, its own root. Before Heaven and earth existed it was there, firm from ancient times. It gave spirituality to the spirits and to God; it gave birth to Heaven and to earth. It exists beyond the highest point, and yet you cannot call it lofty; it exists beneath the limit of the six directions, and yet you cannot call it deep. It was born before Heaven and earth, and yet you cannot say it has been

there for long; it is earlier than the earliest time, and yet you cannot call it old. ("The Great and Venerable Teacher" [*Da zong shi*, 16/6/29], trans. Watson, p. 81)

Yet Zhuangzi also engages in a famous dialogue with a Master Dong-guo, who asks him where the Tao exists. The philosopher responds, "There's no place it doesn't exist," but Master Dongguo insists that he be more specific. When Zhuangzi then answers that "It is in the ant," his questioner doubts that the Way could be found in such a lowly creature, whereupon Zhuangzi states that it is in the panic grass, tiles and shards, and finally, "It is in the piss and shit" ("Knowledge Wandered North" [*Zhi bei you*, 59/22/43]; trans. Watson, pp. 240–41). The Tao, then, can neither be limited to nor separated from phenomena. Though invisible, it manifests itself in the concrete.

In Mahāyāna Buddhist writings this concept expresses itself as a mystical identity of opposites, of the absolute *śūnyatā* and concrete particulars. The *Heart Sūtra*, for example, states that "form is empti-ness and the very emptiness is form; emptiness does not differ from form, form does not differ from emptiness; whatever is form, that is emptiness, whatever is emptiness, that is form, the same is true of feelings, perceptions, impulses and consciousness."[8] Here the five *skandhas*, which constitute the self, are identified with their opposite, the emptiness which transcends individuality. In his commentary on this passage Edward Conze explains that these statements, by equat-ing a term with its negation ("A is what A is not," or "what A is not, that is A"), "obviously violate the logical principle of contradiction." By going through a series of assertions and denials which reveal the "identity of Yes and No" as "the secret of emptiness," logic defeats itself:

> Aristotle pointed out in his "Metaphysics" that the rejection of the prin-ciple of contradiction must lead to the conclusion that "all things are one." This seemed to him manifestly absurd. Here, conversely, the in-sight into the oneness of all is the great goal, and only by contradictions can it be attained. (p. 84)

This insight, of course, is difficult to achieve, and perhaps as an expedient device to resolve a persistent yet delusory tension between the mundane and the transcendental, Nāgārjuna and Jizang devel-oped the system of "double truth" mentioned above. Although pos-iting an ultimate identity between the two realms, these thinkers es-tablished a temporary distinction between a level of absolute truth (*paramārtha-satya*) and one of conventional truth (*sàmvrti-satya*). The former is that intuitive cognition of the real without the distortions of thought categories or points of view, while the latter is only truth so-called for empirical purposes, the conventional realm of reasoning and relativity, where distinctions may exist between subject and object or saṁsāra and nirvāṇa, and A may equal A after all. But this separation is created only for the purpose of transcending itself: because the Mādhyamika system employs a negative dialectic, it must start with that which is to be denied, and this doctrine of double truth is but a means to an end. Murti writes that there is, therefore,

> no difference whatever between Nirvāṇa and Saṁsāra; Noumenon and Phenomenon are not two separate sets of entities, nor are they two states of the same thing. . . . The absolute looked at through the thought-forms of constructive imagination is the empirical world; and conversely, the absolute is the world viewed *sub specie aeternitatis*, without these distorting media of thought. (p. 274)

The Mādhyamika system was particularly influential in the early development of Chan Buddhism, which is also, significantly, the one tradition most often associated with Taoism. Thus we hear an early Chan master giving advice to a student in familiar terminology (*mādhyamika*, literally, means the "middle way"): "Do not abide in the extremity of the Void, but illumine the non-being in the being. It is neither out of the Void nor out of being. Void and being are not conceived of as two. This is called the Middle Way."[9] And the Sixth Chan Patriarch Huineng (638–713) speaks in paradoxical verse to his disciples of the immanence of the transcendental Buddhist law or Dharma:

> From the outset Dharma has been in the world;
> Being in the world it transcends the world.
> Hence do not seek the transcendental world outside,
> By discarding the present world itself.[10]

The Huayan sect, whose major scriptures, the *Avataṁsaka Sūtras*, postulated the interpenetration of particularity and universality such that any particle of dust could contain the entire universe, was also influential in fostering the Chan appreciation of natural phenomena. Thus Dumoulin writes that

> The attitude toward nature peculiar to Zen disciples draws its nourishment from the cosmotheistic world-view set forth so magnificently in the *Avatamsaka Sutras*. The religiously rooted conviction of the divine unity of the universe permits the search for the fulfillment of one's own deepest being by fusion with nature. (p. 41)

But Chan Buddhism gradually moved away from its speculative and logical affinities to Mādhyamika, Tiantai, and Huayan toward a more direct, nonintellectual approach to enlightenment, though without abandoning the shared unitary conception of reality. Although the other sects vigorously postulated the interpenetration of appearance and reality and the identity of noumenon and phenomenon, they were believed by Chan Buddhists to be ultimately unsuccessful in moving from the abstract to the concrete. The latter felt "that these principles are never fully grasped by the intellect alone but must be personally experienced through one's own efforts." Chang Chung-yüan continues by explaining that in pursuing a purely intellectual search for truth, one is necessarily always torn by conflicting pulls of the transcendental and the concrete.

> But for the Ch'an Buddhist nothing is transcendental apart from the concrete. In other words, the man of Ch'an engages in ordinary daily activities and simultaneously transcends them, so that the concrete and the transcendent in his life are one and the same. He lives, as do all men, in time and space, but he is not limited by either. For him the finite dwells within the infinite, the infinite within the finite. They are totally and inseparably identified as one. (p. 91)

Of all the major Mahāyāna sects, then, Chan comes closest to displaying the this-worldly attitude characteristic of Taoism. Those similarities between the two strains of thought which are most frequently noted include: the mystic appreciation of nature; an emphasis on spontaneity and naturalness; an iconoclastic deemphasis on scriptures, rituals, metaphysical speculation, and scholarship; and a preference for a pedagogical method which involves colloquial language, surprise, irrationality, enigma, and silence. Indeed, Chan has been accused of not even being Buddhism at all, but rather a Chinese-Taoist reaction to the foreign religion; it has no Indian counterpart. Zürcher feels, however, that we should consider it as perhaps "the most typically *Chinese* expression of Buddhism" yet still an integral part of the original religious system because "the basic aim of Ch'an, as of Mahāyāna Buddhism as a whole, is the experience of Enlightenment and Emancipation, concepts which even in their Chinese formulations are definitely not inspired by any Chinese creed" ("Buddhism in China," p. 77).

Chan Buddhists are perhaps most famous for their sense that the true doctrine cannot be conveyed in words, a notion which was also shared by other sects. This conviction of the ultimate inadequacy of language constitutes the fourth major similarity between Buddhism and Taoism. The *Dao de jing*, for example, opens with the following dicta:

> The way that can be told
> Is not the constant way;
> The name that can be named
> Is not the constant name.[11]

And scattered throughout the *Zhuangzi* are statements which suggest that words have but limited usefulness, such as the following:

> Men of the world who value the Way all turn to books. But books are nothing more than words. Words have value; what is of value in words is meaning. Meaning has something it is pursuing, but the thing that it is pursuing cannot be put into words and handed down. The world values words and hands down books but, though the world values them, I do not think them worth valuing. ("The Way of Heaven," 36/ 13/64; trans. Watson, p. 157)

We have already seen another anecdote in which Zhuangzi describes words as a fish trap which can be discarded once the "fish" of meaning has been caught. The early Chinese Buddhist Zhu Daosheng (ca. 360–434), also known as Daosheng, turned to the same metaphor in analyzing problems of translating the sūtras:

> The purpose of words is to explain the Truth (*li*), but once Truth has been entered, words may be suspended. Ever since the transmission of the scriptures eastward (to China), their translators have encountered repeated obstacles, and many have been blocked by holding (too narrowly) to the text, with the result that few have been able to see the complete meaning. Let them forget the fish-trap and catch the fish. Then one may begin to talk with them about the Way (*Tao*).[12]

And Daosheng's contemporary Sengzhao (384–414), who developed the first synthesis of the Mādhyamika method and neo-Taoism, employed diction and ideas which seem to have come from the *Zhuangzi* in his treatise "On *Prajñā* Not Being Knowledge":

> Hence the sage is like an empty hollow. He cherishes no knowledge. He dwells in the world of change and utility, yet holds himself to the realm of non-activity (*wu-wei*). He rests within the walls of the nameable, yet lives in the open country of what transcends speech. He is silent and alone, void and open, where his state of being cannot be clothed in language. Nothing more can be said of him. (Quoted Fung, *History*, II, 268)

Yet Daosheng, for one, has also been described as having "treasured and esteemed the sūtras in which everything has its meaning. 'The Buddha does not lie.' He did not lie 'when he substituted the sūtras for himself.'"[13] And certainly, each of the major Mahāyāna sects, including Chan, adopted one or more sūtras as scriptural authorities, although they maintained different opinions about the efficacy of chanting or studying the texts and varying degrees of attachment to them. In general, with the exception of Chan, Mahāyāna Buddhism stressed the relativity and inadequacy of scriptures as "expedient means" (*upāya*) toward the achievement of enlightenment, but it never urged that the writings be abandoned altogether: they were a material medium which conveyed the immaterial.

Even an early Chan master like Yongjia Xuanjue (665–713) did not totally discount the value of words, although his exposition of his position is typically paradoxical and contradictory. In explaining his "ten steps of contemplation," he defines the eighth as clarifying "the meaning of interpretation." While words are incapable of expressing the ultimate truth directly, he says that they may perhaps suggest it indirectly; once they have been correctly interpreted and their meaning gleaned, they may then be transcended:

> The perfect truth is inexpressible, but through words its meaning is revealed. . . . If the true meaning is not revealed, it is because the words have been poorly interpreted. . . . When the meaning has been revealed and the source realized, words and contemplation do not necessarily remain.

In his discussion of the ninth step, however, Xuanjue states that not only can language transmit the "fruits of contemplation," but the two are also totally identified: "When words express contemplation, the two become fused. Then articulation and absolute reality are one. . . . The essence is one and the same; only its names vary. Applying the terms 'word' and 'contemplation' is a mere game." But in moving on to explain the tenth step, he speaks of identifying "the mystic source" and suggests that words are, after all, a hindrance to the understanding of reality and, again, ultimately incapable of approaching the Way:

> Those who are well versed in the doctrine of Buddhism will never be impeded by words and thus fail to understand reality. When reality is understood, the obstacle of words is broken, for what more can words discuss?. . . . That which cannot be contemplated and expressed by words is indeed the essence of Tao.[14]

The true state of nondifferentiation, the contentless intuition of *prajñā*, is, as we have seen, unutterable. Buddhist literature offers at least two famous instances where silences effectively convey the transcendence of all polarities. The first involves the Buddha himself, who is said to have refused to answer a group of fourteen questions now referred to as the *avyākata* or "inexpressibles." These can actually be reduced to four sets of questions concerning the origin, duration, and extent of the world, the immortality of the Buddha, and the relation of soul to body, three of which are tetralemmas, having four alternative answers each. According to Murti, the Buddha's silence indicated his awareness of the limitations of analytical reason, which dogmatically seeks but a single point of view:

That the conflict is not on the empirical level and so not capable of being settled by appeal to facts is realised by the Buddha when he declares them insoluble. Reason involves itself in deep and interminable conflict when it tries to go beyond phenomena to seek their ultimate ground. Speculative metaphysics provokes not only difference but also opposition; if one theorist says "yes" to a question, the other says "no" to the same. . . . [The Buddha] characterises all speculation as diṭṭhi-vāda (dogmatism) and consistently refuses to be drawn into the net (jāla). (p. 40)

By rejecting all the various positions, the Buddha arrived at a non-conceptual knowledge of the absolute and affirmed its inexpressibility.

The second instance is what is referred to as the "thunderous silence" of Vimalakīrti in the ninth chapter of the sūtra spoken by him. A group of bodhisattvas has gathered at his house, and he asks each of them to say something about his understanding of the doctrine of nonduality. One by one they name a traditional pair of opposites—such as birth and death, impurity and purity, form and formlessness, saṃsāra and nirvāṇa, enlightenment and unenlightenment, reality and unreality, joy and sadness—and then state that each can be seen as undifferentiated at some higher level of awareness. Finally Mañjuśrī, who generally appears in sūtras as one of the wisest of the bodhisattvas, offers his viewpoint: "In my opinion, when all things are no longer within the province of either word or speech, and of either indication or knowledge, and are beyond questions and answers, this is initiation into the non-dual Dharma." He then turns to request of Vimalakīrti: "'All of us have spoken; please tell us what is the Bodhisattva's initiation into the non-dual Dharma.'" Vimalakīrti, however, "kept silent without saying a word" (trans. Luk, p. 100). Whereas all the others had uttered examples of polarities, and even Mañjuśrī had *said* that the principle could not be spoken, only Vimalakīrti's silence could communicate the true meaning of nondiscrimination.

Yet the Buddhists, like the Taoists, did not ultimately despair about expressing the inexpressible. They continued to use language, though remaining ever conscious of the inability of a distinction-creating medium to speak of a state beyond distinctions. Like Zhuangzi, who delighted in word play, paradoxes, and non sequiturs, they seem to have felt that the acceptance of contradiction and paradox was a means of simultaneously manifesting the inadequacy of language to answer metaphysical questions or express true reality directly and of approaching the transcendence of all differentiation.

A familiarity with all of these Buddhist-Taoist doctrines cannot but enrich our understanding of Wang Wei's poetry. The indications of his involvement with Buddhism are certainly clear from his biography: his study with the Chan master Daoguang, his conversion of part of his Lantian estate into a monastery, and the dynastic histories' account of his daily activities during the last years of his life. He cannot be identified exclusively with any of the four main sects active during the Tang, and actually, the boundary lines among them were so fluid that the word "sects" is probably inappropriate. Although Wang Wei wrote stele inscriptions for the Chan monks Daoguang and Huineng, his corpus also contains a more general praise of Buddhism and eulogistic essays about the Pure Land ideal, Amīda, the Buddha of the Western Paradise.

Perhaps the most illuminating evidence of Wang Wei's commitment is his choice of cognomen (*zi*), Mojie, already alluded to in poem 49. Combined with his given name Wei, these syllables form the Chinese transliteration of Vimalakīrti's name: Weimojie. We have already seen some of the Indian Buddhist's important utterances— and silence—on such key Mahāyāna tenets as *śūnyatā* and nonduality. The *Vimalakīrti-nirdeśa Sūtra* was especially popular in China because it was said to have been spoken by a layman who successfully practiced his religion while engaged in worldly activities. He affirmed the Mahāyāna ideal of the potential universal Buddhahood of all men and provided an extensive description of the bodhisattva who is not tied to the world but remains in it to help other beings, rather than escaping into nirvāṇa. Moreover, Vimalakīrti also espoused such central Confucian social ideas as filial piety and loyalty to the ruler and demonstrated to the Chinese that the good Buddhist did not necessarily have to abandon his family and retreat to a monastery. As Ch'en observes in *Buddhism in China*:

> Here was a layman rich and powerful, a brilliant conversationalist, a respected householder who surrounded himself with the pleasures of life, but was also a faithful and wise disciple of the Buddha, a man full of wisdom and thoroughly disciplined in his conduct. Indeed the educated elite of Chinese society must have felt that here was a model that they could emulate, for though Vimala was a Buddhist, he could very easily have been taken for a Confucian gentleman. (p. 385)

Ch'en's speculation here could undoubtedly also apply to Wang Wei.

Although generally labeled as a Buddhist poet and, in fact, as the "Poet-Buddha," Wang Wei wrote very few explicitly religious poems. Unlike other Tang poets such as Han Shan or "Cold Mountain" (seventh or ninth century?) and Bo Juyi (772–846), for example, he wrote no completely doctrinal works, such as "hymns of praise or devotional verses patterned after those found in the Chinese translations of Buddhist scriptures and most commonly employing a four-character line."[15] Indeed, though not a *gāthā* or specifically religious song, poem 51, "Kulapati Hu Lay Ill in Bed, so I Sent Some Grain and Presented This Poem to Him," is unusual for its preponderance of doctrine over other elements; there are, in fact, only two other poems in his collection similarly freighted with such allusions, and they are both addressed to the same person ("Kulapati Hu and I Being Ill, I Sent These Two Poems, also Showing Them to the Disciples" [3/2a–b; I, 31–33]).

Instead, as in poems 52–53, Wang Wei sometimes chooses to couch a religious message in allegorical terms. "Suffering from Heat" opens with a graphic description of overwhelming heat which may be read both literally and metaphorically—as the dusty world of suffering, or saṁsāra. The second half of the poem, in which the speaker imagines an escape from the material into ethereal, unbounded spaces, suggests the validity of such an interpretation, for we see that relief from the heat cannot come anywhere within the realm of phenomena, but only "beyond the universe." And in the final four lines it becomes clear that the poem is indeed centered around a distinction between saṁsāra and nirvāṇa, which has not yet been transcended: Wang Wei observes that he is still bound by his body to earthly concerns and therefore suffering, that he has not yet "awakened" or attained enlightenment. The explicit comparison in the last line of nirvāṇa to coolness, of course, confirms a reading of the poem on two levels.

Although "Suffering from Heat" ends with the description of coolness rather than heat, Wang Wei acknowledges that he has not actually achieved the desired release. Poem 53, "Enjoying the Cool," which immediately follows it in the standard edition of his poetry, however, suggests the successful attainment of that state. Certainly the natural imagery throughout presents a clear contrast to that of the preceding poem, the wind and cleansing flow providing the sought-for relief from the heat and dust. There are no explicit references to Buddhism here, although the word "void" (kong) is resonant with abstract implications throughout Wang Wei's work, and the final allusion is a literary one which only hints at the material desires that have been discarded. But it is precisely because the poet does not structure this poem on an overt distinction between saṁsāra and nirvāṇa that he suggests the achievement of transcendence lacking in the first: rather than describing a state of nondifferentiation, the poem embodies it.

Like these two works taken in combination, poem 54, "Climbing to the Monastery of Perception," fuses abstract and concrete levels from beginning to end. While it can be read as a simple description of a physical ascent to the monastery, it also traces the stages of a bodhisattva's movement toward enlightenment. As the journey progresses, the scene becomes more expansive, suggesting the sense of liberation which results from discarding narrow viewpoints and dualities. And the monks are described as dwelling "emptily" atop a cloudy peak; the word *kong* can mean the "sky," their location, or "without any purpose," i.e., lacking conscious, grasping goals, in addition to referring to a nondual intuition of *śūnyatā*. Removed to a realm beyond both the literal and the figurative clouds, they can "contemplate" (the word *guan* in Buddhist literature carries the association of being able to discern illusion from reality) the world with true insight.

Wang Wei's many other descriptions of visits to and from Buddhist recluses and monks are not structured so allegorically as these three poems but simply interweave overtly religious language with personal narrative and natural imagery. In poems 55 through 59, the predominance of doctrinal and historical allusions progressively diminishes, but in all of them some background information—supplied in the many notes—is necessary for an understanding of what is going on. Gradually, however, the discursive or narrative elements give way to the pure presentation of scene; in poem 59, "Visiting the Cloister of Chan Master Fu," for example, Wang Wei simply suggests the length and intensity of his subject's meditation by means of a final image which spatializes time—the monk has become oblivious to the signs of the passing season all about him.

In the next five poems, which continue to describe visits with monks, the references to Buddhist doctrine become even more scarce and essentially insignificant. Poem 60, "A Meal for the Monks of Mt. Fufu," for instance, opens by speaking directly of Wang Wei's belated contact with the religion, but the bulk of the poem presents the serene experience rather than talking about it. Only three other terms here may be referring to the speaker's commitment, and even they could be read in a secular sense. In line 11 "realized" (*wu*) is the Chinese word for enlightenment, and "solitude" (*ji*) often appears in compounds describing the tranquility of nirvāna; the compound "empty void" (*kongxu*) in the last line may also recall the notion of *śūnyatā* or universal emptiness. This concluding statement also serves as an implicit comment on the question about returning that has just been posed, which may have been directed either to the monks or to the poet himself: although night has fallen, he asks them not to bother thinking of their return to the monastery and simultaneously urges himself not to be concerned with thoughts of return to worldly life. And indeed, the final line suggests that all such dualities of place or activity are ultimately "empty," transcended when seen from a higher point of view.

The prose preface to poem 61, "In Qinglong Monastery at Monk Tanbi's Courtyard Assembly," contains much Buddhist terminology, but the poem itself only employs the multivalent word "empty" to

describe the place and person being visited. Here scenic images of
height and expanse evoke the boundlessness and nondiscrimination
of the Buddhist vision, the connection between the two suggested by
the phrase "empty void," which can be read literally as "sky" or again
as the concept of śūnyatā. In the following three parallel couplets
space is covered in all directions: the monk sees horsemen riding to
the south and hears morning cockcries to the north, and the lone
column of smoke rising in the distance fills the vertical dimension,
while a dense growth of trees extends uniformly along the horizon.
Just as the physical objects in the poem extend over a vast expanse,
so the sky—or principle of emptiness—and the monk's mind—which
embraces that principle—are unbounded. The rhetorical questions in
each line where "empty" appears reinforce this sense of limitless-
ness. Wang Wei describes the monk's field of vision as untainted and
pure, free perhaps from worldly attachments but also, as the final
line suggests, from any delusory points of view at all: Tanbi's mind is
"empty," for it goes beyond all distinctions, just as his sight can range
through space.

  Wang Wei uses such natural imagery almost exclusively in the
following three works to evoke Buddhist states of mind. In poem 62,
"Visiting the Mountain Dwelling of Monk Tanxing at Ganhua Mon-
astery," for example, only the allusion to an earlier monk and the
word "sitting" (zuo), which is also used to describe Chan meditation,
belong to an explicitly religious lexicon. Otherwise, the descriptions
of nature and of the monk's harmony with it simply suggest the
peace and tranquility he has attained through his religious life. Wang
Wei also emphasizes this passive reliance on and appreciation of na-
ture in poem 63, "Stone Gate Monastery on Mt. Lantian," to depict
an experience of his own which begins very much like that of the
fisherman in "Song of Peach Blossom Spring" (poem 6). As in the
earlier work, the journey must occur in ignorance; unaware of both
the distance and the course of the route, the speaker finds that each
twist of the stream brings a new and sudden discovery, and even the
arrival at the monastery becomes an almost accidental encounter.
Wang Wei focuses on the solitude and simplicity of the monks' exis-
tence in total harmony with nature: their religious activities are ori-
ented according to features of the surrounding scenery, and human
and natural realms interpenetrate. In the concluding four lines he
returns to the Peach Blossom Spring motif evoked by his opening
description. Unlike the fisherman, the speaker here knows that such
a realm of purity cannot be consciously pursued; although he cannot
remain with the monks now, because he understands the nature of a
successful journey, he can be confident of a return the following
spring, so that the future is contained in the present moment.

  Perhaps the most enigmatic example of such an experience

predicated on an effortless, unconscious union with nature is poem 64, "Visiting the Temple of Gathered Fragrance." Wang Wei opens the poem with a profession of ignorance, which declares that he does not "know" the temple and suggests several possibilities: that he does not know where it is, if it even exists, or that he does not possess a rational knowledge of its significance but rather an intuitive, nondifferentiating awareness. This special kind of ignorance sets the tone for the description of the journey up the mountain; the process is phenomenological, for the speaker moves up the forested peak with no a priori notions of what he will encounter. Each line, therefore, contains images of extreme ambiguity and vagueness. In line 2, for example, "entering" can refer to both the action of the speaker and the location of the monastery, thus implicitly refusing to recognize a distinction between the traveler and his destination, or subject and object. And the obscurity of "cloudy peaks," frequently associated in Wang Wei's poetry with monasteries and ethereal realms in general, suggests the inability of the Temple of Gathered Fragrance to be localized and stresses the inadequacy of merely sensuous perception on such a journey of the spirit.

In the second couplet the poet provides a spare description of the scenery along the way. The phrase "paths without people" (*wu ren jing*, literally "without person path") can also be read as "no paths for people," thus further suggesting the speaker's venture into totally unknown territory which no other humans have traveled; this experience must be his alone. This sense of mystery is evoked again in the question of the following line. As in the first couplet, Wang Wei reveals a distrust of visual perception and purely intellectual cognition. He has presumably heard the sound of a bell from somewhere deep in the mountains, thus confirming, at least, the existence of the monastery (although he does not actually say that he has *heard* a bell at all, so that for us some doubt remains), but is unable to specify its location. So he must continue his ascent without the comforting knowledge of where he is or where he is going.

Although the images in the third couplet are perhaps more specific than those in the first half of the poem, they are both highly ambiguous. As if to continue the denial of the visual implied by the question in line 4, lines 5 and 6 both focus on other sensuous modes of apprehension. "Swallows" (or alternatively, "chokes" [*yan*]) can be read actively and passively, in either case evoking the sound of water rushing over rocks. Similarly, English cannot render the multiple readings of line 6, where the synesthetic effects of the setting sun could also be translated as "The color of the sun is chilled by (or among) green pines" or "The color of the sun leaves green pines to turn cold" (extending the process over time). In both lines the simultaneous activity and passivity of the verbs suggest that the processes occurring cannot be subjected to rational analysis; they can only be apprehended intuitively, as one total experience in which subject and object, the various elements of nature, are indistinguishable. Furthermore, the diction also diminishes the potentially sensuous precision of the couplet. Rather than presenting the concrete nouns, spring and sun, as the agents (or receptors) of each line, Wang Wei speaks of the spring's "*noise*" (*sheng*) and the sun's "*color*" (*se*), so that in each case it is an abstraction and not a particular object that is being described.

The final couplet of "Visiting the Temple of Gathered Fragrance" in no way diminishes the mysterious quality of the journey. Presumably Wang Wei has arrived at the monastery, but he is typically indirect and presents neither buildings nor monks for our observation. Instead he seems to have reached a pond, whose bends and curves continue to recall the winding paths of other spiritual journeys. The pond is "empty"—perhaps dried up, or deserted, or illusory, or transcendent. The last line simply presents a process but does not specify the subject or the precise nature of the object. And the person engaged in "peaceful meditation" may be either a monk from the temple or the poet himself, but since no actual person is named, perhaps Wang Wei is referring to an intangible atmosphere of the place, once again suggesting the fusion of human and natural elements.

The last eleven poems in this chapter are arranged in two groups because of the repeated use of a specific term in each of them. In poems 65–68 the phrase is an explicitly Buddhist one, "nonrebirth" (*wu sheng*), or liberation from the cycle of suffering or eternal rebirth and thus entrance into nirvāṇa. These four works are more directly personal and narrative than many we have seen; where poem 65, "Traveling to Ganhua Monastery," describes a specific visit to a mountain retreat, poem 66, "Visiting Monk Xuan," also provides a more general overview of the poet's rejection of official fame and glory, and both conclude with an affirmation of his commitment to Buddhism. The contexts of poems 67–68 are less exclusively religious. "An Autumn Night, Sitting Alone" concerns itself with some melancholy ruminations on the inevitability of aging—concretized in the dropping of fruits from trees, chirping of autumn cicadas, and whitening of the poet's hair—and the uselessness of popular Taoist formulas for immortality. Wang Wei concludes, therefore, that only Buddhism with its goal of release from the wheel of suffering offers the possibility of transcendence. Poem 68, "Lamenting Yin Yao," uses "nonrebirth" to refer to the poet's tutoring of his friend in Buddhist doctrine; that he had been asked to do so indicates the degree and clarity of his religious conviction.

Poem 69 is another lament for Yin Yao yet differs greatly in both its content and its method. Here, unlike in the preceding work, Wang Wei refrains from any explicit emotional comment on his friend's death, concentrating instead on the depiction of scene and suggesting an attitude which can rise above lament. He begins by describing Yin Yao as going "back" to be buried, thus implying that death, where one achieves the closest, concrete contact with nature, is the original state for man. After the funeral the mourners have also gone "home," not to this same timelessness, however, but to "the realm of men." Yet there is a link between the evergreens and white clouds to which Yin Yao now belongs and the mundane world of his friends: the downward-flowing mountain stream connects the two, enabling Wang Wei to both evoke and transcend his sadness and embody the principle of harmony which underlies his poetic universe.

The image of clouds, and white clouds in particular, recurs in this last group of poems to suggest a Buddhist spirituality, the purity of retreat from government, or, more generally still, the limits of perception and knowledge.[16] "Empty clouded mountains," for example, appear at the end of poem 70, "Sent to the Chongfan Monastery Monk," to describe the subject's isolated retreat. The monk's life is completely at one with nature, for the phrases "door on the stream" and "window facing mountains" literally fuse natural objects and human dwelling. The last couplet is virtually identical to lines 21–22 of poem 6, "Song of Peach Blossom Spring," and notes that just as the monk is oblivious to worldly affairs, so men within society do not know that the mountains are not literally "empty." Here, however, the many Buddhist overtones of the word "empty" enter to suggest that it is the mundane world which is illusory and that true reality belongs to the realm of cloudy mountains.

Poem 71, "In the Mountains, Sent to All My Younger Brothers and Sisters," similarly observes that men of the world are deluded, failing to recognize both what lies within the white clouds and what they represent. Wang Wei presents his fellow Buddhists here as isolated within the mountains yet "forming a group of their own"; his implication is that meditation and sūtra-chanting create a communality more spontaneous, effortless, and thus natural than any more mundane grouping. And the vision of the city residents is a limited one: they can "see" the clouds but possess no insight into what lies within them.

White clouds, then, in Wang Wei's poetry may hide something from view and, at the same time, in effect symbolize what they conceal. By means of this paradox the poet can suggest the limits of merely visual perception when compared to a nondiscriminating, intuitive awareness. In poems 72 and 73 Wang Wei associates this quality with the purity of life in retreat, for each work contains allusions to famous recluses of the past. Although "Given to Wei Mu the

Eighteenth" assumes the likelihood of such a withdrawal for the poet himself, in "Traveling to the Dwelling of Li, Man of the Mountains, and Writing This on His Walls" the possibility is more distant and tantalizing. The ambiguously structured second couplet suggests the hermit's total harmony with nature and ability to define himself in natural terms. Granted, the quasi-question-and-answer format I have chosen is not the only possible translation, but Wang Wei seems to be asking about his friend's age and dwelling place and receiving evasive responses which indicate that Li is just another object in the scene, whose years are those of the pines and whose home is the multitude of bamboos. This integrality is linked by implication to the world of white clouds, which apparently has not yet been attained, yet the connection is not made explicit. By means of this typically open-ended conclusion, Wang Wei suggests that nothing indeed can be posited about them.

One reason why white clouds may remain beyond the grasp of sensuous and rational modes of apprehension is that their realm is limitless. Wang Wei introduces this notion at the end of poem 74, "Farewell," an extremely enigmatic work in which it is impossible to distinguish consistently the two interlocutors. The pronoun "you" (*jun*) does appear in lines 1–3, thus suggesting a clear distinction between an interrogator who offers the wine and an addressee who is going somewhere and answers that he has somehow failed to realize his ambitions. Yet the identity of the speaker of the last two lines cannot be clearly determined. We assume that Wang Wei is bidding farewell here to an unsuccessful friend, yet we must also remember that the poet's own retreat was in Lantian, "at the foot of Southern Mountain." And line 5 appears to have two speakers: the poet urges his disappointed friend to leave, and the latter then requests the former not to question him any more. In either case, the emphatic urgency of the statements is reflected in the tonal pattern of the line, for every word—and this is unusual—belongs to the "oblique" tone category, somewhat more emotive and strident than the "level."

The impossibility of identifying the interlocutors has led many Western critics to conclude that "Farewell" is actually a kind of soliloquy or internal monologue. Wang Wei suggests with sparse detail and simple repetitive language a possible reason behind his desire to retreat—he did not, after all, rise to a very powerful official position—and the traditional association of the Southern Mountains with death further implies that this withdrawal will be a final one. Thus the poem ends with an affirmation of the endlessness of white clouds: there is perhaps something consoling about the purity and peace which they evoke, and they are inexhaustible and timeless, in contrast to the world of limits and time which the traveler is leaving. This statement of limitlessness appropriately concludes an open-ended, puzzling poem. And because of this very boundlessness, the white clouds are indescribable; their true meaning remains inaccessible to both the sense of sight and the intellectual faculties. Nothing can be posited about them, as is also the case for *śūnyatā*, except their limitlessness or essential transcendence of all specific qualities. Wang Wei speaks of it in both temporal, as in "Farewell," and spatial terms. Indeed, he frequently mentions going even "beyond white clouds" when describing, for example, the departure of himself or a friend for a country retreat.

Poem 75, "Answering Pei Di," concludes with this phrase and suggests the only means by which these clouds can be apprehended. The poet opens with a spare depiction of details of the present Wang River scenery and then alludes to a question posed by his friend as to whether Mt. Zhongnan, where they had retreated together before, still exists. Wang Wei affirms that Zhongnan lies somewhere "beyond white clouds": it cannot be localized within space, nor, perhaps, within time, but there is no doubt about its existence. This assurance, moreover, results from the fact that it is his heart that knows; his awareness is intuitive rather than rational. Although "heart" (*xin*) can also be translated as "mind," the line literally reads "Heart/mind knows white clouds beyond" and does not explicitly contain an actual predication about Zhongnan Mountain or, by the same token, a definite object for the verb "knows." This suggests, therefore, that Wang Wei is alluding to a kind of cognition which would not establish such a distinction between the knower and the known. And such a nondiscriminating intuition is associated with the boundless and transcendent white clouds, whose meaning eludes both visual perception and verbal description.

POEM

51

(3/1a; I, 30)

Kulapati Hu Lay Ill in Bed, so I Sent Some
Grain and Presented This Poem to Him

> *Once we clearly observe the four great causes,*
> *What can our original nature possess?*
> *If false calculations are not allowed to arise,*
> 4 *This body will have neither good luck nor ill fortune.*
> *How can we call sound and appearance guests?*
> *Who preserves the* skandhas *and the* dhātu?

If we only speak of the Buddha's lotus eye,
8 *How can we resent the tumor at our elbow?*
Once satiated with fragrant spiritual food,
We will not get tipsy from śrāvaka wine.
Being and nonbeing, we cease to see as before;
12 *Life and death—we receive them all as a dream.*
Falling ill you approach your true form,
Follow emptiness, and calm violent motion.
There is no single dharma that is real;
16 *There is no single dharma that is impure.*
You, Kulapati, have understood all things clearly:
At every chance you perfect your discipline.
You sleep upon a bed without a rug;
20 *Is there any gruel within your pot?*
While fasting, you do not beg for food—
I am certain that you merely rinse your mouth.
For now, take these several pecks of rice:
24 *Accept them to save your floating life.*

NOTES

Title: "Kulapati" (*jushi*) is the term for a householder who practices Buddhism without becoming a monk.

Line 1: The "four great causes" are the elements which combine to form all things, including our bodies: earth (bones and flesh), water (liquids), fire (breath), and wind (movement).

Line 6: The *skandhas* are the five "heaps" or aggregates, the components of an intelligent being: form, feelings, perceptions, impulses and emotions, and acts of consciousness. Buddhism holds that there is no individuality or self which transcends these five heaps. The *dhātu* are the eighteen realms of sense, i.e., the six sense organs (eyes, ears, nose, tongue, body, and mind), their objects or conditions, and their perceptions.

Line 7: The Buddha's eyes were said to resemble the leaves of a lotus.

Line 8: The character *yang*, "willow," in the text is a loan for a similar character meaning "tumor." This is an allusion to a passage in the *Zhuangzi* ("Perfect Happiness" [*Zhi le*], 46/18/20), in which a character reacts to the sprouting of a tumor/willow at his elbow with equanimity, accepting the unceasing processes of change, life, and death.

Line 10: Śrāvaka (*shengwen*, "listeners") is a term for the disciples of Theravāda or Hīnayāna Buddhism, who have grasped many essential doctrinal truths but have not yet attained the selflessness of the bodhisattva, the ideal Mahāyāna Buddhist figure who postpones his own entrance into nirvāṇa until all sentient beings have been enlightened.

Line 15:   The term "dharma" is usually used by Wang Wei in its sense of the Buddhist law or truth, and is thus capitalized in other translations when referring to that concept. Here, however, he is using it in its sense of anything "which has entity and bears its own attributes" (Soothill and Hodous, p. 267) and is referring to the Mahāyāna Buddhist doctrine that all dharmas are at base empty, or devoid of permanent characteristics.

POEM

52

(4/13a; I, 68)

Suffering from Heat

> *The red sun fills sky and earth.*
> *Fiery clouds form mountain peaks:*
> *Grasses and trees are all scorched and shriveled,*
4 > *Streams and marshes entirely dried up.*
> *In light silk, feeling the weight of clothes;*
> *Among dense trees, suffering from scarceness of shade.*
> *Bamboo mats I cannot bear to touch;*
8 > *Linens are washed over and over again.*
> *I long to go out beyond the universe,*
> *Unbounded in a vast expanse.*
> *A distant wind comes from a myriad miles,*
12 > *Rivers and seas cleanse impurities and cares.*
> *But now I see that the body is the trouble*
> *And begin to realize my mind has not yet awakened.*
> *To suddenly enter the Sweet Dew Gate*
16 > *Would be like a pure and cooling joy.*

NOTES

Line 13:   This alludes to a passage in the *Dao de jing*, section 13: "The reason for my great troubles is that I have a body; when I am without a body, what troubles will I have?"

Line 15:   "Sweet dew" (*amṛta*) is a term for the nectar of immortality or nirvāṇa; the entrance to this realm is through the "Sweet Dew Gate."

POEM

53

(4/13b; I, 69)

Enjoying the Cool

Tall trees—more than ten thousand trunks:
A pure flow threading through their midst.
Ahead, above the mouth of the great river,
4   Clear and free comes a distant wind.
Flowing ripples dampen the white sand;
White sturgeon seem to swim in the void.
I lie down upon a large flat rock;
8   Rising billows cleanse my humble body.
I rinse my mouth and then wash my feet,
And face an old fisherman in front of me.
Greedy for bait—how many altogether?
12   Vain thoughts, east of the lotus leaves.

NOTE

Line 12:   This last phrase alludes to an anonymous Han dynasty poem written to music which runs:

South of the river lotus can be picked;
The lotus leaves float neatly on the water.
Fish play amid the lotus leaves.
Fish play east of the lotus leaves.
Fish play west of the lotus leaves.
Fish play south of the lotus leaves.
Fish play north of the lotus leaves.

Included in *Fountain of Ancient Poetry*, 1/34a.

POEM

54

(8/11a; I, 150–51)

Climbing to the Monastery of Perception

A bamboo path leads up from the lowland—
On lotus peaks emerges the Conjured City.

From within a window all three Chu states;
Above the forests the nine level rivers.
On soft grass monks sit cross-legged;
Tall pines echo their chanting sounds.
Emptily dwelling beyond the Dharma cloud,
They contemplate the world, attaining nonrebirth.

NOTES

Title: This monastery was located on Mt. Lu in Hubei province. The poem was probably written during Wang Wei's official mission south in 740.

Line 2:   "Conjured City" alludes to a parable from chapter seven of the *Lotus Sūtra*, in which a guide leads a multitude of people on an arduous journey toward a cache of jewels. When they become weary and frightened and wish to turn back, he conjures up a city in which they can rest temporarily, then dissolves it so that they will move on to their ultimate goal. The parable is used to illustrate the Buddha's "expedient means" or "skill-in-means" (*upāya*), his ability to devise methods of carrying people over the obstacles to enlightenment. The Conjured City is compared in the sūtra to his doctrine that two nirvāṇas exist midway along the path to the ultimate and are thus relatively more quickly attained. After resting and overcoming their discouragement, however, the multitude must press on. For a translation of the parable, see Leon Hurvitz, *Scripture of the Lotus Blossom of the Fine Dharma (The Lotus Sūtra)* (New York: Columbia University Press, 1976), pp. 148–49.

Line 3:   These are the three areas of the ancient kingdom of Chu: Pengcheng in the west, Wu in the east, and Jiangling in the south.

Line 4:   The "nine rivers" are the affluents of the Yangzi.

Line 7:   For "Dharma cloud" (*dharmamegha*), see the Commentary below.

Line 8:   "Nonrebirth" (*wu sheng*, for the Sanskrit *anutpāda*) denotes the liberation from the cycle of eternal rebirth or attainment of nirvāna.

COMMENTARY

Running parallel to the account of an ascent to a mountain monastery here are allusions to the *daśabhūmi* or ten stages of the bodhisattva's progression toward enlightenment. While the "lowland" where the bamboo path begins refers literally to the foot of the mountain, for example, for the Buddhist it simultaneously means *pramuditā*, the initial stage of joy on entering the road to Buddhahood. According to Soothill and Hodous' *Dictionary*, the next eight are *vimalā*, the stage of purity; *prabhākarī*, stage of further enlightenment; *arciṣmatī*, stage of glowing wisdom; *sudurjayā*, mastery of utmost difficulties; *abhimukhī*, the way of wisdom above definitions of purity or impurity; *dūraṁgamā*, going beyond the self to save others; *acalā*, attainment of calmness; and *sādhumatī*, attainment of finest wisdom, thus knowing where and how to save (p. 47). The tenth stage is *dharmamegha*, where the bodhisattva gains the fertilizing powers of the "Dharma cloud" which drops its sweet dew everywhere.

POEM

55   (11/12b; I, 212)

Visiting the Residence of Official Lu and Watching
Him Provide a Meal for Monks; Composed Together

The three virtues differ from the seven graces,
But both look with dark pupils on the blue lotus.
Begging for food, they seek fragrant spiritual meals,
⁴   When cutting garments they copy rice paddy patterns.
Monks bearing flying staffs of tin—
Their benefactor gives them pieces of gold.
They sit cross-legged in the sun beyond the eaves,
⁸   While burning incense wafts smoke below the bamboo.
The cold void: land of the Dharma cloud;
The autumn scene: the five heavens of purity.
Their bodies obey dependent origination,
¹²   But their minds transcend all levels of meditation.
They need not lament the descent of the sun:
Within themselves a lamp is always alight.

NOTES

Line 1:   The "three virtues" (*san xian*) are the three virtuous states of a bod-
hisattva: wisdom, service, and bestowing one's own merit on others. The
"seven graces" (*qi sheng*) are the seven manifestations of holiness in an arhat,
the ideal figure for Theravāda Buddhism: faith, observance of command-
ments, hearing instruction, shame, shame for others, renunciation, and wis-
dom.

Line 2:   The Jin dynasty poet Ruan Ji was said to look with "white eyes"
(i.e., with the whites of his eyes) upon that which he disliked and with "dark
eyes" (i.e., normally, with his pupils) upon that which he approved of. See
the *Jin History*, 49/1361. The *utpala* or blue lotus has leaves which were said
to resemble the eyes of the Buddha; the phrase thus refers to his all-seeing
vision. The lotus flower in general, as an emblem of purity, is associated in
numerous ways with Buddhist doctrine and practice.

Line 4:   The robes of Buddhist monks were typically patched, forming pat-
terns resembling rice paddies crisscrossed by irrigation ditches.

Line 5:   This alludes to a rhymeprose (*fu*) by the fourth-century-A.D. author
Sun Chuo, entitled "Wandering on Mt. Tiantai" (*You Tiantaishan fu*, *Anthology*

of Literature, 11/146–49), which uses Taoist and Buddhist allusions to describe an imaginary ascent of the mountain. One line of the work depicts Buddhist arhats as "Responders-to-truth, with flying tin staffs, treading the void"; monks' staffs had tin rings on them which jangled as they went begging. The rhymeprose has been translated by Burton Watson in *Chinese Rhyme-Prose: Poems in the Fu Form from the Han and Six Dynasties Periods* (New York: Columbia University Press, 1971), pp. 80–85.

Line 9:   For Dharma cloud, see Commentary on poem 54.

Line 10:   The "five heavens of purity" refer to the highest five levels of the eighteen Buddhist heavens and are inhabited by arhats who have escaped the cycle of rebirth.

Line 11:   The doctrine of *hetupratyaya*, "dependent origination," also translated as "conditioned coproduction," is a corollary to the Four Noble Truths of Buddhism which holds that everything begins with ignorance and goes through eleven successively caused stages to decay and death. Once ignorance can be eliminated, then one can escape from the chain of causation. And because all things can be shown to have been produced by causes and conditions external to themselves, they have no independent reality and are "empty" (*śūnya*).

Line 12:   There are four *dhyānas*, or stages of mystic meditation. In the first, the meditator's mind has attained an ecstasy and serenity, although it is still reasoning; in the second, it has been freed from reasoning; in the third, it has been freed of ecstasy; and in the fourth, it has become indifferent to all emotions, transcending them all, and purified. See Soothill and Hodous, p. 459.

POEM

56   (7/10a; I, 129)

On A Summer Day Visiting Qinglong Monastery to Call on the Chan Master Cao

Trudging along, one aged old man
Shuffles to visit a palace of meditation.
Wishing to ask about the principled mind's meaning,
From afar I know the disease of voidness is empty.
Mountains and rivers within the Buddha's eye,
The universe amid the Dharma body:
Do not be surprised when it dissipates burning heat—
It can arouse a wind across this great earth.

NOTES

Title: This monastery was located in the Xinchang ward of Chang'an.

Line 4:   This alludes to the Mahāyāna Buddhist doctrine that all dharmas are empty (śūnya), including the concept of emptiness itself. See, for example, Vimalakīrti's advice to a sick bodhisattva from the sūtra spoken by him, quoted in the introduction to this chapter.

Line 5:   The Buddha's eye, frequently likened to a blue lotus, is able to penetrate all things.

Line 6:   The dharmakāya is the highest of the three "Buddha-bodies," part of a doctrine developed by Mahāyāna Buddhism to explain how the Buddha could be both a historical being and someone transcending time and space. The historical Gautama Buddha was held to be but the first of the three, the nirmāṇakāya ("body of transformation"); the second body, visible to bodhisattvas, was the saṃbhogakāya ("body of bliss"); and the dharmakāya ("Dharma body") was the highest, beyond all predications and spatiotemporal limitations.

POEM

57   (10/10b; I, 188)

_____

Visiting the Chan Master Chengru and the Kulapati Xiao at Their Hermitage on Song Hillock

Asaṅga and Vasubandhu, younger and elder brothers,
Live in a mountain monastery atop a cloudless peak.
At mealtime they follow ringing chimes below the nests of crows;
Walking they tread in the empty woods to the rustle of falling leaves.
They settled by gushing waters which moisten their fragrant table;
In the rain of heavenly flowers they are at peace on beds of stone.
What do these deep caves and tall pines conceal?
Men like the dignified Ancient Master of India.

NOTES

Title: Song Hillock is located in present-day Henan province.

Line 1:   The Indian monk Asaṅga and his younger brother Vasubandhu (fourth and fifth centuries A.D.) wrote hundreds of commentaries on Bud-

dhist sūtras and founded the Yogācāra or Mind-only School, which empha-
sized methods and effects of meditation or trance (*samādhi*).

Line 5: This alludes to a story in the *Jewel Forest in the Garden of the Law*
(*Fayuan zhulin*), a Buddhist encyclopedia completed in 668 by the monk
Daoshi, of how Huiyuan (334–416), founder of the Pure Land sect, chose to
build a monastery by Dragon Spring west of Mt. Lu in Jiangxi province. Hav-
ing found a spot he liked, he decided that its true suitability could only be
confirmed by the water's spirit: this occurred when he hit the ground with
his staff, and water gushed forth from the spring to form a pond. The mon-
astery was completed around the year 386.
Meals of monks are frequently described as "fragrant."

Line 6: This "rain" is the fertilizing power of the lotus, or Buddhist doctrine.

Line 8: "Ancient Master" (*gu xiansheng*) was one name by which the Taoist
sage Laozi was known. Here it refers to the Buddha, and perhaps to one
popular Chinese belief that Laozi, after leaving China, traveled west to India
and became the Buddha Śākyamuni.

POEM
58   (11/11b; I, 210)

Seeking a Night's Lodging at the Monastery of the Chan Master Daoyi

The master of unity lodges on Taibo Mountain,
A lofty peak emerging from clouds and mist.
Chanting flows everywhere through ravines;
4   The flower's rain is only on one peak.
His tracks because of no-mind are concealed;
His name is known because of his instruction.
When birds arrive he speaks of the Dharma again;
8   When guests depart he meditates in peace once more.
By daylight he walks to the end of dewy pines,
In the evening sleeping next to the monastery.
His innermost chamber hidden in deep bamboo,
12   On a clear night he listens to distant streams.
Before this was just amid misty clouds:
Today it is in front of my pillow and mat.
How can I stay just for a while?
16   I should render service for an entire life.

NOTES

Line 1:   The "master of unity" refers to Daoyi, whose name literally means "the Way is one."
Mt. Taibo is located in Shanxi province.

Line 4:   For "flowers' rain," see poem 57, line 6n.

Line 5:   "No-mind" (*wu xin*) is an ideal state attained through meditation in which the mind has been emptied of illusions and purposive thought and is thus capable of effortless action or mystic influences.

POEM

59

(7/9a; I, 127)

Visiting the Cloister of Chan Master Fu

> Through peaks and valleys winds the hidden path;
> In cloudy forests hides the Dharma hall.
> Winged men fly playing music,
> And heavenly women kneel burning incense.
> Beyond the bamboo, peaks are partly aglow;
> In the shade of creepers, water is still cool.
> I wish to know how long he has sat in peace:
> Along the path arises the fragrance of spring.

NOTES

Line 3:   The "Distant Journey" (*Yuan you*), a work dating from the first century B.C. and included in the *Songs of Chu*, 5/269–88, describes a celestial journey which includes encounters with Taoist immortals: "I met the Winged Ones on the Hill of Cinnabar; / I tarried in the ancient land of Immortality" (trans. Hawkes, p. 83). Taoists who succeeded in attaining immortality through diet, breathing exercises, gymnastics, or elixirs were believed to have shed their earthly form, grown wings, and disappeared.

Line 4:   "Heavenly women" (*tian nü*, Sanskrit *apsaras*) were goddesses in Hindu mythology; here they refer to Buddhist nuns.

POEM

60   (3/6b; I, 39)

A Meal for the Monks of Mt. Fufu

Late did I know the clean and pure doctrine,
Daily more removed from the crowd of men.
Now awaiting the distant mountain's monks,
4 Ahead of time I sweep my poor thatched hut.
And truly from within cloudy peaks
They come to my humble home of weeds.
On grass mats we dine on pine nuts,
8 Burn incense, and read books of the Tao.
Light the lamp: daylight's almost gone.
Ring stone chimes: night has just begun.
I have already realized solitude is a joy;
12 This life is more than serene.
Why think seriously of return?
A lifetime is like the empty void.

NOTES

Title: There are many mountains of this name in China; this one was proba-
bly located near Wang Wei's country home in Lantian.

Line 1:   The "clean and pure doctrine" refers to Buddhism.

POEM

61   (11/13b; I, 214)

In Qinglong Monastery at Monk Tanbi's Courtyard Assembly

*Preface: My Elder Brother can open up the depths of darkness;
his understanding pierces beyond phenomena. His power of med-
itation overcomes enemies, and his kindness relieves grim
4 situations. He lives deep in retirement within a community of
monks next to a village of men. Below the high plateau gleams a*

lotus pond, and within the bamboo forest and fruit orchard flour-
ishes a Bodhi tree. When the clouds clear up in all eight
8 *directions and the myriad types of dust disappear, the great void*
is silent and vast. Starting from the Southern Mountains, the
imperial domains become one boundless expanse. The Wei River
penetrates heaven and earth. After walks he meditates, sit-
12 *ting cross-legged and relaxing. Then he steps up into the hall and*
on his prayer mat offers his guests a fragrant meal. He does not
arise, but his contemplation wanders far. No wind blows, but
the air seems clear and cool. He gains the world in a
16 *lotus blossom and records his writings on pattra leaves. At this*
time my Elder Brother Wang Changling of Jiangning brought a
stone tablet and asked me to introduce this [to others]. I wrote
a poem in five rhymes, and, sitting in meditation, I com-
20 *pleted this.*

NOTES

Line 7:   The Bodhi tree is the tree of enlightenment (a *Ficus religiosa* [*pippala*
or *aśvattha*], a type of evergreen), where Śākyamuni Buddha meditated and
gained enlightenment.

Line 8:   Dust here refers to all taints of the mundane world.

Line 16:   The lotus blossom is used as an emblem of Buddhist Dharma or
truth. The leaves of pattra, a kind of palm, were used like parchment for
sūtras.

Line 17:   Wang Changling (698–757), whose cognomen was Shaobo, was a
well-known poet and literary theorist of the Tang dynasty. During his early
years he traveled extensively in the northern and western border regions of
China and wrote several famous frontier poems. After passing the *jinshi* ex-
amination in 727, he embarked on a rather undistinguished government ca-
reer; he is frequently referred to as Wang Jiangning because of a position he
held in Jiangning (near modern Nanjing) from 742–48. He was killed during
the An Lushan rebellion by the prefect Lü Qiuxiao. Brief biographical notices
of Wang Changling are included in the *Old Tang History*, 190c/5050, and the
New Tang History, 203/5780.

High above, a spacious monastery;
The empty void—how can it have limits?
Sitting he sees riders on southern paths;
4 *Below he hears the cocks of Qin city.*
Far away rises a lone column of smoke;
Dense and lush are distant level trees.
Azure mountains lie beyond ten thousand villages,
8 *The setting sun to the west of the Five Mounds.*

His field of vision today is without taint:
Empty-minded, how can he be deluded?

NOTES

Title: Qinglong Monastery was located in a southern ward of Chang'an.

Line 4:   "Qin city" refers to the capital.

Line 8:   These were the burial mounds near Chang'an of five early Han emperors: Changling (of the founding emperor, Gaozu [r. 206–194 B.C.]); Anling (Hui [r. 194–187 B.C.]); Yangling (Jing [r. 156–140 B.C.]); Maoling (Wu [r. 140–86 B.C.]); and Pingling (Zhao [r. 86–73 B.C.]).

POEM

62

(7/9b; I, 128)

Visiting the Mountain Dwelling of Monk Tanxing at Ganhua Monastery

In the evening he grasps a bamboo staff,
Awaiting us at the head of Tiger Creek,
Urging his guests on he listens to mountain echoes;
Returning home he follows the water's flow.
The clustered blossoms of wildflowers are lovely,
The lone cry of a valley bird remote.
Sitting at night in the empty forest, silent,
Pine winds seem like those of autumn.

NOTES

Title: This monastery was located in Lantian, near Wang Wei's estate south of Chang'an.

Line 2:   Tiger Creek is located on Mt. Lu in Jiangxi province. This is an allusion to the monk Huiyuan, who built his Eastern Forest Monastery (*Donglin si*) there (see poem 57, line 5n.). Next to the monastery flowed a creek, and every time Huiyuan saw his guests off to cross it, a tiger would cry out— hence the name.

POEM

63   (3/3a; I, 33–34)

Stone Gate Monastery on Mt. Lantian

In the setting sun, mountains and waters were lovely.
The tossing boat trusted the home-blowing wind.
Enjoying the strangeness, unaware of distance,
4   I followed all the way to the source of the spring.
Afar I loved the lushness of clouds and trees;
At first I thought the route was not the same.
How could I know the clear flow turned?
8   Suddenly I passed through the mountain ahead.
I left the boat and readied my light staff,
Truly satisfied with what I encountered:
Old monks—four or five men,
12   At leisure in the shade of pines and cypress.
At morning chants the forest has not yet dawned;
During night meditation, mountains are even stiller.
Their minds of the Tao reach to shepherd boys;
16   They ask a woodsman about worldly affairs.
At night they lodge beneath the tall forest;
Burning incense, they sleep on clean white mats.
The valley stream's fragrance pervades men's clothes;
20   The mountain moon illumines the stone walls.
Seeking again I fear I'd lose the way;
Tomorrow I will go out to continue my climb.
Smiling I'll leave the men of Peach Blossom Spring:
24   When blossoms are red I will come to see them again.

NOTES

Title: This monastery was located south of Chang'an, in the district of Lantian near Wang Wei's country estate.

Line 23:   For the Peach Blossom Spring, see poem 6.

POEM
64   (7/11b; I, 131)

Visiting the Temple of Gathered Fragrance

I do not know the Temple of Gathered Fragrance,
For several miles, entering cloudy peaks.
Ancient trees, paths without people;
Deep in the mountains, where is the bell?
Noise from the spring swallows up lofty rocks;
The color of the sun chills green pines.
Toward dusk by the curve of an empty pond,
Peaceful meditation controls poison dragons.

NOTES

Title: This monastery was located south of Chang'an.

Line 8:   The "poison dragons" are traditionally interpreted as illusions or passions which may stand in the way of enlightenment, although the source of the allusion has not been definitively determined. Zhao Diancheng cites a passage from the *Nirvāṇa Sūtra* which speaks of the fearsome and harmful dragons in one's dwelling place. Burton Watson, however, suggests that the line may "recall the tale of a poison dragon that lived in a lake and killed passing merchants until it was subdued by a certain Prince P'an-t'o through the use of spells. The dragon changed into a man and apologized for its evil ways" (*Chinese Lyricism*, p. 175).

Still another possible reference may be to the story of the Buddha's conversion of a poisonous dragon in a hermit's cave which occurs in the Sanskrit text, the *Ekottarāgama*. According to Richard Mather, "the dragon, symbolizing hatred, attempted to overwhelm the Buddha with fire from its mouth, but the Buddha, absorbed in a compassionate trance, shone more brilliantly than the dragon and ultimately subdued it." See his "The Landscape Buddhism of the Fifth-Century Poet Hsieh Ling-yün," *Journal of Asian Studies*, Vol. XIII, No. 1 (Nov. 1958), pp. 78–79, n. 65.

POEM

65   (12/7b; I, 227–28)

Traveling to Ganhua Monastery

Kingfisher blue, the incense vapors blend;
Like a green jewel, the precious land is flat.
The dragon palace adjoins beamed dwellings,
4   Tiger caves next to its pillars and eaves.
In the peaceful valley, only the echoes of pines;
Deep in the mountains there are no cries of birds.
Jasper peaks, facing the windows, cleave;
8   The golden stream, piercing the forest, sings.
The road to Ying goes to the end of the clouds;
On rivers of Qin it clears beyond the rain.
The wild goose king holds fruits in his beak as gifts,
12   And the deer woman strolls treading on flowers.
Mustering strength I leave my humble village
To return to the fold and lodge in the Conjured City.
Encircling the hedge wild bracken grows;
16   In the empty building mountain cherries bloom.
A fragrant meal of dark zizania kernels,
Fine vegetables, and green taro-root broth.
I vow to stay until their pure chants end,
20   Sitting correctly to study nonrebirth.

NOTES

Line 2:   The "green jewel" or *vaiḍūrya* (cat's-eye) is one of the seven precious objects named several times in the *Lotus Sūtra*.

Line 3:   "Dragon palace" was a term for a Buddhist monastery.

Line 9:   Ying was the capital of the ancient southern state of Chu.

Line 11:   This alludes to two Buddhist tales, the first included in the *Sūtra of the Buddha's Rewards for Mercy* (*Fo bao en jing*), a text dating from the Latter Han dynasty, about a flock of five hundred wild geese whose king fell into a hunter's net. The other birds were so distraught that one spit blood, and when the hunter saw this and realized that they loved and would die for one another, he freed the king. The second story, in the *Jewel Forest in the Garden of the Law* (*Fayuan zhulin*), tells of a monk named Daduo who meditated all day on a mountain; when it came time for him to eat, birds flew by bearing fruit for him in their beaks.

Line 12:   This alludes to a story in the *Sūtra of the Buddha's Rewards for Mercy* about a girl who was conceived immaculately by a deer and an immortal; wherever she walked, lotus flowers sprang up at her feet.

Line 14:   For "Conjured City," see poem 54, line 2n.

Line 20:   For "nonrebirth," see poem 54, line 8n.

POEM

66

(3/7a; I, 39–40)

Visiting Monk Xuan

Preface: Although this monk is externally but a man, internally he is one with heaven. He is neither inflexible nor disorderly; he can renounce the laws [of visible phenomena] and attain a profound tranquility. With an empty mind he can move with the clouds. He holds with neither form nor emptiness and does not regard objects as objects. His silent language is boundless, for he does not speak in words. Therefore, I have followed him and achieved a spiritual communion. He completely explains mysterious relationships and dives through a sea of virtues. At this time a good rain was just falling and everything in springtime was beautiful. This is explained in the poem and is confirmed by hundreds of other men.

My early years are not worthy of words:
When I saw the Tao I was already old in years.
How can I regret past affairs?
4   The rest of my life luckily can be nurtured.
I vow from now on to cease eating garlic and meat
And never again to get tangled in worldly nets.
Floating fame I shall leave to tassels and girdles:
8   The empty nature has no restraining halter.
I have followed this great guide and master,
Burning incense, I look up to him with reverence.
He lives at ease within a single room,
12   Amid nature's myriad jumbled forms.
Morning orioles sing within tall willows;
Spring rain echoes on the long verandah.
At the foot of his bed is a pair of Ruan Fu's clogs,

16   *In front of the window a staff of strong bamboo.*
About to see the Buddha's countless cloud-bodies,
I scorn the manifestations of heaven and earth.
Singlemindedly within the demands of the Dharma,
20   *I wish to accept the rewards of nonrebirth.*

NOTES

Title: This was a well-known monk who lived at Mt. Zhongnan, south of Chang'an; he had several students, among them Wang Wei and the emperor Xuanzong. This poem was written around the end of 740.

Line 7:   "Tassels and girdles" is a synecdoche for government officials.

Line 15:   Ruan Fu of the Jin dynasty was well known for his reclusive spirit and his fondness for his wooden clogs (see the *Jin History*, 49/1365).

Line 17:   This refers to the notion that the Buddha can take on innumerable forms resembling and hovering like clouds over men, in order to protect and save them.

Line 20:   For "nonrebirth," see poem 54, line 8n.

POEM
67
(9/4a; I, 158)

An Autumn Night, Sitting Alone

Sitting alone I lament my two temples,
In the empty hall, close to the second watch.
Mountain fruits are falling in the rain;
Beneath the lamp insects chirp in the grass.
White hairs in the end are hard to alter,
And yellow gold cannot be produced.
If you wish to know how to shed the illness of age—
There is only the study of nonrebirth.

NOTES

Line 2:   The "second watch" was the period between 9–11 p.m.

Line 6:   This alludes to popular Taoist attempts at alchemy and developing methods for achieving immortality.

Line 8:   For "nonrebirth," see poem 54, line 8n.

POEM
68
(5/11b; I, 86)

Lamenting Yin Yao

How long can a human lifetime last?
In the end we return to formlessness.
I think of you, waiting only to die:
4 *Ten thousand things can grieve a person's heart.*
Your kind mother has not yet been buried,
Your only daughter is just ten years old.
In the vast expanse beyond the chilly wilds,
8 *Desolate, I hear the sounds of lament.*
Floating clouds fill the boundlessness;
Flying birds are unable to sing.
How lonely are the traveling men!
12 *The white sun turns bitter cold.*
I regret that when you were still alive
And asked to study nonrebirth with me,
My exhortations sadly came too late
16 *And caused you to end without success.*
Old friends all have gifts to bestow
But also could not reach you in your lifetime.
I failed you in more ways than one:
20 *Crying in pain I return to my brushwood gate.*

NOTES

Title: Yin Yao (709–48), a native of Danyang in Jiangsu province, was a minor official, poet, and fellow Buddhist.

Line 14: For "nonrebirth," see poem 54, line 8n.

POEM
69
(14/7a; I, 266)

Lamenting Yin Yao

We send you back for burial on Stone Tower Mountain.
Pines and cypresses green on green: the guests have ridden home.

Your bones buried among white clouds will be there forever,
Only leaving the water to flow toward the realm of men.

NOTE

Line 1:   Stone Tower Mountain is located near Chang'an.

POEM
70
(6/9a; I, 101–2)

Sent to the Chongfan Monastery Monk

The Chongfan monk
The Chongfan monk
In autumn goes home to Fufu, in spring will not return.
Falling flowers and calling birds are numerous and confused.
A door on the stream, a window facing mountains: quiet and at
*   peace.*
Amid these gorges who knows that human affairs exist?
Within the commandery one gazes afar at empty clouded moun-
*   tains.*

NOTE

Line 3:   For Mt. Fufu see poem 60, title note.

POEM
71
(13/la; I, 239)

In the Mountains, Sent to All My Younger
Brothers and Sisters

In the mountains many companions in the Dharma
Meditate and chant, forming a group of their own.
From a citywall, if men gaze at them from afar,
They should only see white clouds.

NOTE

Line 1: "Companions in the Dharma" is a term for Buddhist monks and nuns.

POEM

72

(13/1b; I, 240)

Given to Wei Mu the Eighteenth

We are both "dark-pupiled" travelers
And share a longing for white clouds.
If we do not go to the eastern mountain,
Each day we'll let the spring grass grow deep.

NOTES

Line 1: For "dark-pupiled," see poem 55, line 2n.

Line 3: This is an allusion to the famous Jin dynasty recluse Xie An; see poem 40, line 3n.

Line 4: This alludes to an anonymous second-century-B.C. poem entitled "Summons for a Recluse Gentleman" (*Zhao yinshi*) and included in the *Songs of Chu*, 12/381–85. Presumably addressed to an official who had withdrawn from service, it presents a lengthy and vivid description of the various perils and fearsome aspects of nature in an effort to entice him to return to civilized society. Early in the poem the speaker mentions deep, flourishing spring grass as part of the wilds from which the recluse has not yet returned; here, however, Wang Wei obviously reverses the thrust of the original poem. For a translation of the "Summons," see Hawkes, pp. 119–20.

POEM

73

(9/1b; I, 154)

Traveling to the Dwelling of Li, Man of the Mountains, and Writing This on His Walls

The world is completely like a dream.
In a wild mood he sometimes sings to himself.
Ask about years: Pine trees are old.

Has he land? Bamboo forests aplenty.
He asks Han Kang to sell him some herbs;
He'll let Master Xiang pass through his door.
Yet he resents, lying on pillow and mat:
What can be done about white clouds?

NOTES

Line 5:   Han Kang, cognomen Boxiu, was a native of Baling, near Chang'an in present-day Shaanxi province, who sold herbal medicines in the capital and never changed his prices. One day when a woman identified him by name, he despaired because he had wanted to remain obscure; he left the city and escaped into the mountains around Baling. See the *History of the Latter Han*, 83/2770–71.

Line 6:   Xiang (or Shang) Chang, cognomen Ziping, was a native of Chaoge in Henan who was well known for his familiarity with the *Classic of Changes* and various Taoist texts. Despite repeated entreaties, he refused to hold government office, and during the Jianwu reign period (A.D. 25–56), after marrying off his children, he disappeared into the mountains. See the *History of the Latter Han*, 83/2758–59.

POEM

74
(3/12a; I, 48)

Farewell

Dismounting I give you wine to drink,
And inquire where you are going.
You say you did not achieve your wishes
And return to rest at the foot of Southern Mountain.
But go—do not ask again:
White clouds have no ending time.

POEM

75
(13/la; I, 239)

Answering Pei Di

Vast and broad, the wide cold current;
Gray and bleak, the dark autumn rain.

You ask about Zhongnan Mountain:
My heart knows beyond white clouds.

COMMENTARY

This poem was written in response to one by the poet's friend which describes the obscuring darkness of the rain at Wang Wei's Wang River estate and inquires at the end if Mt. Zhongnan, unseen, still exists. Pei Di's poem is entitled "At Wang Valley Being Met by Rain, Remembering Zhongnan Mountain and Presenting a Quatrain" and is included in Wang Wei's collection on the same page. It has been cited as evidence that Wang Wei's retreat to Mt. Zhongnan antedated the one to his Wang River estate in Lantian.

Notes to Chapter Four

1. *A History of Zen Buddhism* (Boston: Beacon, 1971), p. 55. For more extensive accounts of the adaptation of Buddhism in China, see Kenneth K. S. Ch'en, *Buddhism in China: A Historical Survey* (Princeton: Princeton University Press, 1964) and his *The Chinese Transformation of Buddhism*. E. Zürcher's *The Buddhist Conquest of China: The Spread and Adaptation of Buddhism in Early Medieval China* (Leiden: E. J. Brill, 1959) focuses on the assimilation of Buddhism in southern and central China during the fourth and fifth centuries A.D. and emphasizes the importance of the social and cultural environment.

2. *The Central Philosophy of Buddhism: A Study of the Mādhyamika System* (London: Allen and Unwin, 1955), pp. 214, 220.

3. Derk Bodde, in Fung Yu-lan, *A History of Chinese Philosophy*, trans. Derk Bodde (Princeton: Princeton University Press, 1953; 2 vols.), II, 295.

4. For an explanation of *skandhas*, see Edward Conze, *Buddhism: Its Essence and Development* (New York: Harper and Row, 1959), p. 14 and *passim*.

5. *The Vimalakīrti Nirdeśa Sūtra*, trans. Charles Luk (Berkeley: Shambala, 1972), pp. 53–54.

6. *The Buddhist Teaching of Totality: The Philosophy of Hwa-Yen Buddhism* (University Park, Pa.: Pennsylvania State University Press, 1971), pp. 88–90.

7. "Buddhism in China," in *The Legacy of China*, ed. Raymond Dawson (Oxford: Oxford University Press, 1964), p. 70. See also Chapter Three of his *The Buddhist Conquest of China*, pp. 81–179, and Kenneth K. S. Ch'en, *Buddhism in China*, pp. 61–65.

8. Trans. Edward Conze, *Buddhist Wisdom Books* (New York: Harper and Row, 1972), p. 81.

9. From the biography of Niutou Fayong (594–657) in *The Transmission of the Lamp (Jingde chuan deng lu* [*Taishō*, Vol. 51, No. 2076, 4/228a]); trans. Chang Chung-yüan, *Original Teachings of Ch'an Buddhism* (New York: Vintage, 1971), p. 24.

10. Trans. Philip B. Yampolsky, *The Platform Sutra of the Sixth Patriarch* (New York: Columbia University Press, 1967), p. 161. He provides the original on p. 18 of the Chinese text.

11. Trans. D. C. Lau, *Tao Te Ching* (Baltimore: Penguin, 1963), p. 57.

12. From his biography in the *Biographies of Lofty Monks* (*Gao seng zhuan*), quoted in Fung Yu-lan, II, 270.

13. W. Liebenthal, "The World Conception of Chu Tao-sheng," *Monumenta Nipponica*, XII (1956), p. 98; quoted in Dumoulin, p. 62.

14. From his biography in *The Transmission of the Lamp* (*Taishō*, Vol. 51, No. 2076, 5/242b); trans. Chang Chung-yüan, pp. 33–34.

15. Watson, *Chinese Lyricism*, p. 170. And in his discussion of the most apparent influence of Buddhism on the literary life of China, Kenneth K. S. Ch'en devotes only four pages to translations of poems by Wang Wei and fifty-five to Bo Juyi. See *The Chinese Transformation of Buddhism*, pp. 179–239.

16. G. W. Robinson has also noted that this image has "an important non-literal significance." He writes that "the white clouds or, sometimes, *beyond* the white clouds, represent some incorporeal, ideally pure country of the spirit. . . ." See his *Poems of Wang Wei* (Baltimore: Penguin, 1973), p. 18. Indeed, the association of white clouds with eremitic retreat was an established poetic convention by Wang Wei's time.

FIVE

Nature Poems

W E have now come to the poems for which Wang Wei has be-
come ˙justly famous—his impassive depictions of tranquil nature
scenes, often written while on temporary retreat from service at
court. Although, as I hope has been made clear, they do not make up
the entirety of his *oeuvre* by any means, they do embody the type of
vision most characteristic of and best expressed by him. They are also
more immediately accessible to Western readers by virtue of the rela-
tively less significant role played by literary, historical, and religious
allusions in them than in other works, although it is important to
remember that most of these would have been thoroughly familiar to
Wang Wei's own audience. In most cases notes are only necessary to
supply geographical information. For these reasons, and also be-
cause these evocations of scene tend to be rather brief, more transla-
tions have been included here than in any other chapter.

I have arranged these poems according to certain patterns of
perception and thought which underlie Wang Wei's mode of appre-
hending the world, but the distinctions are certainly not hard and
fast ones. The first four poems continue along the lines suggested at
the end of the last chapter, revealing an implicit denial of the visual
which is striking in the work of someone who has been singled out
for the visual immediacy and precision of his concrete images by
most Western critics. This is not surprising, however, when the
philosophical and religious underpinnings, with their emphasis on
intuitive rather than sensuous perception, are considered. In poem
76, "Written on Crossing the Yellow River to Qinghe," for example,
Wang Wei explicitly frames the presentation of precise details of a
natural scene by statements which suggest a more powerful haziness
of vision. Sky and earth seem to have merged in the opening of this
poem, and the speaker can distinguish nothing within this vast ex-

panse of river and clouds. Although the uniformity momentarily dis-
perses to offer a view of some elements of his surroundings, he sees
no really distinct objects; even during this brief period of clarity his
sense of sight is unreliable, for he only "seems to" spot mulberry
trees and hemp plants on the shore. And in the final couplet, as the
poet turns to look back on the course he has traveled, he finds his
view blocked once again: a huge watery mist encloses and obscures
everything in the scene.

Wang Wei again suggests the bounds of visual perception in
poem 77, "Mt. Zhongnan," which also opens with a depiction of con-
nectedness and distance. The "celestial capital" which the mountain
adjoins may refer to an imaginary stellar as well as to the actual im-
perial center, so it simultaneously looms up into the heights and
overlooks Chang'an. The following hyperbolic image (the range was
actually limited to the inland province of Shaanxi) conveys the sense
of horizontal, in addition to this vertical, extension. It is above all in
the second couplet that Wang Wei evokes the contingent and limited
nature of perception. Each line contains a verb of sight coupled with
another active verb, which is then followed by an implicit denial of
the ability to actually see anything at all. As he turns to gaze into the
distance behind him, white clouds unite to obstruct his view. And as
he proceeds forward, the azure mists which he had once perhaps
perceived as a distinct entity have suddenly, now that he has pene-
trated them, disappeared or become "nothing" (wu). In both direc-
tions his view is blocked, by an enclosing barrier of clouds behind
and undefined "nothingness" ahead; the neo-Taoist implications of
wu, of course, also suggest that the true basis of reality is something
that cannot be "looked" at.

Another way in which Wang Wei renders apparently precise im-
agery curiously unvisualizable is by using a few key abstract nouns,
as in poem 78, "Sailing down the Han River." Here again the second
couplet emphasizes the intangibility of the scene, with the subject in
each case an abstraction ("flow" and "color") rather than a concrete
noun, creating a sense of elusive otherworldliness. The river's flow
extends "beyond heaven and earth" and is thus inaccessible to nor-
mal human perception. Likewise, the mountain's hue lies some-
where "between [or within] being and nonbeing," a description
which can hardly be considered visually immediate. Furthermore,
the terminology here recalls the Buddhist notions of the apparent
illusoriness of all things yet also their ultimate reality in the unity of
emptiness. The word for "color" (se), for example, is also the Chinese
translation for the Sanskrit rūpa, the Buddhist term for form, appear-
ance, and phenomenon. Wang Wei is thus implying here that no dis-
tinctions can be made between the concrete and the abstract, or exis-
tence and nonexistence; rūpa and śūnyatā are identical, as phrased in

the *Heart Sūtra* quoted above (p. 117): "form is emptiness and the very emptiness is form." And after presenting elements of the scene in terms that cannot be visually apprehended, Wang Wei goes on to suggest the fundamental relativity of perception. The cities in line 5 seem to be floating on the shore because the observer himself is not stationary, but passing by in his boat, and what appears to be the sky moving among the waves is actually only its reflection. The ethereality of the scene is further heightened when we remember that the word for sky here (*kong*) also means emptiness.

Poem 79, "Zhongnan Retreat," similarly uses abstractions to suggest a certain evanescent, unvisualizable quality of the concrete. Wang Wei opens in an unusually discursive manner, evoking the freedom and spontaneity of life in reclusion and then ambiguously suggesting an ideal mode of cognition in line 3. "Splendid things" (*sheng shi*) may be interpreted, somewhat paradoxically, as either "worldly affairs" or "beautiful scenes," or it may also refer to "affairs of the past," as in the phrase *sheng chao*, which means "the past dynasty." In any case, for Wang Wei these "splendid things" seem to represent any aspects of the phenomenal world which men habitually value but which he, in contrast, knows to be "empty." "Empty knowledge," of course, is the nondual awareness of *śūnyatā*, the transcendence of distinctions through the intuitive apprehension of an underlying oneness of all things. Wang Wei continues to undermine the reliability of normal perception in the third couplet, where the object of each verb is not a concrete noun but an abstraction: "place" and "time." He defines his destination in negative, imprecise terms: it is simply "the place where the water ends," all other scenic details remaining unspecified, and he watches not the clouds themselves moving in the sky but "the time when clouds rise." The action of the clouds has been frozen, but that does not make them more stable, concrete, and easily apprehended. Rather, time itself seems to have been hypostatized and transformed into an object of perception which by nature cannot be visually perceived.

This refusal to concentrate detail on specific objects also characterizes the dominant temporal patterns underlying Wang Wei's depictions of natural scenes and illustrated in the next four poems. His preference for the unknowable, unspecifiable, and vague emerges especially clearly in his focus on extended moments of transition, whether on a daily or a seasonal scale, when temporal flux prevents the isolation of particular moments or objects. Yet at the same time, although this concern concentrates on time as linear movement and change, by becoming the very object of focus it paradoxically stops the flow and results in the sense of stasis and timelessness typical of the poet's works. Poem 80, "Dwelling in the Mountains: Impromptu Lines," for example, is situated at two transitional moments—of the

season and of the day. Bamboos "hold new powder," the promise of
the future, while lotuses shed their petals or "old clothes," remnants
of the past. Similarly, the lighting of fires signals the beginning of the
night while the return of the water chestnut pickers ends the day. In
each case the juxtaposition serves to hypostatize a moment in the
natural cycle, embracing temporal distinctions only to transcend
them. The last four lines of poem 81, "Recluse Li's Mountain Dwell-
ing," create a similar extended moment.

Poem 82, "Rejoicing that Zu the Third Has Come to Stay," refers
simultaneously to present, past, and future moments in the poet's
friendship, and the next poem to the same person also creates a sense
of stasis through the juxtaposition of temporal adverbs, which ap-
pear in all but two lines. In the first line "just" evokes the briefness
of the friends' visit together; they have seemed "only" to have had
the time to smile once, and this has "just" occurred in the immediate
past. "Still" in line 2 also links past and present, but with the oppo-
site implications: while their happiness has been fleeting, their sad-
ness is prolonged indefinitely. The farewell banquet has occurred in
the past, but "already" indicates the speaker's painful awareness of
the future, and "again" in line 4 brings the past into the present, with
its notion of recurrence also suggesting a cyclical stasis. Line 7 evokes
the speed of Zu's departure, collapsing time into a moment which
embraces both present and past. Wang Wei's friend has, by implica-
tion, just untied his boat and set off, yet he is "already far away": his
travel, then, seems to have taken "no time." And the last line explic-
itly depicts the motionlessness developed throughout the poem; tem-
poral and physical stasis are linked, for Zu Yong is actually still stand-
ing still.

Spatial parallels to this all-embracing temporal stasis in Wang
Wei's poetry can be seen in poems 84–87. Just as he focuses on tran-
sitional moments to obliterate clear distinctions in time, so he often
presents landscapes in which locations and directions of movement
are juxtaposed and balanced. Granted, in "Written at Qi River Fields
and Gardens," for example, the parallelism of regulated verse would
demand the oppositions in space of the middle two couplets, which
seem to cancel each other out, but the first and last couplets also
contribute to the creation of a vast tableau devoid of motion. In the
next four poems, verbs which express location or contiguity rather
than transitive action—such as "overlooks," "joins," "connects"—
and place words which simply locate things in relation to each
other—such as "beyond," "amid," "above," "below," etc.—similarly
create the impression of motionlessness. Furthermore, this mode of
presentation evokes the sense of a fundamentally interconnected
universe and avoids concentration on the specific description of any

one particular object, as might be expected from Wang Wei's aware-
ness of perceptual limitations and his preference for vagueness. For
example, in poem 85, "Recent Clearing: An Evening View," we seem
to have been given a number of visualizable details, but the poet
actually provides no specific information, except for colors, about the
physical characteristics and contours of elements in the scene. Rather
than focus on an extended description of one object in each line, he
merely names it and places it in relation to another. Nor does he
specify where each pair should be placed within the total scene; he is
concerned less with painting a detailed canvas than with evoking his
particular sense of space.

Farewell poems provide a predictably apt context for develop-
ing notions of time and space, and Wang Wei's many works written
on such occasions are no exception. Poems 88–97 were all composed
on the departures of various friends and colleagues, mostly for gov-
ernment posts in the provinces. In almost every case Wang Wei char-
acteristically traces the path or events his addressee will soon tra-
verse and experience, thus in effect collapsing time and space into an
all-encompassing whole. Poem 89, "Farewell to Yuan the Second on
His Mission to Anxi," is a notable exception, for its last line drifts off
into the unknown. This sense of incompletion must have been ap-
parent to traditional audiences, however, for when the poem became
a popular farewell song, the last line was repeated three times.

The next few poems do typically display a knowledge of immi-
nent events which joins disparate moments—not only present and
future, but also the past, by way of historical allusion—in a timeless
whole. Wang Wei combines this with frequently verbless evocations
of the landscape as a vast enclosed entity in which all elements, and
by implication poet and friend, too, are linked, thus transcending
distance in space as well. Poem 95, "Farewell to Senior Officer Yang
Going to Office in Guozhou," for example, begins by exaggerating
the difficulties of the friend's journey and indirectly suggests that
Yang should perhaps abandon such impossible travels. The second
couplet contains no verbs, creating the sense of both spatial and tem-
poral expanse. The path of one thousand Chinese miles is one which
only birds should be flying; by implication, the actual distance which
men must traverse, winding up, down, and around the mountains,
would be much greater. And temporally the journey would also seem
unending, for gibbons' cries, traditionally interpreted as mournful,
would be heard relentlessly all day, every day. Yet this space is si-
multaneously one in which Wang Wei and Yang are connected, here
by the image of the moon they share. And the cuckoo's call in the last
line alludes by convention to the prospect of return: this final image
brings the poem back to its point of departure and, coupled with the

reference to the moon and the opening mention of the impossibility
of travel, creates the impression that Yang has never left, that no
movement has occurred at all.

In the next three poems Wang Wei specifically invokes the span-
ning of distances by coupling the word "from afar" (*yao*) with verbs
of cognition or recognition. Despite the vastness soon to separate
speaker and addressee in poem 96, "Farewell to Judiciary Inspector
Wei," the former knows from afar the latter's feelings and percep-
tions. The same phrase recurs in poem 98, "Written on Climbing
Candidate Pei Di's Little Pavilion," and to the same effect. The open-
ing lines here describe a peaceful life amid the fullness of nature,
with interesting transpositions in the second couplet similar to those
of poem 84: although we would generally expect to find the smaller
or more quickly moving objects, the birds, defined in relation to the
larger sun, here Wang Wei presents them as an unmoving point of
reference next to the usually imperceptible downward movement of
the star. Similarly, in the following line he attributes what is normally
considered a human quality—being at leisure—to the autumn plain.
In both cases, the two actions or states are typically depicted as con-
tiguous or linked, and the reversals, furthermore, suggest an ab-
stract, underlying unity of man and nature that would enable such
interchangeability of description.

This poem was not written, of course, on the occasion of a
friend's departure, but the situation is similar, if somewhat ambigu-
ous, because of the implied separation. From the title we know that
Wang Wei is at Pei Di's pavilion, but the whereabouts of the latter is
unclear. He may also be there as host, but the mention of someone
on the forest's edge suggests that Pei Di is probably there instead and
thus unable to "see within these eaves" and know of his friend's
presence. One could also translate the third couplet as: "From afar I
know you are at the edge of the distant woods,/ And I do not see you
within these eaves." Or Wang Wei may simply be speaking of what is
the case when *he* is at his own country home, from which he cannot
see Pei's pavilion. In any case, the poet is simultaneously expressing
his awareness of the distance between two locations—and possibly
men—and transcending that very separation by imaginatively put-
ting himself in both places at the same time, an act achieved in his
early work, poem 3. The ambiguity of the final couplet here rein-
forces this impression, for the traveler could be interpreted as either
Pei Di arriving at the pavilion or Wang Wei returning home. Move-
ment occurs, then, in both directions, which cancel each other out
and create the sense of a spatially enclosed and interconnected uni-
verse.

The harmony between self and world implicit in this poem un-
derlies, of course, Wang Wei's work as a whole. His poetry reveals a

thoroughgoing fusion of emotion and scene: nature and man can be presented in the same terms, so that the depiction of one simultaneously speaks of the other. This integration manifests itself in various ways. In poems 99 and 100, for instance, although the detailed focus on one object in each is unusual, the poet typically relates both birds and bamboo to human activities, while stressing at the same time the superiority of purely natural phenomena. Thus the morning cries of the hundred-tongued birds are preferable to those of the domesticated cock, and bamboos growing freely by a Taoist altar are finer than those employed for practical functions.

Wang Wei occasionally suggests the integrality of man and nature by means of a pathetic fallacy, the transference of human emotions to natural objects. This is true of poem 101, "The Red Peony," where the poet further indicates that his understanding of the flower's true feelings can penetrate its deceptively gay exterior. Similarly, he presents the river and rain as grieving in the next poem, and the willow blossoms teasing the late spring in poem 104.

The painful contrast which opens poem 103, "Farewell to Qiu Wei on His Return East of the Yangzi after Failing the Examination"— between internal and external situations, the friend's disappointment and the lushness of spring—is rare in Wang Wei's poetry. Much more common is the interpenetration of the two realms indicated in the third couplet of poem 105, "On a Spring Day Going with Pei Di to Xinchang Ward to Visit the Hermit Lu and Not Encountering Him." And if the poet makes explicit comparisons between man and nature, he is more likely to emphasize likeness rather than difference. Thus he compares thoughts of his friend to the ubiquitous colors of spring in poem 106, "Farewell to Shen Zifu Returning East of the Yangzi," his heart to a peaceful river in the following work, and vice versa in the next. In poem 109 the relationship is not so much one of likeness as of effect: the arrival at a mountaintop after a journey through dense foliage produces both a physical and an emotional liberation.

Such overt comparisons, however, are the exception rather than the rule in Wang Wei's poetry, for his notion of the integrality of man and nature generally remains unstated. This is especially true of the many works written while he was on retreat from court service, which constitute the remainder of the translations in this chapter. To be sure, the degree of discursiveness and emotionality, as opposed to the pure depiction of scene with human presences deemphasized though always there, varies even within this group, and this is reflected in my selection. Thus poems 110, "Written in Early Autumn in the Mountains," and 111, "In Response to the Visit of Several Gentlemen," are imbued with a sense of melancholy which in the latter even suggests an unhappiness with life in seclusion. This is not an attitude traditionally associated with "Wang Wei the recluse poet,"

yet it is not altogether surprising when his commitment to govern-
ment service is recalled. Even poem 112, "Drifting on the Front
Pond," therefore, which otherwise presents images of the mutual se-
renity of man and nature, concludes with a statement about the
poet's "irresolute" attitude toward remaining there or returning, pre-
sumably to court.

The next four poems were all written at Wang Wei's country
estate on the Wang River in Lantian and embody a movement from
this implicit uncertainty to a thoroughgoing tranquility of life amid
nature. Poem 113, "Written after Prolonged Rain at Wang River Es-
tate," opens with a depiction of a placid summer scene and of the
speaker's own appropriately ascetic practices. But whereas the first
of the two concluding allusions asserts the certainty of his with-
drawal, the second undermines it: in protesting the seagulls' refusal
to trust him, Wang Wei suggests that they might indeed have reasons
for doubting the sincerity of his rejection of the court world. The
images in the third couplet of poem 114, "Written on Returning to
Wang River," are equally unsettling. The tendrils and catkins are frail
and fleeting, evocative of the ephemerality of natural beauty and of
life in general, as well as of a corresponding instability in the poet
himself. He is a complex of conflicting doubts: about the likelihood of
attaining a purity of mind and freedom from worldly trammels (he
has not yet reached the realm of white clouds but is only heading
"toward" them); about his desire to live in extreme solitude; and,
most basically, about the strength of his wish to retreat at all. This
irresolution, along with the implied contrast between old age and the
youthful spring grasses, may account for the sadness of the final line.
Although Wang Wei seems to close both the gate and the poem with
a reassuring finality, he has opened up many questions for both him-
self and his readers.

In poems 115, "Wang River Retreat," and 116, "At My Wang
River Retreat, Presented to Candidate Pei Di," however, we see none
of these doubts, and only peaceful evocations of life in retreat with
the companionship of like-minded recluses. This is also true of the
next two poems, among Wang Wei's best known works. "Dwelling in
the Mountains: An Autumn Evening" opens with a description of the
mountains as "empty," yet we find later that they are by no means
devoid of human presences. The adjective thus evokes the tranquility
of the poet's country home and also calls to mind its many Buddhist
implications about the nature of reality. The choice of such transi-
tional periods as evening and autumn is characteristic, as are the in-
terrelationships among natural objects implied in the second couplet.
In each case Wang Wei disrupts normal syntax to place the verb at
the end of the line, thus presenting the phenomena not as acting

upon one another in an agent-receptor relationship, but as existing side by side in total harmony, without clear subject–object distinctions. And just as there are no privileged objects in nature, so man does not occupy a privileged point of view. In the third couplet the observer apprehends movements in nature without prior knowledge of their causes: the effects—rustling among the bamboos and lotuses—are noticed before their causes—washerwomen and fishermen coming down the river—are discovered. Throughout the poem Wang Wei refrains from obtruding an active, dominating subjectivity upon the scene and suggests instead the integrality and equivalence of man and nature, and the concluding allusion allows him to comment on and reinforce this sense in an indirect manner. By reversing the meaning of the ancient poem written to summon a recluse back to court, Wang Wei indicates that he is oblivious to the passage of time, to be signaled by the withering of spring grasses, and reveals an attitude of quiet contentment and submergence of the self in nature.

Poem 118, "In Response to Vice-Magistrate Zhang," similarly embodies this fundamental integration. It opens discursively, apparently from the perspective of one who has chosen a life of quiet seclusion over involvement in mundane affairs, but then shifts to more imagistic language. In the third couplet Wang Wei presents some typical scenes and pleasures of the hermit, phrased with ambiguous syntax. In addition to the reading I have given it, each line may be read as two juxtaposed clauses ("Pine winds blow; I loosen my belt. / The mountain moon shines; I pluck my zither"); as one clause with a compound verb of causation ("Pine winds blow and loosen my belt. / The mountain moon shines and plucks my zither"); or as one clause without a direct indication of activity on the part of the human subject ("Pine winds blow on my loosened belt. / The mountain moon shines on my plucked zither"). Certainly, all four possibilities evoke an immediate, harmonious relationship between man and nature.

In the concluding couplet Wang Wei turns to address his friend Zhang, like him an official. The latter has apparently questioned the poet about the reasons underlying failure and success, or about the principle of universal change—both meanings are possible—and, in any case, he is interested in discovering how one should relate to the vicissitudes of the world. The final image, Wang Wei's "response," suggests at least three interpretations. In the first place, it may be regarded as a non-answer in the tradition of the Chan or Zen *kōan* (*gongan* in Chinese), by means of which a Buddhist master attempts to bring a student to enlightenment by answering a rational question with a non sequitur, thus jolting the latter out of practiced, logical, categorical modes of thought and liberating his mind to facilitate a sudden intuitive realization of truth. Wang Wei's answer, in this case, would deliberately bear no relationship to Zhang's query, seeking instead to reject such cognitive concerns.

Or secondly, because the fisherman, along with the woodcutter, is a favorite Taoist figure who represents a rustic, pure life in harmony with nature, we may read this final line as a simple suggestion to Zhang to follow the example of such men and escape from official life to the freedom and serenity of country living. This is a realm, moreover, where such distinctions as the failure and success of one's career will have no meaning.

Yet a third interpretation of this line comes to mind when we consider that it may allude to a specific fisherman's song, the "Fisherman" (*Yu fu*), included in the *Songs of Chu*, 7/295–98. In this earlier poem, a rustic fisherman converses with the fourth-century-B.C. poet Qu Yuan, who had been a loyal minister to the king of Chu and committed to the Confucian ideal of service but who was slandered by others at court and banished. He remained self-righteous about his inflexible moral purity and later chose suicide over an acceptance of the contemporary situation. In this song, when Qu Yuan meets the fisherman, he explains that he has been exiled because he was "clear" and "sober," while the rest of the world was "muddy" and "drunk." The fisherman, however, suggests that it might have been more circumspect to adapt to the circumstances and move with the times:

> "The Wise Man is not chained to material circumstances," said the fisherman, "but can move as the world moves.
> "If all the world is muddy, why not help them to stir up the mud and beat up the waves?
> "And if all men are drunk, why not sup their dregs and swill their lees?
> "Why get yourself exiled because of your deep thoughts and your fine aspirations?"

When Qu Yuan insists that he would rather drown in the river than compromise and hide his "shining light in the dark and dust of the world," the fisherman departs with a gentle mocking reply:

> The fisherman, with a faint smile, struck his paddle in the water and made off.
> And as he went he sang: "When the Ts'ang-lang's waters are clear, I can wash my hat strings in them;
> "When the Ts'ang-lang's waters are muddy, I can wash my feet in them."
> With that, he was gone, and did not speak again.
> (Trans. Hawkes, pp. 90–91)

Unlike the self-righteous Qu Yuan, the fisherman, by adjusting to the conditions he finds, paradoxically can remain freer of their influence. Ultimately, perhaps, he realizes that when seen from a larger perspective, the waters are all the same. With this allusion, then, Wang Wei affirms the unifying vision and transcendence of distinctions that constitute the key principle of coherence in his poetic universe.

The last poems in this chapter were composed in three groups, all situated in a country retreat. The seven quatrains entitled "Joys of Fields and Gardens" (poems 119–25) employ a rarely used hexasyllabic line; the resulting impression of extreme symmetry, reinforced by the strict parallelism within couplets observed in each poem, provides a syntactic counterpart to the thematic contrast between service and reclusion which runs through the entire group. And the five "Miscellaneous Poems Written at Huangfu Yue's Cloud Valley" (126–30) all focus on isolated places and events at a friend's estate.

By far the most famous group of poems, however, is Wang Wei's *Wang River Collection* (131–50), written in the company of his friend Pei Di. The preface explains the background of the collection; the twenty quatrains Pei wrote to harmonize with these are included in the Qing dynasty edition of Wang's works. Wang Wei is also said to have painted a long continuous scroll which depicted the same twenty scenic spots on his Lantian estate, but unfortunately, this work is no longer extant, although there are numerous imitations dating from later dynasties.

The order of the poems in the collection seems to be determined by nothing other than the geographical layout of the Wang River estate, if even that, but the sequence as a whole does resume the key modes of consciousness of the poet's entire *oeuvre*. We find here the same transcendence of temporal distinctions, the awareness of boundlessness, the emphasis on perceptual and cognitive limitations, and, running throughout, a sense of the harmony of man and nature. Very few of the poems concentrate on merely providing visual, "painterly" details of a scenic spot but instead indirectly convey these characteristic notions.

The first quatrain (131), for example, could hardly be described as an exhaustive representation of Meng Wall Cove. On the contrary, the juxtaposition of "new home" to "ancient trees" in the first couplet suggests a more abstract concern with time. The distinction between new and old would generally evoke the idea of temporal flux, but Wang Wei then implies that, though others may accept it, he does not. He projects himself into the future to imagine the arrival of a new owner of the estate, who will follow him as inevitably as he did Song Zhiwen, and he visualizes him grieving over "former men's possessions," the most important of which was probably life itself.

Such laments are in vain, first, because what any man may have been or had is ultimately inconsequential when viewed in terms of the larger scheme of things, and second, because such distinctions between people and times are meaningless, since the process will keep recurring. "Meng Wall Cove" itself contains the present, past, and future to create a timeless whole in which all is the same. Several other poems in the group employ allusions to legend or history to the same effect.

Poem 132, "Huazi Hill," presents another familiar notion in Wang Wei's poetry, the sense of almost overwhelming boundlessness. Birds are seen flying off "endlessly" (*bu qiong*, literally, "inexhaustibly"), which could be interpreted either spatially or temporally, or both, and the scene is filled entirely by "continuous mountains," which Wang Wei describes only vaguely as possessing the colors of autumn. Wandering up and down the hill over an undefined space and time, the speaker remarks enigmatically about his sadness. Although he provides no cause for these feelings, their limitlessness corresponds to the qualities of the scene. Moreover, the question without an answer provides an appropriately open-ended nonconclusion to this depiction of the inexhaustible.

"Grained Apricot Lodge" (133) similarly ends on an inconclusive note which also emphasizes the element of ignorance. Wang Wei suggests the same distinction between a realm of clouds (or cloudy mountains) and that of men which has appeared in many other poems. Here he also implies, however, that there may be a link between them, for the clouds may indeed travel to the world of men and make rain. But he states that he does not know if such is the case, so the quatrain concludes with an unanswered question.

A similar phrase, "cannot be known," occurs at the end of the fourth poem in the group, "Clear Bamboo Range" (134), and here the ignorance is even more enigmatic because Wang Wei does not state what it is about the woodcutters that remains unknowable or why. He speaks of "secretly" entering the mountain road, possibly referring to the earlier recluses (the "Four Whiteheads") or perhaps to his own seclusion. Whatever the case, "Clear Bamboo Range" opens with an emphasis on vividness and sharp definition, but the ambiguity and mystery of this couplet are characteristic of both this collection and Wang Wei's work as a whole.

"Southern Hillock" (140), for example, emphasizes the limits of vision; the poet gazes afar at houses on the other shore, but there is no mutual recognition over the distance. And "Magnolia Enclosure" (136) also stresses the vagaries of perception. As in so many other poems, Wang Wei sets the scene during a transitional period—an autumn twilight—when only the last rays of daylight linger on. Through this dimness brilliant colors can be glimpsed but intermittently; this inconstant clarity of vision is also suggested in the last line of "Northern Hillock" (146), where the waters are seen as alternately "Bright and dim to the edge of the azure forest." In "Magnolia Enclosure," furthermore, the evening mists are curiously described as "without a place to be." This suggests a number of possibilities: that nature has somehow provided no place for them to rest; that they are always moving and therefore have no established location; or that they are intangible and thus literally unlocalizable, essentially nowhere. In any case, the image is typical because of its vague reference and negative phrasing.

Poem 135, "Deer Enclosure," is probably the most famous of the entire collection and perhaps even of Wang Wei's work as a whole. Here again we find a denial of the visible and extremely enigmatic language. The poet opens with his familiar adjective, "empty" (*kong*), which may denote the unpopulated state of the mountain and simultaneously imply both its illusory nature and also its ultimate reality.

In neither the first nor the second line does Wang Wei specify the subject, and critics have often commented on the resulting ambiguity and apparent contradiction. Actually, since Chinese poets rarely use personal pronouns, the absence of subjects is not a particularly striking feature of this couplet, and the problem may simply be one that arises only in translation into Western languages. Nevertheless, many readers find it extremely paradoxical that no men are seen, yet human voices are heard. The contradiction can, however, be resolved in an apparently simplistic manner, yet one which would accord with the predominant concerns of Wang Wei's poetry. The other "empty mountains" in his poems have also been found to be occupied by people, certainly the poet himself, at least, and often recluses and monks, which suggests the appropriateness of a Buddhist reading of the term "empty," although we do not need to deny its concomitant implication of a general solitude amid nature. That people cannot be seen, though their voices are heard, simply reminds us of Wang Wei's persistent affirmation of the limits of sight. Hearing may be somewhat more reliable, closer to a nondifferentiating intuition; here, of course, it is also vague: the voices are, in fact, only indistinct "echoes." There is in fact no real contradiction between the two sensory (visual and auditory) messages—just the suggestion, perhaps, of their shared delusory nature.

This lack of perceptual clarity is partly explained by the second couplet, which places the scene at sunset, when the source of light itself is vanishing. Here Wang Wei moves from the massive mountain to focus on a small mossy glade, the deer enclosure of the title. He glimpses the last rays of sunlight, which penetrate the deep forest and cast a final glow. The phrase "reflected light," like the "echoes" in line 2, emphasizes the insubstantiality of what is being perceived, a reflection of what is already intangible—light—and thus two steps removed from the concrete sun. Yet, as anyone who has walked in the woods late in the day well knows, it also aptly characterizes the peculiar quality of fading sunlight there: since its source cannot actually be seen through the trees, the light seems to be emanating from and mutually illuminating the various objects themselves. Its intensity is diminished, but it seems to possess a whiteness of its own which causes the color of the foliage to pale slightly.

The last word of "Deer Enclosure" has also been the subject of much critical discussion. *Shang* is normally read as a place word meaning "upon" or "above"; in another tone, however, it becomes a verb meaning "to ascend," and this is the same tone as that of its rhyme-word "echoes" (*xiang*). Yet both possible tones of *shang* belong to the "oblique" tone category, as does *xiang*, so that there is no serious breach of tonal regulations if the line is read as its quite normal word order would indicate. Nevertheless, although I have attempted to suggest the most likely interpretations of each line in this poem, the number and variety of possibilities demonstrate Wang Wei's typical reliance on ambiguity and avoidance of distinctions.

The voices in "Deer Enclosure," even if they are only echoes, remind us that man is not excluded from the world of the Wang River Collection. "White Rock Rapids" (145), for example, describes a natural scene in terms of human actions: the rushes were once graspable, and the stream itself is presented as the functional site of many families' moonlit washing. Nor does the poet remain in constant and total seclusion. Indeed, poems 137–39 all bring in preparations for the possibility or actual arrival of guests: the brewing of a dogwood blossom infusion, the sweeping of the path, and the welcoming of a traveler from across the lake. In "Lake Yi" (141) the scene is one of parting, which again suggests an immediately prior period of companionship. And "Willow Waves" (142) brings in a more populated world by distinguishing the trees on the country estate from those on the imperial moat in the capital, whose twigs would be broken off in a traditional gesture of parting.

Finally, although "Bamboo Lodge" (147) stresses the speaker's isolation from others, Wang Wei certainly does not deny his own presence in the scene and in fact reveals here the fundamental self-world relationship of his poetry as a whole, one which does not neglect the personal to focus only on the natural, but which is grounded in a strong mutuality of man and nature. Like many other poems in the group, the quatrain opens with an allusion to one of the *Nine Songs* in the ancient southern anthology, the *Songs of Chu*, but without its mood of loneliness or lament. Rather, his solitude here is a choice, and one in which he can enjoy those activities most suggestive of harmony with nature: playing music and voicing the special kind of

Taoist whistle. In line 3 Wang Wei again evokes both the dark denseness of the bamboo grove and the ignorance of other men which may have made his solitude possible. The object of "men do not know" is not clearly specified, for "the deep wood," which may be an inverted object, could also simply be a locative phrase. What others "do not know," then, may be the existence of the grove itself, as well as its meaning, or, more likely, the fact of the speaker's presence there and its significance. By means of this vagueness of reference Wang Wei can emphasize the condition of ignorance itself, the limitations of rational cognition which have been suggested so frequently in his work.

At the same time, however, he may be hinting at another, intuitive mode of knowledge which structures his particular relationship with nature and which other men do not share: they do not truly "know" the woods as he does. And this intuitive relationship is one of complete integration of self and world: the poet has expressed his sense of harmony through his music and his whistle, and nature seems to reciprocate, for the moon comes to shine on him. This image of the moon may also serve as a symbol for a sudden, instantaneous enlightenment occurring after a period of solitary contemplation in the darkness. Certainly, as we have seen, for the Chan Buddhist the realization of spiritual truth is intimately connected with the experience of nature. And it is this intimacy, this dissolution of boundaries between self and world, which is evoked in "Bamboo Lodge" and which has emerged as the fundamental principle of coherence in the world of Wang Wei's poetry.

POEM

76   (4/13a; I, 68)

Written on Crossing the Yellow River to Quinghe

A boat sailing on the great river—
The gathered waters reach to the end of the sky.
Sky and waves suddenly split asunder:
A commandery city—a thousand, ten thousand homes.
Farther on I see a city market again;
There seems to be some mulberry and hemp.
Looking back at my old home country:
The water's expanse joins the clouds and mist.

NOTE

Title: The district of Qinghe was located in present-day Hebei province.

POEM

77

(7/7a; I, 124)

Mt. Zhongnan

Taiyi nears the celestial capital;
Continuous mountains arrive at the edge of the sea.
White clouds, as I turn and gaze, merge.
Azure mists, as I enter and look, disappear.
The whole expanse shifts at the central peak.
Shadow and light differ in every valley.
Wishing to seek lodging among men,
I cross the water to ask an old woodsman.

NOTES

Line 1:   "Taiyi" refers to Mt. Zhongnan, as well as to the whole Zhongnan range south of Chang'an.

Line 5:   The "whole expanse" (*fen ye*, literally, "dividing the wilds") refers to both the mass of constellations which had once been used to demarcate areas of land and that very territory itself.

POEM

78

(8/10b; I, 150)

Sailing down the Han River

On the Chu frontier the three Xiangs come together.
At Jingmen the nine streams pass through.
The river's flow is beyond heaven and earth;
The mountain's color between being and nonbeing.
Commandery cities float on the shore ahead;
Ripples and waves stir the distant sky.
At Xiangyang the lovely scenery
Will let old Master Shan get drunk.

NOTES

Title: The Han River begins its flow in Shaanxi and flows southeast into the Yangzi at Hankou. This poem was probably written during Wang Wei's southern tour of duty in 740.

Line 1:   The "three Xiangs" are the tributaries of the Xiang River, which flows from Hunan in the ancient southern state of Chu.

Line 2:   The "nine streams" are the branches of the Yangzi, which flow through the Jingmen Pass in Hubei.

Line 8:   "Old Master Shan" (*Shan weng*, or, possibly, "Old Man of the Mountains," since *shan* means "mountain") is an allusion to a certain Shan Jian, cognomen Jilun (253–312), who, after an illustrious career spent governing four prefectures, retired to a pastoral area in Xiangyang and became famous for his penchant for drinking. His biography is in the *Jin History*, 43/1228–30.

POEM
79
(3/4a; I, 35)

Zhongnan Retreat

In middle years I am rather fond of the Tao;
My late home is at the foot of Southern Mountain.
When the feeling comes, each time I go there alone.
That splendid things are empty, of course, I know.
I walk to the place where the water ends
And sit and watch the time when clouds rise.
Meeting by chance an old man of the forest,
I chat and laugh without a date to return.

POEM
80
(7/7a; I, 124)

Dwelling in the Mountains: Impromptu Lines

In solitude I close my brushwood gate,
In the vast expanse, facing lowering light.
Cranes nest in pine trees all around;
Men visiting my wicker gate are few.

Tender bamboos hold new powder,
And red lotuses shed old clothes.
At the ford lantern fires are lit:
Everywhere water chestnut pickers come home.

POEM

81

(3/4b; I, 35–36)

Recluse Li's Mountain Dwelling

Gentlemen swell the imperial ranks;
The common man gladly excuses himself.
Now I follow the alchemist wanderer
To his mountaintop home above the forest.
Against the range flowers have not yet blossomed;
Entering clouds, trees are thick and thin.
In broad daylight he keeps to himself and sleeps on;
Mountain birds warble from time to time.

POEM

82

(7/5a; I, 120)

Rejoicing that Zu the Third Has Come to Stay

Before my gate a visitor from Luoyang
Dismounts his horse and brushes off traveling clothes.
Not in vain has an old friend come riding,
Though usually my gate is closed.
Travelers come back from the end of the lane;
Gathered snow carries a lingering glow.
Since early years we have been intimate friends:
Where will your fine carriage return?

NOTES

Title: Zu Yong of Luoyang received his *jinshi* degree in 725 and was a poet and essayist; he was appointed as Officer in the Bureau of Military Equipment (*jiabu yuanwai lang*) by Zhang Yue (667–730).

Line 7:   For "intimate friends," the text reads literally "those sharing a robe,"
an allusion to a song in the *Classic of Poetry* (poem no. 133), whose first stanza
is as follows:

How can you say you have no clothes?
I will share my robe with you.
The king raises his army;
We ready our lances and axes.
I will share enemies with you.

POEM

83
(4/1a; I, 49)

At Qizhou, Bidding Farewell to Zu the Third

Meeting each other, there's just one smile;
Seeing you off, still shedding tears.
At the farewell banquet already pained by parting,
Grieving I enter the desolate city again.
The sky is cold and the distant mountains pure.
Sun dusks, and the long river rushes on.
You loosen the rope and are already far away:
I gaze at you, still standing in place.

NOTE

Title: For Zu the Third, see poem 82.
Qizhou was the name of a commandery in present-day Henan province.

POEM

84
(7/8b; I, 126)

Written at Qi River Fields and Gardens

Life in retreat by the Qi River:
The eastern wilds are vast, no mountains in sight.
The sun is hidden beyond the mulberries,
And the river gleams between the villages.
Herdboys leave gazing afar at their hamlets;

Hunting dogs return following men.
A peaceful man—what is there to do?
The brushwood gate is closed all day long.

NOTE

Title: The Qi is a branch of the Wei River, in present-day Henan province.
Some biographers speculate that Wang Wei spent time in retreat there during
the 740s.

POEM

85
(4/9b; I, 62)

Recent Clearing: An Evening View

A recent clearing: the plains and wilds are vast;
To the limits of sight there is no dust or dirt.
The citywall gate overlooks the ford;
Village trees adjoin the mouth of the creek.
White waters gleam beyond the fields,
And emerald peaks emerge behind the mountains.
In a farming month there are no idle men:
Families pour out to work the southern fields.

POEM

86
(3/4a; I, 35)

To Cui Jizhong of Puyang, Inspired by the Mountains Ahead

Autumn colors inspire fine feelings—
How much more at peace above the pond.
In the distance below the western woods,
We easily recognize mountains in front of the gate.
A thousand miles are crossed by darkest colors;
Several crags emerge from the midst of clouds.

Jagged peaks face the state of Qin,
8 Crowded together, hiding the Jing Pass.
In lingering rain the slanting sun shines;
Through evening mists flying birds return.
My old friend today is as before,
12 But I sigh over my haggard face.

NOTES

Title: Cui Jizhong was Wang Wei's cousin on the maternal side. This poem was written after the autumn of 752, when Cui was named prefect of the commandery of Puyang, in Shandong province.

Line 7:   The area around the capital of Chang'an once constituted the ancient kingdom of Qin, in present-day Shaanxi.

Line 8:   Jing Pass is also located in Shaanxi province.

POEM
87
(6/15b; I, 112)

Written on the Cold Food Festival East of the City

The clear creek threads all the way through peach and plum trees.
Under flowing ripples and green rushes lies fragrant white angelica.
Above the gorge are people's homes: how many all together?
Falling flowers have half dropped into eastward-flowing waters.
Kicked balls frequently pass above the flying birds;
Rope swings vie to emerge from within the drooping willows.
By the vernal equinox youthful ones are already rambling about,
Not needing to wait until Qingming or Lustration Festival time.

NOTES

Title: For the Cold Food Festival, see poem 40, line 7n. People commonly enjoyed swinging on rope swings during this holiday.

Line 7:   The vernal equinox occurred during the second lunar month.

Line 8:   Qingming occurred immediately after the Cold Food Festival, at the beginning of the third lunar month, and was marked by the sweeping of graves. For the Spring Lustration Festival, see poem 30.

POEM

88   (10/12a; I, 190)

Farewell to the Taoist Master Fang on His
Return to Mt. Song

> The immortal official is about to travel to Nine Dragon Pond.
> With tasseled scepter and crimson pennants he leans on the stone
>   shrine.
> The mountain peak thrusts into the heavens, halfway to the top
>   of the sky;
> Caves pierce beneath the river, emerging south of the water.
> By the waterfall firs and pines often carry rain;
> In the setting sun brilliant greens suddenly turn into mist.
> May I ask if the twin white cranes coming to welcome you
> Once in the past at Heng Mountain led Su Dan away?

NOTES

Title: Mt. Song, the central sacred peak, is in Henan province.

Line 1:   Nine Dragon Pond was located to the east of Mt. Song.

Line 8:   The *Record of Spirits and Immortals* (*Shen xian zhuan*) by Ge Hong
(fourth-century A.D.) includes a story about a certain Su Dan of Bin (in
Hunan) who received a summons to prepare for the arrival of a group of
immortals. A flock of white cranes then descended from the purple mists,
changed into youths, and took him away to become an immortal; he is re-
ferred to as Su the Immortal Duke. Mt. Heng is one of the five sacred peaks,
located in Hunan. There is another anecdote about Su Dan in the *Water Classic*
(*Shui jing*), but it does not mention Mt. Heng or the white cranes.

POEM

89   (14/5a; I, 263)

Farewell to Yuan the Second on His Mission
to Anxi

> In Wei City morning rain dampens the light dust.
> By the travelers' lodge, green upon green—the willows' color is
>   new.

I urge you to drink up yet another glass of wine:
Going west from Yang Pass, there are no old friends.

NOTE

Title: The protectorate of Anxi was located in modern Xinjiang. The city of Wei (line 1) was in Shaanxi province, and Yang Pass (line 4) in Dunhuang district of Gansu province.

POEM

90

(8/3a; I, 137–38)

Farewell to Subprefect Qian on His Return to Lantian

The color of grass grows more lovely each day;
Fewer people leave for the Peach Blossom Spring.
In your hand you hold Zhang Heng's rhymeprose;
My eyes follow your colorful Laolai robe.
Each time you wait for mountain cherries to bloom;
Sometimes together with sea swallows you return.
This year by the Cold Food Festival
You should be able to reach your brushwood gate.

NOTES

Title: Qian Qi was a native of Wuxing who received his *jinshi* degree around 750. He has a brief biographical notice in the *New Tang History*, 203/5786.

Line 2:   For Peach Blossom Spring, see poem 6.

Line 3:   This alludes to a work by Zhang Heng, cognomen Pingzi (78–139), entitled "Rhymeprose on Returning to the Country" (*Gui tian fu*); it is included in the *Anthology of Literature*, 15/206–7.

Line 4:   Laolaizi was a recluse noted for his extreme filial piety: even at the age of 70, he would dress in colorful clothes and play like a child in order to amuse his aged parents. In his *Records of the Historian* (63/2141), Sima Qian speculates that Laolaizi and the Taoist sage Laozi were the same person.

Line 7:   For the Cold Food Festival, see poem 40, line 7n.

POEM

91   (8/6b; I, 143)

Farewell to District Magistrate Wei of Fangcheng

From afar I think of the border of reeds and rushes,
The deserted expanse where Chu natives travel.
High birds on the long Huai River,
Flat wasteland by the old Ying citywall.
From your envoy's carriage let nesting pheasants breed;
The district's drums will answer the crows of the cock.
If you see the provincial magistrate,
Do not resent a greeting with tablet in hand.

NOTES

Title: Fangcheng district was located in present-day Henan and in the ancient kingdom of Chu, of which Ying was the capital.

Line 5:   This alludes to Lu Gong, district magistrate of Zhongmou (in Henan province) during the Latter Han dynasty. When it became known that Lu's district had escaped being infested by a plague of destructive grain-eating moths, his superior Yuan An sent Fei Qin to investigate the reasons. After walking through the fields, Lu and Fei rested under a mulberry tree and saw both a pheasant and a young boy nearby. Fei asked the youth why he did not trap the pheasant, and the boy responded that the bird was about to give birth. Fei was amazed and concluded that it was Lu's benevolence, extending through his good influence down to the population, that had spared his district from the plague. The story is given in the *History of the Latter Han*, 25/874.

Line 6:   This is another allusion to a virtuous official, Deng You, cognomen Bodao, a native of Xiangyang during the Jin dynasty. After being appointed governor of the commandery of Wu, Deng became known for the fairness of his administration and the contentment of the populace. When it came time for him to leave his post, the people tried to keep his boat from departing, so that he had to slip out during the night. The people of Wu sang a song about him which ran:

> Bang, bang, beat five drums:
> At cockcrow the sky is about to dawn.
> Marquis Deng has been transferred and cannot stay;
> Prefect Xie has retired and cannot leave.

Deng's biography is included in the *Jin History*, 90/2338–40.

Line 8: Officials presented reports to their superiors on tablets whose material (jade, ivory, bamboo, wood, etc.) would vary depending on the position of the higher official.

POEM

92   (8/9a; I, 147)

Farewell to Xing of Guizhou

Hand bells and pipes will clamor at Jingkou:
On wind-blown waves you go down to Lake Dongting.
From Purple Divide approaching the Crimson Bank,
You'll strike the billows and open the window again.
The sun sets, and river and lake are white.
At high tide, sky and earth turn dark.
Bright pearls will return to Hepu—
They should follow the emissary stars.

NOTES

Title: Xing Ji was appointed Censor of General Affairs (*shiyushi*) of Guizhou (in modern Guangxi) in 761. The four places mentioned in lines 1–3 would have been encountered on the southward journey to his post and are located in Jiangsu, Hunan, Anhui, and Jiangsu provinces, respectively. This poem has been cited as evidence that Wang Wei must not have died until sometime in 761, and not 759, a commonly given date.

Line 7: This alludes to an anecdote related in the *History of the Latter Han* (76/2473). Meng Chang, cognomen Bozhou, was appointed prefect of Taian in Hepu (present-day Guangdong province), a region that did not raise agricultural products but produced pearls for trade with its neighbor, Jiaozhi. When he arrived, he found that because of corruption, the pearls were disappearing from Hepu, trade had fallen off, and the people were dying of starvation. Within a year of his taking office, however, he had managed to correct the situation, bring the pearls back into the market, and restore the original livelihood of the populace.

Line 8: This is an allusion to Li He of the Latter Han dynasty, who was skilled at reading natural signs. During the reign of emperor He (r. 88–106), Li was visited at his home in Yizhou (Sichuan province) by two imperial messengers in disguise, and he astonished them by recognizing their true identities. When queried as to how he had known, he replied that it was because two "messenger" (i.e., shooting) stars had just appeared in the sky, moving in the direction of Yizhou. See the *History of the Latter Han*, 82A/2717–18.

POEM

93   (3/11a; I, 46)

Farewell to Prefect Yuwen
Going to Office in Xuancheng

> Scattered and silent, the mountains beyond the clouds:
> Far into the distance enjoy them from your boat.
> Hand bells and pipes will play as you go up the Yangzi,
4 Echoing clearly through the autumn void.
> The land is distant, the old citywall overgrown;
> The moon is bright and the cold tide vast.
> At times they give thanks to the spirit of Jingting Mountain
8 And then release the nets of fishermen.
> Where can I send my thoughts of you?
> The southward wind strongly fills the sails.

NOTES

Line 7: Jingting Mountain is located in the north of the district of Xuan-cheng, in present-day Anhui province. There was a temple there where offerings were made to its spirit, known as the Lord of Zihua.

Line 10: In the original, this line reads: "The south wind blows the 'five-ounces.'" A "five-ounces" (*wu liang*) consisted of a bunch of chicken feathers of that weight which was tied to the mast of a boat and used to gauge the strength of the wind: a breeze moving the "five-ounces" would be strong enough to fill the sails.

POEM

94   (8/7a; I, 144)

Farewell to Prefect Li of Zizhou

> In ten thousand ravines trees penetrate the sky,
> And cuckoos echo on a thousand peaks.
> The mountains' midst is half-filled with rain,
> From tips of trees doubling a hundred streams.
> Han women will bring tong cloth in tribute

And men of Ba dispute about taro fields.
Wen Weng was a civilizing influence:
Do you dare not follow this ancient sage?

NOTES

Title: Zizhou was located in present-day Sichuan.

Line 2: The call of the cuckoo (*cuculus poliocephalus*) is supposed to sound like a phrase which means "It's better to return" (*bu ru guiqu*), hence it is a frequent motif in farewell poems. Also, there is a legend that a king of Shu (Sichuan) named Du Yu died of shame after a love affair with his chief minister's wife; his soul was metamorphosed into the cuckoo (sometimes translated as nightjar) and is said to shed bloody tears in late spring.

Line 5: "Han" refers here not to the dynasty or the main ethnic subgroup of China, but to a small tribe living on the Jialing River in Sichuan, which was formerly known as the West Han River. The flowers of the tong tree growing in the area were used to make cloth, which had been offered as tribute to the central government for centuries.

Line 6: Ba was the name of an ancient state which once occupied part of Sichuan province.

Line 7: Wen Weng was appointed prefect of Shu during the Han dynasty. When he arrived there, he discovered that the people were living barbarian lives by Chinese standards; he made successful efforts to educate and civilize them and became known as a humane, enlightened reformer. See the *History of the Former Han*, 89/3625–26.

Line 8: As Zhao Diancheng points out, the order of the first two characters in this line should be changed from *bu gan* ("you do not dare") to *gan bu* ("do you dare not").

POEM

95

(8/8b; I, 146–47)

Farewell to Senior Officer Yang Going to Office in Guozhou

Baoxie Valley will not hold a carriage:
Where then will you be going?
A bird's path for a thousand miles,
And gibbons' cries all hours of the day.
By the official bridge, travelers offer wine;

Amid mountain trees, a shrine to the Young Maid.
After parting we will share the bright moon:
You should hear the cuckoo's call.

NOTES:

Title: In one edition of Wang Wei's poems the name Ji appears after the title "Senior Officer"; Yang Ji is known to have been sent to the frontier in 766 (well after this poem must have been written) to foster friendly relations with the Tibetan people (*Old Tang History*, 196B/5243). Guozhou is in Sichuan province.

Line 1:   Baoxie Valley, so named because its southern entrance was called Bao and its northern entrance Xie, was part of the narrow and precipitous route from the capital to Guozhou.

Line 5:   This refers to the ancient practice of offering wine and meat as sacrifices to the spirits to ensure a safe journey.

Line 6:   This shrine was located at the foot of a mountain of the same name near Baoxie Valley and was said to have been erected to the daughter of Zhang Lu, a military leader during the Latter Han dynasty.

Line 8:   For "cuckoo," see poem 94, line 2n.

POEM

96   (14/5b; I, 264)

Farewell to Judiciary Inspector Wei

You are about to follow the general in capturing Youxian:
On the sandy battleground galloping horses head toward Juyan.
From afar I know the Han envoy beyond Xiao Pass
Grieves to see the lone citywall next to the setting sun.

NOTES

Line 1:   Youxian was the title of a Xiongnu king who was pursued by Han dynasty troops far from the border. One night, believing that he was beyond reach, he got drunk and did not notice that Chinese troops had managed to surround him. He managed to escape with his favorite concubine and some warriors, but most of his chieftains were taken prisoner; he himself was never captured. The story is in the *History of the Former Han*, 94A/3767.

Line 2:   Juyan and Xiao Pass (in line 3) are both located on the northwest frontier.

POEM

97

(8/8a; I, 145)

Farewell to a Friend Returning South

For a myriad miles spring should have ended;
On the three rivers wild geese are also scarce.
Joining the sky, the Han River is broad.
A lone traveler returns to the city of Ying.
In the country of Yun paddy sprouts are lush;
Among people of Chu zizania grains are plump.
I imagine your parents will lean on their gate and gaze
And recognize your Laolai robe from afar.

NOTES

Line 2: The "three rivers" may refer to the Xiang, Pu, and Yangzi Rivers, or to the Min, Li, and Xiang Rivers—all of which are located in southern regions of China.

Line 4: Ying was the capital of the ancient southern kingdom of Chu.

Line 5: Yun was a state during the Spring and Autumn period (722–481 B.C.), located in present-day Hubei.

Line 8: For "Laolai robe," see poem 90, line 4n.

POEM

98

(9/2a; I, 155)

Written on Climbing Candidate
Pei Di's Little Pavilion

Living in peace you don't go out of doors;
You fill your eyes by gazing at cloudy mountains.
The setting sun, alongside the birds, sinks down;
The autumn plain, away from men, is at rest.
From afar I know at the distant forest's edge
One cannot see within these eaves.
A seasoned traveler often goes out by moonlight:
Gatekeeper, do not bolt the door.

NOTE

Title: Wang Wei refers to Pei Di as, literally, a "budding talent" (*xiucai*), a
polite way of addressing a candidate for the *jinshi* examination at the time.

POEM

99   (10/13b; I, 193)

Listening to the Hundred-Tongued Birds

Outside the gate of Orchid Temple grass grows in profusion.
Inside Weiyang Palace they roost amid the flowers.
At times they follow one another past the Imperial Park;
I do not know which one of them heads for Gold Embankment.
When spring comes they know how to speak a thousand different
    tongues;
As day breaks their cries are heard before a hundred birds.
The myriad homes and thousand families should all know it has
    dawned:
At Jianzhang Palace why need we listen for the crowing cock?

NOTES

Title: This was a type of sparrow which could twist its tongue to imitate the
calls of several different species of birds.

Line 1:   Orchid Temple was a belvedere located in the Imperial Park to the
east of Chang'an.

Line 2:   Weiyang Palace near Chang'an was built by the first Han emperor
(r. 206–194 B.C.).

Line 8:   Jianzhang Palace was built during the reign of the Han emperor Wu
in 104 B.C. and was located to the west of Weiyang Palace.

POEM
100 (11/9b; I, 207)

At Advisor Shen the Fourteenth's Place for Reading Sūtras, Where New Bamboos Are Growing; Harmonizing with Poems by Several Gentlemen

> Life in retreat: each day is pure and tranquil;
> The tall bamboos are beautiful and dense.
> At tender joints remain shells of young shoots,
> 4   While new clusters emerge by the old fence.
> Among slender branches, the wind's jumbled echoes;
> Through scattered shadows the cold gleam of the moon.
> The Music Bureau fashions them into imperial flutes,
> 8   And fishermen cut them down as fishing poles.
> How can they compare, inside the gate of the Tao,
> With those azure greens that brush immortal altars?

NOTE

Line 10:   This refers to the Immortal Stone Mountain (*Xianshishan*) in Yongjia (Zhejiang province), so named because legend had it that someone who had abstained from eating grains had grown wings and become a Taoist immortal there. There was a large flat stone on its peak, some eight hundred feet square, which was named Immortal Altar; four bamboos grew around it and made music when the wind blew through them.

POEM
101 (13/10b; I, 253–54)

The Red Peony

> Green beauty, tranquil and at leisure;
> Red garments, light then dark again.
> The flower's heart grieves, about to break:
> From spring colors, how can the heart be known?

POEM

102
(8/8a; I, 146)

Farewell to the Nephew of Official Hesui

In the southern states there is a returning boat:
Through Jingmen Pass it travels up the river.
Far and wide beyond the reeds and rushes
Lie cloudy waters and Zhao's burial mound.
The mast carrying citywall crows departs;
The river joining the evening rain grieves.
Who can bear to hear the gibbons' cries?
Do not wait for fall in the mountains of Chu.

NOTE

Line 4:   The tomb of King Zhao of the ancient southern state of Chu was
located in Dangyang (Hubei province); the Jingmen Pass was also located in
this area.

POEM

103
(8/10b; I, 149–50)

Farewell to Qiu Wei on His Return East of the Yangzi after Failing the Examination

I pity that you did not achieve your wishes—
How much more in the springtime of willow branches!
For traveling your funds have been exhausted;
As you go home, white hairs are new.
At the Five Lakes one half-acre dwelling;
From a myriad miles, a lone returning man.
Knowing you are like Ni but unable to recommend you,
I am ashamed to be a censorate official.

NOTES

Title: Qiu Wei (694–ca. 789) was a native of Jiaxing (Suzhou) who was known for his filial piety. He passed the *jinshi* examination fairly late and held, among other offices, the post of Court Censor (*shiyushi*) from 735–36.

Line 5:   The five Lakes are located near Suzhou, where Qiu's family lived.

Line 7:   This alludes to Ni Heng, cognomen Zhengping, whose talents (unlike Qiu Wei's) were recognized by others. He was brought to the attention of court by Kong Rong (153–208), one of the Seven Masters of the Jian'an reign period. See the *History of the Latter Han*, 80B/2652–58.

POEM

104   (8/3b; I, 138–39)

Farewell to Qiu Wei Going to Tangzhou

Wan district and Luoyang are windblown and dusty:
Your journey will cause much bitter pain.
My "Four Griefs" will reach the Han river;
Your family now will live among people of Sui.
The color of sophoras shades the clear daylight,
And willow catkins tease the end of spring.
Court officials have come to bid farewell:
Our ruler has favored you with embroidered robes.

NOTES

Title: Tangzhou and Suizhou (line 4) were both located in present-day Hubei province.

Line 1:   The district of Wan, now known as Nanyang, was located in Henan province, between Luoyang and Tangzhou.

Line 3:   This alludes to a set of four poems by Zhang Heng (78–139) entitled "The Four Griefs Poems" (*Si chou shi*) and included in the *Anthology of Literature*, 29/406–7.

Line 8:   These were robes worn by a court censor, a post held by Qiu Wei.

POEM

105   (10/11a; I, 189)

On a Spring Day Going with Pei Di to Xinchang Ward to Visit the Hermit Lu and Not Encountering Him

The Peach Blossom Spring has always been cut off from wind and
    dust.
At the southern edge of Willow Market we visit a recluse friend.
Arrived at his gate we do not dare to write "common bird."
Seeing bamboo why do we need to ask about our host?
Outside the city azure mountains are almost inside the room;
From eastern homes flowing waters enter the western environs.
Behind closed doors he has written books for several years and
    months:
The pines he planted have aged with him and grown a scaly bark.

NOTES

Title: Xinchang Ward was located in the capital city of Chang'an.

Line 1:   For Peach Blossom Spring, see poem 6.

Line 2:   This market was located in the southwestern part of Chang'an.

Line 3:   This alludes to a story in the *New Account of Tales of the World* (*Shishuo xinyu* [*Xin bian zhuzi jicheng* (Taipei: Shijie, 1974), VIII, 24/200]) about Xi Kang (223–62) and Lü An (d. 262), good friends who would travel long distances to see each other. Once Lü went to visit Xi but the latter was not at home; his elder brother Xi Xi went out to greet Lü, who refused to enter the house but only wrote the word "phoenix" (*feng*) on the door and left. Xi Xi was delighted, thinking that Lü meant thereby to compliment him by comparing him to the lofty bird. Actually, however, Lü was criticizing him, saying that he was no more than a "common bird" (*fan niao*), two words which can be formed from the character *feng*.

Line 4:   This is an allusion to Wang Huizhi (d. 388), a son of the famous calligrapher Wang Xizhi (321–79). Huizhi once stopped to admire the bamboos in the yard of a friend, Wu Zhongyi, but refused his host's entreaties to come in and visit. Wu finally had to close the gate behind Wang to induce him to stay. See the *Jin History*, 80/2103.

POEM
106 (14/5b; I, 264)

Farewell to Shen Zifu Returning East of the Yangzi

By willows at the edge of the ford, travelers are scarce.
The fisherman swings his oar toward the winding shore.
There are only thoughts of you like the colors of spring:
South of the Yangzi, north of the Yangzi—sending you home.

NOTES

Line 1: Willows are traditionally associated with parting in Chinese poetry: since the Han dynasty it had been customary to break a willow twig to give to a departing friend.

Line 4: The geography of this poem may seem puzzling, for Shen is returning "east of the Yangzi," yet the river must run an east-west course if it can be bordered on both north and south by "the colors of spring." In fact, it does so through most of central China but then swings northward as it approaches the Pacific. "East of the Yangzi," then, would refer to the present-day provinces of southern Anhui and Zhejiang.

POEM
107 (9/1b; I, 154)

Written on Climbing the Hebei Citywall Tower

Divided fields above Fu's grotto:
A traveler's stop within the clouds and mist.
On the high citywall I gaze at the far setting sun;
To the end of the reach azure mountains gleam.
Fire on the shore: a lone skiff rests for the night.
Fishermen's homes: evening birds return.
Vast and distant, the sky and earth at dusk:
My heart and the broad river are at peace.

NOTES

Title: Hebei City was located in the Pinglu district of Shanzhou, in present-day Henan province.

Line 1:   The term "divided fields" literally means "well-city," referring to the Zhou dynasty system of dividing a plot of land into nine sections resembling the character for "well" (*jing*—two horizontal lines intersecting two vertical lines). The eight outside portions would be owned and cultivated by eight families, who would farm the central section for the state. "Fu's grotto" refers to the residence of Fu Yue: according to legend, the first emperor of the Shang/Yin dynasty, Tang (r. 1766–1753 B.C.), had a dream about Fu, searched all over for him, and made him his chief minister when he finally found him.

POEM

108

(3/3b; I, 34)

Green Creek

> To enter into Yellow Flower River,
> Always follow Green Creek's waters.
> Along the mountains for a myriad turns,
> 4 Yet traveling no more than a hundred miles.
> Noises deafen amid a jumble of rocks,
> And colors are tranquil deep within the pines.
> Tossing lightly, water chestnuts float;
> 8 Clear and still, reeds and rushes gleam.
> My heart has always been serene:
> The clear river is equally at peace.
> Let me stay atop a large flat rock
> 12 And dangle a fishhook from now on.

NOTE

Line 1:   Yellow Flower River is located in Shaanxi province.

POEM

109

From Dasan Pass Going through Deep Forests and Dense Bamboo on a Winding Path for Forty or Fifty Miles to Brown Ox Peak and Seeing Yellow Flower River

A precipitous path—how many thousands of turns?
Just a few miles, yet resting three times.
Now and then I see my companions
4   *Vanish and appear behind a wooded hill.*
Splashing and gusting, the rain upon the pines;
Flowing on, the stream amid the rocks.
Tranquil words are deep within the creek,
8   *Long whistles high atop the mountain.*
Gazing I see south of Southern Mountain,
The white sun beclouded in the distance.
An azure marsh is beautiful and still;
12   *Green trees are dense as if afloat.*
I have always hated being enclosed:
Boundlessness dissipates men's cares.

NOTE

Line 8: A "whistle" (*xiao*) was probably a combination of Taoist breathing techniques and whistling which was said to express feelings and was associated with harmonizing with nature and achieving immortality; the word has also been translated as "humming," "singing," and "crooning." The tradition of the *xiao* began during the Jin dynasty and has always been linked with Taoism. Its most famous practitioner was Sun Deng, a friend of the poet Ruan Ji, whose *xiao* was said to sound like a phoenix (see poem 46, line 11n.). By the Tang dynasty there were apparently twelve different types of *xiao*. For further details see Zhuang Shen, pp. 97–101 and p. 107, n. 15 and Donald Holzman, *Poetry and Politics: The Life and Works of Juan Chi (A.D. 210–263)* (Cambridge: Cambridge University Press, 1976), pp. 150–52.

POEM

110

(10/9b; I, 187)

Written in Early Autumn in the Mountains

Untalented, I do not dare to burden a glorious era:
I long to head for the eastern creek and keep the old bamboo fence.
Not despising Shang Ping's marrying his daughters off early,
I do object to Magistrate Tao's leaving office so late.
In the grassy court crickets' echoes quicken with autumn's approach.
Within the mountains cicada sounds lament as evening nears.
In solitude by the brushwood gate where no one else arrives,
In an empty grove I meet alone with the white clouds.

NOTES

Line 3:   Shang Ping is Shang Chang, cognomen Ziping; his last name is also sometimes given as Xiang. See poem 73, line 6n.

Line 4:   Magistrate Tao is Tao Qian, who actually only served as magistrate (*ling*) of Pengze in Jiangxi province for eighty days.

POEM

111

(1/5b; I, 8)

In Response to the Visit of Several Gentlemen

Alas, I have not yet died,
Lamenting this lonely life.
In reclusion at Lantian,
4   On sterile land I plow the fields,
At year's end paying taxes
In order to offer millet sacrifices.
Mornings I go to the eastern marsh
8   Before the dew dries on the grass.
At dusk I watch smoke from cooking fires,
Shouldering a pole, coming home.
I heard there were guests,

12   *Went and swept the brushwood gate.*
One small dish—will that do?
A melon slice, ripe jujubes.
I gaze up at this venerable group,
16   *Silvery-white, an old man;*
Ashamed I have no fine bamboo,
Spreading rushes in place of mats.
By rippling waves, we climb the bank,
20   *Plucking those lotus flowers,*
Quietly watch the silvery sturgeon;
The white sand gleams below.
Mountain birds fly together,
24   *The sun obscured by light rosy clouds.*
They climb on carriages, mount horses
And suddenly disperse like rain.
Sparrows chirp in the desolate village,
28   *Cocks crow in the empty house.*
Once more I am alone again:
Doubled sobs, repeated sighs.

COMMENTARY

This is Wang Wei's only poem written in the archaic tetrasyllabic meter of the *Classic of Poetry*, the 305 songs, ballads, and hymns said to have been collected by Confucius himself. Several of the ancient poems are complaints about hardship, loneliness, and poverty, and much of the lament in this poem, as well as its directness of expression, may be attributed to the poet's awareness of this tradition. Commentators also believe that the "sigh" in the first line over not yet having died suggests that the poem was written shortly after the death of either Wang Wei's wife or his mother. In any case, a considerable amount of posing is involved, for the poet was never poor, and it is doubtful if he ever toiled in the fields himself. Nevertheless, the emotion pervasive here does recur in other poems on life in retreat.

POEM

112

(9/1a; I, 153)

Drifting on the Front Pond

The autumn sky gleams into the distance—
And even more, remote from the midst of men:
Traversed by cranes on the edge of the sand

And joining with mountains beyond the clouds.
The limpid waves are tranquil as night approaches;
The clear moon is white and serene.
This evening I will trust to my single oar,
Irresolute, not yet to return.

POEM

113

(10/10a; I, 187)

Written after Prolonged Rain at
Wang River Estate

A prolonged rain in the empty woods: cookfire smoke rises slowly,
As we steam pigweed and stew millet to feed those on the eastern
  fields.
Over vast and boundless paddies fly the white herons;
In dense, dark summer trees warble yellow orioles.
Within the mountains practicing peace I watch the morning hi-
  biscus.
Beneath the pines in a cleansing fast I cut off a dewy sunflower.
The rustic old man has done with the struggle to win a place on
  the mat:
Seagull, for what reason are you still suspicious of me?

NOTES

Line 7: This alludes to a story of how the Taoist Yang Zhu, having been rebuked by Laozi for his arrogance, succeeded so well in modifying his demeanor that the people at the inn where he happened to be staying, who had once humbly given him a mat to himself, ended up daring to struggle with him for a place on it. The anecdote is recorded in the *Zhuangzi*, "Imputed Words" (*Yu yan*, 76/27/25), and in another Taoist text, the *Liezi* (*Xin bian zhuzi jicheng*, IV, 2/25).

Line 8: This refers to the another story in the same section of the *Liezi* (2/21) of a man who used to roam freely with the gulls by the sea. One day, however, his father asked him to catch one for him; when the man went to the beach the next day, the gulls refused to fly to him.

POEM
114
(7/6b; I, 123)

Written on Returning to Wang River

In the mouth of the valley a bell stirs, remote.
Woodsmen and fishermen gradually grow scarce.
Far away the distant mountain dusks;
Alone toward white clouds I return.
Water chestnut tendrils are weak and hard to still;
Willow catkins are light and easily fly.
On the eastern marsh, the color of spring grass:
Sadly I close the brushwood gate.

POEM
115
(10/9b; I, 186)

Wang River Retreat

I haven't gone to the eastern hills for close to a year.
Returning home I have just had time to seed the spring fields.
In the rain the grasses' color turns green, like a dye.
Above the water peach blossoms redden, ready to blaze.
Youlü the mendicant is the scholar of sūtra studies,
And old Master Hunchback is the provincial village worthy.
Throwing on clothes and losing my sandals, I rush out to greet
    them:
Together we like to talk and laugh before my humble door.

NOTES

Line 5:   This refers to Uruvilva Kaśpaya (Youloupinluo Jiaye), one of
Śākyamuni Buddha's main disciples.

Line 6:   This is an allusion to an anecdote in the *Zhuangzi* ("Mastering Life,"
48/19/17) about an encounter between Confucius and a wise hunchback of
Chu, who impressed the sage with the skill, concentration, and ease with
which he caught cicadas on the tip of a sticky pole.

Line 7:   The phrase "losing (or dropping) my sandals" alludes to a story in the *Chronicle of the Three Kingdoms* (*Wei*, 21/597). When the poet Wang Can (177–217), one of the Seven Masters of the Jian'an Period, arrived at Chang'an, he attracted the attention of Cai Yong (133–92), an official well known for his talents and erudition and highly respected at court. Despite his lofty position, when the latter heard that Wang Can was at his gate, he lost his sandals in his hurry to greet him.

POEM

116

(7/5b: I, 122)

At My Wang River Retreat, Presented to Candidate Pei Di

> Cold mountains turn deep green,
> Autumn waters daily flowing on.
> I lean on my staff outside the brushwood gate
> And listen to evening cicadas in the wind.
> At the ford lingers a setting sun;
> From the deserted village rises one wisp of smoke.
> Again I meet a drunken Jieyu
> Madly singing in front of Five Willows.

NOTES

Title: For an explanation of "Candidate," see poem 98, title note.

Line 7:   For Jieyu, see poem 44, line 1n.

Line 8:   "Five Willows" alludes to the poet Tao Qian; see poem 38, line 10n.

POEM

117

(7/6a; I, 122–23)

Dwelling in the Mountains: An Autumn Evening

> Empty mountains after a recent rain:
> The air, since evening, turns autumnal.
> The bright moon, amid the pines, shines.

The clear stream, over rocks, flows.
Bamboos rustle: washerwomen return.
Lotuses move: fishing boats come downstream.
As it wishes spring's fragrance may cease:
This prince naturally can stay.

NOTE

Line 8:   For the allusion here, see poem 72, line 4n.

POEM

118   (7/4b; I, 120)

In Response to Vice-Magistrate Zhang

In late years I care for tranquility alone—
A myriad affairs do not concern my heart.
A glance at myself: there are no long-range plans.
I only know to return to the old forest.
Pine winds blow, loosening my belt;
The mountain moon shines as I pluck my zither.
You ask about reasons for success and failure:
A fisherman's song enters the shore's deeps.

POEMS

119–25   (14/1a–b; I, 257–58)

Joys of Fields and Gardens

119.

Coming and going through thousands of gates, a myriad homes,
I have traversed northern villages, southern environs.
What is the purpose of ambling horses' tinkling pendants?
At Kongtong who is that man with disheveled hair?

NOTE

Line 4:   This alludes to a story in the *Zhuangzi*, "Let It Be, Leave It Alone" [*Zai you*, 26/11/28] about a hermit named Master Guang Cheng who lived on Kongtong Mountain. When the mythical Yellow Emperor visited there to study the Tao with him in order to better govern others, Guang Cheng refused. Only when the Emperor, after three months in solitary retirement, returned and requested help in governing his own body did the Master agree to instruct him.

120.

Meeting again, enfeoffed as the marquis of ten thousand homes,
Standing and talking, bestowed with two discs of jade.
How can that surpass tilling southern fields side by side?
Or compare with sleeping high by the eastern wall?

NOTES

Line 2:   This is an allusion to Yu Qing of the ancient kingdom of Zhao, who met King Xiaocheng of Zhao three times: on his first visit he was given gold and a pair of white jade discs; the second time he was appointed minister of Zhao; and the third time he was enfeoffed as a marquis of ten thousand homes. See the *Records of the Historian*, 76/2370ff.

Line 3:   This alludes to Changju and Jieni, two men who plowed fields together. Once when Confucius passed by and sent his disciple Zilu to ask them where a nearby river could be forded, Changju refused to tell him, insisting that if Confucius were a real sage, he should already know the location. Then Jieni chided Zilu for following a man who was trying in vain to change the world, rather than escape from it. See the *Analects*, XVIII.6.

Line 4:   "Sleeping high" is a phrase denoting a life of ease and freedom from anxiety.

121.

They pick water chestnuts at the head of the ford, where the wind
*   is sharp*
And ply their staffs to the west of the village, in slanting sun.
By the side of Apricot Altar, a fisherman;
Within Peach Blossom Spring, the homes of men.

NOTES

Line 3:   This alludes to an anecdote in the *Zhuangzi* ("The Old Fisherman" [*Yu fu*, 86/31/1]), in which a fisherman comes upon Confucius playing his zither at Apricot Altar and, in a lengthy conversation, chides him for his officious meddling in the affairs of others. He convinces the sage that one should not be concerned about the observance of propriety and rites, which are but creations of man, but rather about following the Way of Heaven.

Line 4:   For Peach Blossom Spring, see poem 6.

122.

Dense and lush, fragrant grass in the green of spring;
High and thick, tall pines in the summer cool.
Oxen and sheep return by themselves to the village lane.
Children do not know officials' gowns and caps.

123.

Beneath the mountain one wisp of smoke in a distant village;
On the edge of the sky a lone tree on the high plain.
A "One-Gourd" Yan Hui in a rustic lane;
The "Master of Five Willows" just across the way.

NOTES

Line 3:   One of Confucius' favorite disciples, Yan Hui, or Yan Yuan, was known for his remarkable frugality and good nature: he would be satisfied with a handful of rice, a gourd of water, and a humble home. See the *Analects*, VI.9.

Line 4:   For "Master of Five Willows," see poem 38, line 10n.

124.

Peach blossoms are red and also hold last night's rain.
Willows are green and carry, too, the spring mist.
Flowers fall; the servant boy has not yet swept.
Orioles chirp; the mountain guest is still asleep.

125.

Pouring wine we meet above the spring's waters.
Holding zithers we like to lean on tall pines.
The southern garden's dewy mallows are cut each morning;
The eastern valley's yellow grain is pounded at night.

POEMS

126–30

Miscellaneous Poems Written at Huangfu Yue's Cloud Valley

126. Bird Call Valley

Man at leisure, cassia flowers fall.
The night still, spring mountain empty.
The moon emerges, startling mountain birds:
At times they call within the spring valley.

127. Lotus Flower Bank

Every day they leave to pluck lotuses.
Islets are far; many return at dusk.
In plying poles do not splash the water:
I fear you'll dampen red lotus dresses.

128. Cormorant Bank

Suddenly dipping among red lotus flowers,
It emerges again from the clear shore and soars.
Standing alone—how new are its plumes?
A fish in its beak, atop the ancient log.

129. Upper Peace Field

Mornings they till Upper Peace Field;
Evenings they till Upper Peace Field.
May I ask the one who asked at the ford:
How can we know the virtue of Ju and Ni?

NOTE

Line 4:   Ju and Ni refer to Changju and Jieni; see poem 120, line 3n.

130. Duckweed Pond

The spring pond is deep and wide.
For a while I await the light skiff's return.
Ever so slowly green duckweed comes together;
The drooping willows sweep it open again.

POEMS

131–50

The Wang River Collection

Preface: My retreat is in the Wang River mountain valley. The places to walk to include: Meng Wall Cove, Huazi Hill, Grained Apricot Lodge, Clear Bamboo Range, Deer Enclosure, Magnolia Enclosure, Dogwood Bank, Sophora Path, Lakeside Pavilion, Southern Hillock, Lake Yi, Willow Waves, Luan Family Shallows, Gold Powder Spring, White Rock Rapids, Northern Hillock, Bamboo Lodge, Magnolia Bank, Lacquer Tree Garden, and Pepper Tree Garden. When Pei Di and I were at leisure, we each composed the following quatrains.

131. Meng Wall Cove
A new home at the mouth of Meng Wall:
Ancient trees, the last withered willows.
The one who comes again—who will it be?
Grieving in vain for former men's possessions.

132. Huazi Hill
Flying birds leave endlessly.
On continuous mountains autumn colors return.
Up and down Huazi Hill:
Melancholy—what limits to these feelings?

133. Grained Apricot Lodge
Grained apricot cut for beams;
Fragrant reeds woven for a roof.
I do not know if clouds within the rafters
Go to make rain among men.

NOTE

Line 3:   These last two lines allude to the second of Guo Pu's (276–324) "Seven Poems on Traveling with Immortals" (*You xian shi qi shou, Anthology of Literature,* 21/292–95), whose second couplet reads: "Clouds arise within the rafters; / Winds emerge from the windows and doors." This is a description of the residence of a Taoist priest, to whom Wang Wei is thus suggesting a comparison.

134. Clear Bamboo Range

Tall and dense, they gleam by the empty riverbend;
Azure-green, billowing, flowing waves.
Secretly enter the Shang Mountain road:
Woodcutters cannot be known.

NOTE

Line 3:   This refers to the famous hermits known as the "Four Whiteheads,"
who, when the First Qin Emperor came to power in 221 B.C., retired to Mt.
Shang in Shaanxi province and refused to serve in his autocratic government.
See the *Records of the Historian*, 55/2045.

135. Deer Enclosure

Empty mountain, no man is seen.
Only heard are echoes of men's talk.
Reflected light enters the deep wood
And shines again on blue-green moss.

136. Magnolia Enclosure

Autumn mountains embrace the lingering light.
Flying birds follow companions ahead.
Brilliant blue-green—at times distinct and clear;
Evening mists without a place to be.

137. Dogwood Bank

They bear fruit both red and green,
And then, like flowers, blossom once again.
In the mountains, if guests are to stay,
Prepare this dogwood cup.

138. Sophora Path

The bypath is shaded by sophoras;
In secluded shadows, green moss is thick.
But the gatekeeper sweeps it in welcome
In case the mountain monk should come.

139. Lakeside Pavilion

A light bark greets the honored guest,
Far and distant, coming across the lake.
On the porch, each with goblets of wine:
On all four sides lotuses bloom.

140. Southern Hillock

A light skiff leaves for Southern Hillock.
To Northern Hillock, wide waters are hard to cross.
On the other shore I gaze at people's houses:
Far and distant, we do not know each other.

141. Lake Yi

Blowing flutes cross to the distant shore.
At day's dusk I bid farewell to you.
On the lake with one turn of the head:
Mountain green rolls into white clouds.

142. Willow Waves

Separate rows of fine trees next to each other
Cast their shadows into clear ripples.
Not like those on the imperial moat,
Where the spring wind is wounded by farewells.

143. Luan Family Shallows

Brisk gusts in the autumn rain;
Rushing on, the stream pours over rocks.
Leaping waves naturally splash each other:
White egrets are startled, then descend again.

144. Gold Powder Spring

Drink each day at Gold Powder Spring
And you should have a thousand years or more:
To soar on an azure phoenix with striped dragons,
And with plumes and tassels attend the Jade Emperor's court.

NOTE

Line 3: The allusions in this couplet are to the mythical figures of the Queen Mother of the West (*Xi wang mu*), who was said to have ridden in an azure phoenix chariot pulled by striped animals, and the Jade Emperor, supreme deity in the Taoist pantheon. Gold was believed by Taoists to confer immortality, hence their many alchemical experiments.

145. White Rock Rapids

Clear and shallow, White Rock Rapids.
Green rushes once could be grasped.
Families live east and west of the water,
Washing silk beneath the bright moon.

146. Northern Hillock

Northern Hillock north of the river's water;
Various trees vivid against crimson railings.
Winding about, the Southern River's waters:
Bright and dim to the edge of the azure forest.

147. Bamboo Lodge

Alone I sit amid the dark bamboo,
Play the zither and whistle loud again.
In the deep wood men do not know
The bright moon comes to shine on me.

NOTES

Line 1: This alludes to a poem entitled "The Mountain Spirit" (*Shan gui*),
the ninth of the *Nine Songs* in the *Songs of Chu*, 2/140–42. There the speaker
grieves over the failure of his lady (the spirit) to arrive, and he waits in sor-
rowful solitude in a dense and gloomy bamboo grove.

Line 2: For an explanation of this "whistle," see poem 109, line 8n.

148. Magnolia Bank

On the tips of trees "lotus" flowers
In the mountains produce red calices.
The mouth of the valley is silent without men.
In all directions they open, then fall.

NOTE

Line 1: This alludes to "The Xiang River Princess" (*Xiang jun*), the third of
the *Nine Songs* in the *Songs of Chu*, 2/113–19, in which the shaman-speaker
laments the impossibility of meeting with his goddess-love. He compares
this with the likelihood of finding wild figs in the water or lotuses on tree-
tops. Here, however, Wang Wei turns the factual impossibility into a legiti-
mate metaphor: the magnolia blossoms do indeed resemble lotus flowers
growing on tree branches.

149. Lacquer Tree Garden

The ancient man was not a haughty official,
Naturally lacking experience of worldly affairs.
He happened to lodge in a humble post,
Among the lifeless, many-branched trees.

NOTES

Line 1: This "ancient man" was Zhuangzi, who is said to have served some time as Keeper of the Lacquer Tree Garden (*qiyuan li*) in the state of Meng (*Records of the Historian*, 63/2143).

Line 4: The phrase translated here as "lifeless" (*posuo*) has many meanings, but Zhao Diancheng believes that it alludes to a passage in the biography of Yin Zhongwen (d. 407): after coming upon an old sophora tree, Yin contemplated it for some time and sighed: "This tree is lifeless, with no intention of reviving" (*Jin History*, 99/2605).

150. Pepper Tree Garden

Cinnamon wine greets the Son of Heaven;
Sweet pollia is bestowed on the lovely person.
Pepper broth libations on the jeweled mat—
We wish to bring down the Lord Within the Clouds.

NOTE

Line 4: This is a spirit to whom the second of the *Nine Songs* in the *Songs of Chu*, 2/105–12, is addressed. The other images in this quatrain also appear frequently throughout this southern anthology.

Chinese Text of Poems

1　題友人雲母障子

君家雲母障。持向野庭開。自有山泉入。非因彩畫來。

2　過秦皇墓

古墓成蒼嶺。幽宮象紫臺。星辰七曜隔。河漢九泉開。
有海人寧渡。無春雁不迴。更聞松韻切。疑是大夫哀。

3　九月九日憶山東兄弟

獨在異鄉爲異客。每逢佳節倍思親。遙知兄弟登高處。
徧插茱萸少一人。

4　洛陽女兒行

洛陽女兒對門居。纔可顏容十五餘。良人玉勒乘驄馬。
侍女金盤膾鯉魚。畫閣朱樓盡相望。紅桃綠柳垂簷向。
羅帷送上七香車。寶扇迎歸九華帳。狂夫富貴在青春。
意氣驕奢劇季倫。自憐碧玉親教舞。不惜珊瑚持與人。
春牕曙滅九微火。九微片片飛花璅。戲罷曾無理曲時。
妝成祇是薰香坐。城中相識盡繁華。日夜經過趙李家。
誰憐越女顏如玉。貧賤江頭自浣紗。

5　賦得清如玉壺冰

藏冰玉壺裏。冰水類方諸。未共銷丹日。還同照綺疏。
抱明中不隱。含淨外疑虛。氣似庭霜積。光言砌月餘。
曉凌飛鵲鏡。宵映聚螢書。若同夫君比。清心尚不如。

6　桃源行

漁舟逐水愛山春。兩岸桃花夾古津。坐看紅樹不知遠。

行盡青溪不見人。山口潛行始隈隩。山開曠望旋平陸。
遙看一處攢雲樹。近入千家散花竹。樵客初傳漢姓名。
居人未改秦衣服。居人共住武陵源。還從物外起田園。
月明松下房櫳靜。日出雲中雞犬喧。驚聞俗客爭來集。
競引還家問都邑。平明閭巷掃花開。薄暮漁樵乘水入。
初因避地去人間。更聞成仙遂不還。峽裏誰知有人事。
世中遙望空雲山。不疑靈境難聞見。塵心未盡思鄉縣。
出洞無論隔山水。辭家終擬長游衍。自謂經過舊不迷。
安知峯壑今來變。當時只記入山深。青溪幾度到雲林。
春來徧是桃花水。不辨仙源何處尋。

7　李陵詠

漢家李將軍。三代將門子。結髮有奇策。少年成壯士。
長驅塞上兒。深入單于壘。旌旗列相向。簫鼓悲何已。
日暮沙漠陲。戰聲烟塵裏。將令驕虜滅。豈獨名王侍。
既失大軍援。遂嬰穹盧恥。少小蒙漢恩。何堪坐思此。
深衷欲有報。投軀未能死。引領望子卿。非君誰相理。

8　息夫人

莫以今時寵。能忘舊日恩。看花滿眼淚。不共楚王言。

9　燕支行

漢家天將才且雄。來時謁帝明光宮。萬乘親推雙闕下。
千官出餞五陵東。誓辭甲第金門裏。身作長城玉塞中。
衛霍纔堪一騎將。朝廷不數貳師功。趙魏燕韓多勁卒。
關西俠少何氣呼勃。報讎只是聞嘗膽。飲酒不曾妨刮骨。
畫戟雕戈白日寒。連旗大旆黃塵沒。疊鼓遙翻瀚海波。
鳴笳亂動天山月。麒麟錦帶佩吳鉤。颯踏青驪躍紫騮。

拔劍已斷天驕臂。歸鞍共飲月支頭。漢兵大呼一當百。
虜騎相看哭且愁。教戰須令赴湯火。終知上將先伐謀。

10　西施詠

艷色天下重。西施寧久微。朝爲越溪女。暮作吳宮妃。
賤日豈殊衆。貴來方悟稀。邀人傅脂粉。不自着羅衣。
君寵益驕態。君憐無是非。當時浣紗伴。莫得同車歸。
持謝鄰家子。效顰安可希。

11　魚山神女祠歌二首

迎神曲

坎坎擊鼓。魚山之下。吹洞簫。望極浦。女巫進。紛屢
舞。陳瑤席。湛清酤。風凄凄兮夜雨。神之來兮不來。
使我心兮苦復苦。

12　　　　　送神曲

紛進拜兮堂前。目眷眷兮瓊筵。來不語兮意不傳。作暮
雨兮愁空山。悲急管。思繁絃。靈之駕兮儼欲旋。倏雲
收兮雨歇。山青青兮水潺潺。

13　榆林郡歌

山頭松柏林。山下泉聲傷客心。千里萬里春草色。黃河
東流流不息。黃龍戍上游俠兒。愁逢漢使不相識。

14　隴頭吟

長城少年游俠客。夜上戍樓看太白。隴頭明月迴臨關。
隴上行人夜吹笛。關西老將不勝愁。駐馬聽之雙淚流。

身經大小百餘戰。麾下偏裨萬戶侯。蘇武纔爲典屬國。
節旄空盡海西頭。

15　少年行四首

新豐美酒斗十千。咸陽遊俠多少年。相逢意氣爲君飲。
繫馬高樓垂柳邊。

16

出身仕漢羽林郎。初隨驃騎戰漁陽。孰知不向邊庭苦。
縱死猶聞俠骨香。

17

一身能擘兩彫弧。虜騎千重只似無。偏坐金鞍調白羽。
紛紛射殺五單于。

18

漢家君臣歡宴終。高議雲臺論戰功。天子臨軒賜侯印。
將軍佩出明光宮。

19　從軍行

吹角動行人。喧喧行人起。笳悲馬嘶亂。爭渡金河水。
日暮沙漠垂。戰聲烟塵裏。盡係名王頸。歸來報天子。

20　送平淡然判官

不識陽關路。新從定遠侯。黃雲斷春色。畫角起邊愁。
瀚海經年別。交河出塞流。須令外國使。知飲月支頭。

21　使至塞上

單車欲問邊。屬國過居延。征蓬出漢塞。歸雁入胡天。

大漠孤烟直。長河落日圓。蕭關逢候騎。都護在燕然。

22 出塞作

居延城外獵天驕。白草連天野火燒。暮雲空磧時驅馬。
秋日平原好射鵰。護羌校尉朝乘障。破虜將軍夜渡遼。
玉靶角弓珠勒馬。漢家將賜霍嫖姚。

23 早朝

皎潔明星高。蒼茫遠天曙。槐霧暗不開。城鴉鳴稍去。
始聞高閣聲。莫辨更衣處。銀燭已成行。金門儼鵷鷺。

24 和賈舍人早朝大明宮之作

絳幘雞人送曉籌。尚衣方進翠雲裘。九天閶闔開宮殿。
萬國衣冠拜冕旒。日色纔臨仙掌動。香烟欲傍袞龍浮。
朝罷須裁五色詔。珮聲歸向鳳池頭。

25 敕借岐王九成宮避暑應敎

帝子遠辭丹鳳闕。天書遙借翠微宮。隔窗雲霧生衣上。
卷慢山泉入鏡中。林下水聲暄語笑。巖間樹色隱房櫳。
仙家未必能勝此。何事吹笙向碧空。

26 華嶽

西嶽出浮雲。積翠在太清。連天疑黛色。百里遙青冥。
白日爲之寒。森沉華陰城。昔聞乾坤閉。造化生巨靈。
右足踏方山。左手推削成。天地忽開拆。大河注東溟。
遂爲西峙嶽。雄雄鎮泰京。大君包覆載。至德被羣生。

上帝佇昭告。金天思奉迎。人祇望幸久。何獨禪云亭。

27　和僕射晉公扈從溫湯

天子幸新豐。旌旗渭水東。寒山天仗裏。溫谷慢城中。
奠玉羣仙座。焚香太乙宮。出游逢牧馬。罷獵有非熊。
上宰無爲化。明時太古同。靈芝三秀紫。陳粟萬箱紅。
王禮尊儒教。天兵小戰功。謀猷歸哲匠。詞賦屬文宗。
司諫方無闕。陳詩且未工。長吟吉甫頌。朝夕仰清風。

28　奉和聖製從蓬萊向興慶閣道中留春
雨中春望之作應制

渭水自縈秦塞曲。黃山舊繞漢宮斜。鑾輿迥出仙門柳。
閣道迴看上苑花。雲裏帝城雙鳳闕。雨中春樹萬人家。
爲乘陽氣行時令。不是宸游重物華。

29　奉和聖製暮春送朝集使歸郡應制

萬國仰宗周。衣冠拜冕旒。玉乘迎大客。金節送諸侯。
祖席傾三省。褰帷向九州。楊花飛上路。槐色蔭通溝。
來預鈞天樂。歸分漢主憂。宸章類河漢。垂象滿中州。

30　奉和聖製與太子諸王三月三日龍池春禊應制

故事修春禊。新宮展豫游。明君移鳳輦。太子出龍樓。
賦掩陳王作。杯如洛水流。金人來捧劍。畫鷁去迴舟。
苑樹浮宮闕。天池照冕旒。宸章在雲漢。垂象滿皇州。

31　奉和聖製重陽節宰臣及羣臣上壽應制

四海方無事。三秋大有年。百工逢此日。萬壽願齊天。

芍藥和金鼎。茱萸插玳筵。玉堂開右个。天樂動宮懸。
御柳疏秋影。城鴉拂曙烟。無窮菊花節。長奉柏梁篇

32　大同殿生玉芝龍池上有慶雲百官共睹
　　聖恩便賜宴樂敢書即事

欲笑周文歌宴鎬。遙輕漢武樂橫汾。豈如玉殿生三秀。
詎有銅池出五雲。陌上堯樽傾北斗。樓前舜樂動南薰。
共歡天意同人意。萬歲千秋奉聖君。

33　旣蒙宥罪旋復拜官伏感聖恩竊書鄙意
　　兼奉簡新徐使君等諸公

忽蒙漢詔還冠冕。始覺殷王解網羅。日比皇明猶自暗。
天齊聖壽未云多。花迎喜氣皆知笑。鳥識歡心亦解歌。
聞道百城新佩印。還來雙闕共鳴珂。

34　菩提寺禁裴迪來相看說逆賊等
　　凝碧池上作音樂供奉人等舉聲
　　便一時淚下私成口號誦示裴迪

萬戶傷心生野煙。百官何日再朝天。秋槐葉落空宮裏
凝碧池頭奏管弦。

35　口號又示裴迪

安得捨塵網。拂衣辭世喧。悠然策藜杖。歸向桃花源

36　贈從弟司庫員外絿

少年識事淺。強學干名利。徒聞躍馬年。苦無出人智

即事豈徒言。累官非不試。既寡遂性歡。恐招負時累。
清冬見遠山。積雪凝蒼翠。皓然出東林。發我遺世意。
惠連素清賞。風語塵外事。欲緩攜手期。流年一何駛。

37　戲贈張五弟諲三首

吾弟東山時。心尚一何遠。日高猶自臥。鐘動始能飯。
領上髮未梳。牀頭書不卷。清川興悠悠。空林對偃蹇。
青苔石上淨。細草松下軟。窗外鳥聲閑。階前虎心善。
徒然萬像多。澹爾太虛緬。一知與物平。自顧為人淺。
對君忽自得。浮念不煩遣。

38

張弟五車書。讀書仍隱居。染翰過草聖。賦詩輕子虛。
閉門二室下。隱居十年餘。宛是野人也。時從漁父魚。
秋風日蕭索。五柳高且疏。望此去人世。渡水向吾廬。
歲晏同攜手。只應君與予。

39

設置守麌兔。垂釣伺游鱗。此是安口腹。非關慕隱淪。
吾生好清靜。蔬食去情塵。今子方豪蕩。思為鼎食人。
我家南山下。動息自遺身。入鳥不相亂。見獸皆相親。
雲霞成伴侶。虛白侍衣巾。何事須夫子。邀予谷口真。

40　送綦毋潛落第還鄉

聖代無隱者。英靈盡來歸。遂令東山客。不得顧採薇。
既至君門遠。孰云吾道非。江淮度寒食。京洛縫春衣。
置酒臨長道。同心與我違。行當浮桂棹。未幾拂荊扉。

樹遠帶行客。孤城當落暉。吾謀適不用。勿謂知音稀。

41　送綦母校書棄官還江東

明時久不達。棄置與君同。天命無怨色。人生有素風。
念君拂衣去。四海將安窮。秋天萬里淨。日暮澄江空。
清夜何悠悠。扣舷明月中。和光魚鳥際。澹爾蒹葭叢。
無庸客昭世。衰鬢白如蓬。頑疎暗人事。僻陋遠天聰。
微物縱可採。其誰爲至公。余亦從此去。歸耕爲老農。

42　酬賀四贈葛巾之作

野巾傳惠好。茲覩重兼金。嘉此幽棲物。能齊隱吏心。
早朝方暫挂。晚沐復來簪。坐覺囂塵遠。思君共入林。

43　酬郭給事

洞門高閣靄餘暉。桃李陰陰柳絮飛。禁裏疎鐘官舍晚。
省中啼鳥吏人稀。晨搖玉珮趨金殿。夕奉天書拜瑣闈。
強欲從君無那老。將因臥病解朝衣。

44　偶然作六首

楚國有狂夫。茫然無心想。散髮不冠帶。行歌南陌上。
孔丘與之言。仁義莫能獎。未嘗肯問天。何事須擊壤。
復笑採薇人。胡爲乃長往。

45

田舍有老翁。垂白衡門裏。有時農事閒。斗酒呼鄰里。
喧聒茅簷下。或坐或復起。短褐不爲薄。園葵固足美。

動則長子孫。不曾向城市。五帝與三王。古來稱天子。
干戈將揖讓。畢竟何者是。得意苟爲樂。野田安足鄙。
且當放懷去。行行沒餘齒。

46

日夕見太行。沉吟未能去。問君何以然。世網嬰我故。
小妹日成長。兄弟未有娶。家貧祿既薄。儲蓄非有素。
幾迴欲奮飛。踟躕復相顧。孫登長嘯臺。松竹有遺處。
相去詎幾許。故人在中路。愛染日已薄。禪寂日已固。
忽乎吾將行。寧俟歲云暮。　　　　。

47

陶潛任天眞。其性頗耽酒。自從棄官來。家貧不能有。
九月九日時。菊花空滿手。中心竊自思。儻有人送否。
白衣攜壺觴。果來遺老叟。且喜得斟酌。安問升與斗。
奮衣野田中。今日嗟無負。兀傲迷東西。蓑笠不能守。
傾倒彊行行。酣歌歸五柳。生事不曾問。肯愧家中婦。

48

趙女彈箜篌。復能邯鄲舞。夫婿輕薄兒。鬬雞事齊主。
黃金買歌笑。用錢不復數。許史相經過。高門盈四牡。
客舍有儒生。昂藏出鄒魯。讀書三十年。腰下無尺組。
被服聖人教。一生自窮苦。

49

老來懶賦詩。惟有老相隨。當代謬詞客。前身應畫師。
不能捨餘習。偶被世人知。名字本皆是。此心還不知。

50　留別山中溫古上人幷示舍弟縉

解薜登天朝。去師偶時哲。豈惟山中人。兼負松上月。
宿昔同游止。致身雲霞末。開軒臨潁陽。臥視飛鳥沒。
好依盤石飯。屢對瀑泉歇。理齊少狎隱。道勝寧外物。
舍弟官崇高。宗兄此削髮。荊扉但灑掃。乘閒當過拂。

51　胡居士臥病遺米因贈

了觀四大因。根性何所有。妄計苟不生。是身孰休咎。
色聲何謂客。陰界復誰守。徒言蓮花目。豈惡楊枝肘。
既飽香積飯。不醉聲聞酒。有無斷常見。生滅幻夢受。
即病即實相。趣空定狂走。無有一法眞。無有一法垢。
居士素通達。隨宜善抖擻。床上無氈臥。鐺中有粥否。
齋時不乞食。定應空漱口。聊持數斗米。且救浮生取。

52　苦熱

赤日滿天地。火雲成山嶽。草木盡焦卷。川澤皆竭涸。
輕紈覺衣重。密樹苦陰薄。莞簟不可近。絺綌再三濯。
思出宇宙外。曠然在寥廓。長風萬里來。江海蕩煩濁。
却顧身爲患。始知心未覺。忽入甘露門。宛然清涼樂。

53　納涼

喬木萬餘株。清流貫其中。前臨大川口。豁達來長風。
漣漪涵白沙。素鮪如游空。偃臥盤石上。翻濤沃微躬。
漱流復濯足。前對釣魚翁。貪餌凡幾許。徒思蓮葉東。

54　登辨覺寺

竹徑從初地。蓮峯出化城。窗中三楚盡。林上九江平。

輭草承趺坐。長松響梵聲。空居法雲外。觀世得無生。

55　過盧員外宅看飯僧共題

三賢異七聖。青眼慕青蓮。乞飯從香積。裁衣學水田。
上人飛錫杖。檀越施金錢。趺坐簷前日。焚香竹下烟。
寒空法雲地。秋色淨居天。身逐因緣法。心過次第禪。
不須愁日暮。自有一燈然。

56　夏日過青龍寺謁操禪師

龍鍾一老翁。徐步謁禪宮。欲問義心義。遙知空病空。
山河天眼裏。世界法身中。莫怪銷炎熱。能生大地風。

57　過乘如禪師蕭居士嵩邱蘭若

無着天親弟與兄。嵩邱蘭若一峯晴。食隨鳴磬巢烏下。
行踏空林落葉聲。迸水定侵香案濕。雨花應共石牀平。
深洞長松何所有。儼然天竺古先生。

58　投道一師蘭若宿

一公棲太白。高頂出雲烟。梵流諸壑遍。花雨一峯偏。
迹為無心隱。名因立教傳。鳥來還語法。客去更安禪。
晝涉松露盡。暮投蘭若邊。洞房隱深竹。清夜聞遙泉。
向是雲霞裏。今成枕席前。豈惟留暫宿。服事將窮年。

59　過福禪師蘭若

巖壑轉微逕。雲林隱法堂。羽人飛奏樂。天女跪焚香。
竹外峯偏曙。藤陰水更涼。欲知禪坐久。行路長春芳。

60　飯覆釜山僧

晚知清淨理。日與人羣踈。將候遠山僧。先期掃敝廬。
果從雲峯裏。顧我蓬蒿居。藉草飯松屑。焚香看道書。
燃燈晝欲盡。鳴磬夜方初。已悟寂爲樂。此生閒有餘。
思歸何必深。身世猶空虛。

61　靑龍寺曇壁上人兄院集 幷序

吾兄大開蔭中。明徹物外。以定力勝敵。以惠用解嚴。
深居僧坊。傍俯人里。高原陸地。下映芙蓉之池。竹林
果園。中秀菩提之樹。八極氛霽。萬彙塵息。太虛寥廓。
南山爲之端倪。皇州蒼茫。渭水貫於天地。經行之後。
跌坐而閑。升堂梵筵。餌客香飯。不起而游覽。不風而
清涼。得世界於蓮花。記文章於貝葉。時江寧大兄持片
石命維序之。詩五韻。坐上成。

高處敝招提。虛空詎有倪。坐看南陌騎。下聽秦城雞。
渺渺孤烟起。芊芊遠樹齊。靑山萬井外。落日五陵西。
眼界今無染。心空安可迷。

62　過感化寺曇興上人山院

暮持筇竹杖。相待虎溪頭。催客聞山響。歸房逐水流。
野花叢發好。谷鳥一聲幽。夜坐空林寂。松風直似秋。

63　藍田山石門精舍

落日山水好。漾舟信歸風。玩奇不覺遠。因以緣源窮。
遙愛雲木秀。初疑路不同。安知清流轉。偶與前山通。
捨舟理輕策。果然愜所適。老僧四五人。逍遙蔭松柏。
朝梵林未曙。夜禪山更寂。道心及牧童。世事問樵客。

暝宿長林下。焚香臥瑤席。澗芳襲人衣。山月映石壁。
再尋畏迷誤。明發更登歷。笑謝桃源人。花紅復來覿。

64　過香積寺

不知香積寺。數里入雲峯。古木無人徑。深山何處鐘。
泉聲咽危石。日色冷青松。薄暮空潭曲。安禪制毒龍。

65　遊感化寺

翡翠香烟合。瑠璃寶地平。龍宮連棟宇。虎穴傍簷楹。
谷靜惟松響。山深無鳥聲。瓊峯當户折。金澗透林鳴。
郊路雲端迴。秦川雨外晴。雁王銜果獻。鹿女踏花行。
抖擻辭貧里。歸依宿化城。繞籬生野蕨。空館發山櫻。
香飯青菰米。嘉蔬綠芋羹。誓陪清梵末。端坐學無生。

66　謁璿上人　并序

上人外人內天。不定不亂。捨法而淵泊。無心而雲動。
色空無得。不物物也。默語無際。不言言也。故吾徒得
神交焉。玄關大啟。德海羣泳。時雨既降。春物俱美。
序于詩者。人百其言。

少年不足言。識道年已長。事往安可悔。餘生幸能養。
誓從斷葷血。不復嬰世網。浮名寄纓珮。空性無羈鞅。
夙從大導師。焚香此瞻仰。頹然居一室。覆載紛萬象。
高柳早鶯啼。長廊春雨響。牀下阮家屐。牕前筇竹杖。
方將見身雲。陋彼示天壤。一心在法要。願以無生獎。

67　秋夜獨坐

獨坐悲雙鬢。空堂欲二更。雨中山果落。燈下草蟲鳴。

白髮終難變。黃金不可成。欲知除老病。惟有學無生。

68　哭殷遙

人生能幾何。畢竟歸無形。念君等爲死。萬事傷人情。
慈母未及葬。一女纔十齡。泱漭寒郊外。蕭條聞哭聲。
浮雲爲蒼茫。飛鳥不能鳴。行人何寂寞。白日自淒清。
憶昔君在時。問我學無生。勸君苦不早。令君無所成。
故人各有贈。又不及生平。負爾非一途。痛哭返柴荊。

69　哭殷遙

送君返葬石樓山。松柏蒼蒼賓馭還。埋骨白雲長已矣。
空餘流水向人間。

70　寄崇梵僧

崇梵僧。崇梵僧。秋歸覆釜春不還。落花啼鳥紛紛亂。
澗戶山窗寂寂閒。峽裏誰知有人事。郡中遙望空雲山。

71　山中寄諸弟妹

山中多法侶。禪誦自爲群。城郭遙相望。惟應見白雲。

72　贈韋穆十八

與君青眼客。共有白雲心。不向東山去。日令春草深。

73　游李山人所居因題屋壁

世上皆如夢。狂來或自歌。問年松樹老。有地竹林多。

藥倩韓康賣。門容向子過。翻嫌枕席上。無那白雲何。

74　送別

下馬飲君酒。問君何所之。君言不得意。歸臥南山陲。
但去莫復問。白雲無盡時。

75　答裴迪

淼淼寒流廣。蒼蒼秋雨晦。君問終南山。心知白雲外。

76　渡河到清河作

汎舟大河裏。積水窮天涯。天波忽開拆。郡邑千萬家。
行復見城市。宛然有桑麻。迴瞻舊鄉國。淼漫連雲霞。

77　終南山

太乙近天都。連山到海隅。白雲迴望合。青靄入看無。
分野中峯變。陰晴眾壑殊。欲投人處宿。隔水問樵夫。

78　漢江臨汎

楚塞三湘接。荊門九派通。江流天地外。山色有無中。
郡邑浮前浦。波瀾動遠空。襄陽好風日。留醉與山翁。

79　終南別業

中歲頗好道。晚家南山陲。興來每獨往。勝事空自知。
行到水窮處。坐看雲起時。偶然值林叟。談笑無還期。

80　山居即事

寂寞掩柴扉。蒼茫對落暉。鶴巢松樹徧。人訪蓽門稀。
嫩竹含新粉。紅蓮落故衣。渡頭燈火起。處處採菱歸。

81　李處士山居

君子盈天階。小人甘自冤。方隨鍊金客。林上家絶巇。
背嶺花未開。入雲樹深淺。清晝猶自眠。山鳥時一囀。

82　喜祖三至留宿

門前洛陽客。下馬拂征衣。不枉故人駕。平生多掩扉。
行人返深巷。積雪帶餘暉。早歲同袍者。高車何處歸。

83　齊州送祖三

相逢方一笑。相送還成泣。祖帳已傷離。荒城復愁入。
天寒遠山淨。日暮長河急。解纜君已遙。望君猶佇立。

84　淇上即事田園

屏居淇水上。東野曠無山。日隱桑柘外。河明閭井間。
牧童望村去。獵犬隨人還。靜者亦何事。荊扉乘晝關。

85　新晴晚望

新晴原野曠。極目無氛垢。郭門臨渡頭。村樹連溪口。
白水明田外。碧峯出山後。農月無閒人。傾家事南畝。

86　崔濮陽兄季重前山興

秋色有佳興。況君池上閒。悠悠西林下。自識門前山。

千里橫黛色。數峯出雲間。嵯峨對秦國。合杳藏荊關。
殘雨斜日照。夕嵐飛鳥還。故人今尚爾。歎息此頹顏。

87　寒食城東即事

清溪一道穿桃李。演漾綠蒲涵白芷。谿上人家凡幾家。
落花半落東流水。蹴踘屢過飛鳥上。鞦韆競出垂楊裏。
少年分日作遨遊。不用清明兼上已。

88　送方尊師歸嵩山

仙官欲往九龍潭。旄節朱旛倚石龕。山壓天中半天上。
洞穿江底出江南。瀑布杉松常帶雨。夕陽彩翠忽成嵐。
借問迎來雙白鶴。已曾衡嶽送蘇耽。

89　送元二使安西

渭城朝雨裛輕塵。客舍青青柳色新。勸君更盡一杯酒。
西出陽關無故人。

90　送錢少府還藍田

草色日向好。桃源人去稀。手持平子賦。目送老萊衣。
每候山櫻發。時同海燕歸。今年寒食酒。應得返柴扉。

91　送方城韋明府

遙思葭菼際。寥落楚人行。高鳥長淮水。平蕪故郢城。
使車聽雉乳。縣鼓應雞鳴。若見州從事。無嫌手板迎。

92　送邢桂州

饒吹喧京口。風波下洞庭。趨圻將赤岸。擊汰復揚舲。
日落江湖白。潮來天地青。明珠歸合浦。應逐使臣星。

93　送宇文太守赴宣城

寥落雲外山。迢遙舟中賞。饒吹發西江。秋空多清響。
地迴古城蕪。月明寒潮廣。時賽敬亭神。復解琵師網。
何處寄相思。南風吹五兩。

94　送梓州李使君

萬壑樹參天。千山響杜鵑。山中一半雨。樹杪百重泉。
漢女輸橦布。巴人訟芋田。文翁翻教授。敢不倚先賢。

95　送楊長史赴果州

褒斜不容幰。之子去何之。鳥道一千里。猿啼十二時。
官橋祭酒客。山木女郎祠。別後同明月。君應聽子規。

96　送韋評事

欲逐將軍取右賢。沙塲走馬向居延。遙知漢使蕭關外。
愁見孤城落日邊。

97　送友人南歸

萬里春應盡。三江雁亦稀。連天漢水廣。孤客郢城歸。
鄖國稻苗秀。楚人菰米肥。懸知倚門望。遙識老萊衣。

98　登裴迪秀才小臺作。

端居不出戶。滿目望雲山。落日鳥邊下。秋原人外閒。
遙知遠林際。不見此簷間。好客多乘月。應門莫上關。

99　聽百舌鳥

上蘭門外草萋萋。未央宮中花裏栖。亦有相隨過御苑。
不知若箇向金隄。入春解作千般語。拂曙能先百鳥啼。
萬戶千門應覺曉。建章何必聽鳴雞。

100　沈十四拾遺新竹生讀經處同諸公之作

閒居日清靜。修竹自檀欒。嫩節留餘籜。新叢出舊欄。
細枝風響亂。疎影月光寒。樂府裁龍笛。漁家伐釣竿。
何如道門裏。青翠拂仙壇。

101　紅牡丹

綠艷閒且靜。紅衣淺復深。花心愁欲斷。春色豈知心。

102　送賀遂員外外甥

南國有歸舟。荊門泝上流。蒼茫葭菼外。雲水與昭邱。
檣帶城烏去。江連暮雨愁。猿聲不可聽。莫待楚山秋。

103　送邱爲落第歸江東

憐君不得意。況復柳條春。爲客黃金盡。還家白髮新。
五湖三畝宅。萬里一歸人。知禰不能薦。羞爲獻納臣。

104 送邱爲往唐州

宛洛有風塵。君行多苦辛。四愁連漢水。百口寄隨人。
槐色陰清晝。楊花惹暮春。朝端肯相送。天子繡衣臣。

105 春日與裴迪過新昌里訪呂逸人不遇

桃源一向絕風塵。柳市南頭訪隱淪。到門不敢題凡鳥。
看竹何須問主人。城外青山如屋裏。東家流水入西鄰。
閉戶著書多歲月。種松皆老作龍鱗。

106 送沈子福歸江東

楊柳渡頭行客稀。罟師盪槳向臨圻。惟有相思似春色。
江南江北送君歸。

107 登河北城樓作

井邑傅巖上。客亭雲霧間。高城眺落日。極浦映蒼山。
岸火孤舟宿。漁家夕鳥還。寂寥天地暮。心與廣川閒。

108 青溪

言入黃花川。每逐青溪水。隨山將萬轉。趣途無百里。
聲喧亂石中。色靜深松裏。漾漾汎菱荇。澄澄映葭葦。
我心素已閒。清川澹如此。請留盤石上。垂釣將已矣。

109 自大散以往深林密竹蹬道盤曲四五十里
　　　　至黃牛嶺見黃花川

危徑幾萬轉。數里將三休。迴環見徒侶。隱映隔林丘。
颯颯松上雨。潺潺石中流。靜言深溪裏。長嘯高山頭。

望見南山陽。白日靄悠悠。青皋麗已淨。綠樹鬱如浮。
曾是厭蒙密。曠然消人憂。

110 早秋山中作

無才不敢累明時。思向東溪守故籬。不厭尚平婚嫁早。
却嫌陶令去官遲。草堂蛩響臨秋急。山裏蟬聲薄暮悲。
寂寞柴門人不到。空林獨與白雲期。

111 酬諸公見過

嗟余未喪。哀此孤生。屏居藍田。薄地躬耕。歲晏輸稅。
以奉粢盛。晨往東皋。草露未晞。暮看煙火。負擔來歸。
我聞有客。足掃荊扉。簞食伊何。副瓜抓棗。仰厠羣賢。
皤然一老。媿無莞簟。班荊席薰。汎汎登陂。折彼荷花。
淨觀素鮪。俯瞰白沙。山鳥羣飛。日隱輕霞。登車上馬。
儵忽雨散。雀噪荒村。雞鳴空館。還復幽獨。重欷累嘆。

112 汎前陂

秋空自明迥。況復遠人間。暢以沙際鶴。兼之雲外山。
澄波澹將夕。清月皓方閒。此夜任孤棹。夷猶殊未還。

113 積雨輞川莊作

積雨空林烟火遲。蒸藜炊黍餉東菑。漠漠水田飛白鷺。
陰陰夏木囀黃鸝。山中習靜觀朝槿。松下清齋折露葵。
野老與人爭席罷。海鷗何事更相疑。

114 歸輞川作

谷口疎鐘動。漁樵稍欲稀。悠然遠山暮。獨向白雲歸。

菱蔓弱難定。楊花輕易飛。東皋春草色。惆悵掩柴扉。

115　輞川別業

不到東山向一年。歸來纔及種春田。雨中草色綠堪染。
水上桃花紅欲然。優婁比邱經論學。傴僂丈人鄉里賢。
披衣倒屣且相見。相歡語笑衡門前。

116　輞川閒居贈裴秀才迪

寒山轉蒼翠。秋水日潺湲。倚杖柴門外。臨風聽暮蟬。
渡頭餘落日。墟里上孤烟。復值接輿醉。狂歌五柳前。

117　山居秋暝

空山新雨後。天氣晚來秋。明月松間照。清泉石上流。
竹喧歸浣女。蓮動下漁舟。隨意春芳歇。王孫自可留。

118　酬張少府

晚年惟好靜。萬事不關心。自顧無長策。空知返舊林。
松風吹解帶。山月照彈琴。君問窮通理。漁歌入浦深。

119　田園樂七首

出入千門萬戶。　　　　經過北里南鄰。
蹀躞鳴珂有底。　　　　崆峒散髮何人。

120

再見封侯萬戶。　　　　立談賜璧一雙。

詎勝耦耕南畝。   何如高臥東窗。

121

採菱渡頭風急。   策杖村西日斜。
杏樹壇邊漁父。   桃花源裏人家。

122

萋萋芳草春綠。   落落長松夏寒。
牛羊自歸村巷。   童稚不識衣冠。

123

山下孤烟遠村。   天邊獨樹高原。
一瓢顏回陋巷。   五柳先生對門。

124

桃紅復含宿雨。   柳綠更帶春烟。
花落家僮未掃。   鶯啼山客猶眠。

125

酌酒會臨泉水。   抱琴好倚長松。
南園露葵朝折。   東谷黃粱夜舂。

126　　皇甫岳雲谿雜題五首

鳥鳴磵

人閒桂花落。夜靜春山空。月出驚山鳥。時鳴春澗中。

127   蓮花塢

日日採蓮去。洲長多暮歸。弄篙莫濺水。畏濕紅蓮衣。

128   鸕鷀堰

乍向紅蓮沒。復出清浦颺。獨立何褵褷。銜魚古查上。

129   上平田

朝畊上平田。暮畊上平田。借問問津者。寧知沮溺賢。

130   萍池

春池深且廣。會待輕舟迴。靡靡綠萍合。垂楊掃復開。

輞川集 并序

余別業在輞川谷。其遊止有孟城坳、華子岡、文杏館、斤竹嶺、鹿柴、木蘭柴、茱萸沜、宮槐陌、臨湖亭、南垞、欹湖、柳浪、欒家瀨、金屑泉、白石灘、北垞、竹里館、辛夷塢、漆園、椒園等。與裴迪閒暇。各賦絕句云爾。

131   孟城坳

新家孟城口。古木餘衰柳。來者復爲誰。空悲昔人有。

132   華子岡

飛鳥去不窮。連山復秋色。上下華子岡。惆悵情何極。

133　文杏館

文杏裁爲梁。香茅結爲宇。不知棟裏雲。去作人間雨。

134　斤竹嶺

檀欒映空曲。青翠漾漣漪。暗入商山路。樵人不可知。

135　鹿柴

空山不見人。但聞人語響。返景入深林。復照青苔上。

136　木蘭柴

秋山斂餘照。飛鳥逐前侶。彩翠時分明。夕嵐無處所。

137　茱萸沜

結實紅且綠。復如花更開。山中儻留客。置此茱萸杯。

138　宮槐陌

仄徑蔭宮槐。幽陰多綠苔。應門但迎掃。畏有山僧來。

139　臨湖亭

輕舸迎上客。悠悠湖上來。當軒對樽酒。四面芙蓉開。

140　南垞

輕舟南垞去。北垞淼難即。隔浦望人家。遙遙不相識。

141 歌湖

吹簫凌極浦。日暮送夫君。湖上一迴首。山青卷白雲。

142 柳浪

分行接綺樹。倒影入清漪。不學御溝上。春風傷別離。

143 欒家瀨

颯颯秋雨中。淺淺石溜瀉。跳波自相濺。白鷺驚復下。

144 金屑泉

日飲金屑泉。少當千餘歲。翠鳳翔文螭。羽節朝玉帝。

145 白石灘

清淺白石灘。綠蒲向堪把。家住水東西。浣紗明月下。

146 北垞

北垞湖水北。雜樹映朱欄。逶迤南川水。明滅青林端。

147 竹里館

獨坐幽篁裏。彈琴復長嘯。深林人不知。明月來相照。

148 辛夷塢

木末芙蓉花。山中發紅萼。澗戶寂無人。紛紛開且落。

149   漆園

古人非傲吏。自闕經世務。偶寄一微官。婆娑數株樹。

150   椒園

桂尊迎帝子。杜若贈佳人。椒漿奠瑤席。欲下雲中君。

Chinese Names, Titles, and Key Terms

A Glossary

Column 1 provides an alphabetically arranged list, in pinyin romanization, of proper names, place names, official titles, book and chapter titles, and key terms mentioned in the poems and main text of this volume. Column 2 gives them in Wade-Giles romanization, and Column 3 provides the Chinese characters.

Pinyin	Wade-Giles	Characters
An Lushan	An Lu-shan	安祿山
Anxi	An-hsi	安西
Ba	Pa	巴
Baishi daoren shi-shuo	Pai-shih tao-jen shih-shuo	白石道人詩說
Baitou yin	Pai-tou yin	白頭吟
Ban Chao	Pan Ch'ao	班超
Bao Zhao	Pao Chao	鮑照
Baoxie	Pao-hsieh	襃斜
Ben shi shi	Pen-shih shih	本事詩
Biyu	Pi-yü	碧玉
Bo Juyi	Po Chü-i	白居易
Bo Yi	Po I	伯夷
Boliang	Po-liang	柏梁
Boling	Po-ling	博陵
Bunkyō hifuron (Jap.)		文鏡秘府論
Cai Yong	Ts'ai Yung	蔡邕
Cai Ze	Ts'ai Tse	蔡澤
Canglang shihua	Ts'ang-lang shih-hua	滄浪詩話
Cao Cao	Ts'ao Ts'ao	曹操
Cao Jiping	Ts'ao Chi-p'ing	曹濟平
Cao Zhi	Ts'ao Chih	曹植
Cen Shen	Ts'en Shen	岑參
chan	ch'an	禪
Chang Jian	Ch'ang Chien	常建
Chang'an	Ch'ang-an	長安

Pinyin	Wade-Giles	Characters
Chang'an zhi	Ch'ang-an chih	長安志
Changdao	Ch'ang-tao	長道
Changju	Ch'ang-chü	長沮
chanyu	ch'an-yü	單于
Chen	Ch'en	陳
Chen Yixin	Ch'en I-hsin	陳貽焮
Cheng	Ch'eng	成
Chengzhai ji	Ch'eng-chai ji	誠齋集
Chongdan	Ch'ung-tan	冲淡
Chongfan	Ch'ung-fan	崇梵
Chu	Ch'u	楚
Chu ci	Ch'u-tz'u	楚辭
Chu ci buzhu	Ch'u-tz'u pu-chu	楚辭補註
Chun qiu	Ch'un-ch'iu	春秋
Congshu jicheng	Ts'ung-shu ji-ch'eng	叢書集成
Cui Fuda	Ts'ui Fu-ta	崔傅答
Cui Jizhong	Ts'ui Chi-chung	崔季重
Cui Xiyi	Ts'ui Hsi-i	崔希逸
Da sheng	Ta sheng	達生
Da xu	Ta hsü	大序
da ya	ta ya	大雅
ta yuecheng	ta yüeh-ch'eng	大樂丞
Da zong shi	Ta tsung-shih	大宗師
Daduo	Ta-to	達多
Dajianfu	Ta-chien-fu	大薦福
Daming	Ta-ming	大明
Dasan	Ta-san	大散
Datong	Ta-t'ung	大同
Dai Shulun (Rongzhou)	Tai Shu-lun (Jung-chou)	戴叔倫（容州）

Pinyin	Wade-Giles	Characters
Daijingtang shihua	Tai-ching-t'ang shih-hua	帶經堂詩話
Daizong	Tai-tsung	代宗
Dao de jing	Tao-te-ching	道德經
Daoguang	Tao-kuang	道光
Daoshi	Tao-shih	道世
Daoyi	Tao-i	道一
Deng Kuiying	Teng K'uei-ying	鄧魁英
Deng You (Bodao)	Teng Yu (Po-tao)	鄧攸（伯道）
dianzhong shiyushi	tien-chung shih-yü-shih	殿中侍御史
Ding Fubao	Ting Fu-pao	丁福保
Dingyuan hou	Ting-yüan hou	定遠侯
Diwang shiji	Ti-wang shih-chi	帝王世紀
Dong Shi	Tung Shih	東施
Dongting	Tung-t'ing	洞庭
Dou Hong	Tou Hung	竇鴻
Dou Xian	Tou Hsien	竇憲
Du Fu (Shaoling)	Tu Fu (Shaoling)	杜甫（少陵）
Du Yu	Tu Yü	杜宇
Ershi	Er-shih	貳師
Ershisi shipin	Er-shih-ssu shih-p'in	二十四詩品
Fan Mingyou	Fan Ming-yu	范明友
Fan Wenlan	Fan Wen-lan	范文瀾
Fangcheng	Fang-ch'eng	方城
Fangzhang	Fang-chang	方丈
Fayuan zhulin	Fa-yüan chu-lin	法苑珠林
Fei Qin	Fei Ch'in	肥親
Fen	Fen	汾
Fo bao en jing	Fo-pao-en-ching	佛報恩經
fu	fu	賦

Pinyin	Wade-Gilea	Characters
Fu Chai	Fu Ch'ai	夫差
Fu Donghua	Fu Tung-hua	傅東華
Fu Yue	Fu Yüeh	傅說
Fuchun	Fu-ch'un	富春
Fufu	Fu-fu	覆釜
Ganhua	Kan-hua	感化
gao miao	kao-miao	高妙
Gao seng zhuan	Kao-seng chuan	高僧傳
Ge Hong	Ko Hung	葛洪
gongan	kung-an	公案
Gongsun Ao	Kung-sun Ao	公孫敖
Gou Jian	Kou Chien	勾踐
Guan Yu	Kuan Yü	關羽
Guangcheng	Kuang-ch'eng	廣成
Gui tian fu	Kuei-t'ien fu	歸田賦
Gui yuantian qu	Kuei yüan-t'ien ch'ü	歸園田去
Guizhou	Kuei-chou	桂州
Gukou	Ku-k'ou	谷口
Guo Bogong	Kuo Po-kung	郭伯恭
Guo Chenggu	Kuo Ch'eng-ku	郭承叚
Guo Maoqian	Kuo Mao-ch'ien	郭茂倩
Guo Pu	Kuo P'u	郭璞
Guo Shaoyu	Kuo Shao-yü	郭紹虞
Guozhou	Kuo-chou	果州
Gushi yuan jianzhu	Ku-shih yüan chien-chu	古詩源箋註
guti shi	ku-t'i shih	古體詩
Han (dynasty)	Han	漢
Han (kingdom)	Han	韓
Han Ju	Han Chü	韓駒

Pinyin	Wade-Giles	Characters
Han Kang (Boxiu)	Han K'ang (Po-hsiu)	韓康（伯休）
Han Shan	Han Shan	寒山
Han shu	Han shu	漢書
Han Weijun	Han Wei-chün	韓維鈞
Han Yu (Tuizhi)	Han Yü (T'ui-chih)	韓愈（退之）
Handan	Han-tan	邯鄲
Hanxu	Han-hsü	含蓄
Hao	Hao	鎬
Haofang	Hao-fang	豪放
He	Ho	和
He Wenhuan	Ho Wen-huan	何文煥
Hebei	Ho-pei	河北
Heng	Heng	衡
Henzō Kinkō (Jap.)		遍照金剛
Hepu	Ho-p'u	合浦
Hexi	Ho-hsi	河西
Hong Xingzu	Hung Hsing-tsu	洪興祖
Hongdao	Hung-tao	宏道
Hou Han shu	Hou Han shu	後漢書
Hua	Hua	華
Huai	Huai	淮
huai gu	huai ku	懷古
Huang Tingjian (Shangu)	Huang T'ing-chien (Shan-ku)	黃庭堅（山谷）
Huangfu Yue	Huang-fu Yüeh	皇甫岳
Huayan	Hua-yen	華嚴
Hui	Hui	惠
Hui Shi	Hui Shih	惠施
Huineng	Hui-neng	慧能

Pinyin	Wade-Giles	Characters
Huiyuan	Hui-yüan	慧遠
Huo Qubing	Huo Ch'ü-ping	霍去病
ji	chi	寂
Jia Zhi	Chia Chih	賈至
Jia Zong	Chia Tsung	賈琮
jiabu yuanwailang	chia-pu yüan-wai-lang	駕部員外郎
Jian'an	Chien-an	建安
jiancha yushi	chien-ch'a yü-shih	監察御史
Jiang Kui	Chiang K'uei	姜夔
Jianwu	Chien-wu	建武
Jianyuan	Chien-yüan	建元
Jianzhang	Chien-chang	建章
Jiaoran	Chiao-jan	皎然
Jiaping	Chia-p'ing	嘉平
Jiashi tanlu	Chia-shih t'an-lu	賈氏談錄
jiedu dashi	chieh-tu ta-shih	節度大使
Jieni	Chieh-ni	桀溺
Jifu	Chi-fu	吉甫
Jili	Chi-li	綺麗
Jilu	Chi-lu	雞鹿
Jin	Chin	晉
Jin Ding	Chin Ting	金丁
Jin shu	Chin shu	晉書
jing (well)	ching	井
jing (scene)	ching	景
Jingde chuan deng lu	Ching-te ch'uan-teng lu	景德傳燈錄
Jingjian	Ching-chien	勁健
Jingkou	Ching-k'ou	京口
Jingmen	Ching-men	荆門

Pinyin	Wade-Giles	Characters
Jingting	Ching-t'ing	敬亭
jinshi	chin-shih	進士
jinti shi	chin-t'i shih	近體詩
jishizhong	chi-shih-chung	給事中
Jiu Tang shu	Chiu T'ang shu	舊唐書
Jizang	Chi-tsang	吉藏
Jizhou	Chi-chou	濟州
Jiu ge	Chiu ko	九歌
Jiucheng	Chiu-ch'eng	九成
juan	chüan	卷
jueju	chüeh-chü	絕句
Juling	Chü-ling	巨靈
jushi	chü-shih	居士
Juyan	Chü-yen	居延
Kaiyuan	K'ai-yüan	開元
Kangxi	K'ang-hsi	康熙
kong	k'ung	空
Kong Rong	K'ung Jung	孔融
konghou	k'ung-hou	箜篌
Kongtong	K'ung-t'ung	崆峒
kubu langzhong	k'u-pu lang-chung	庫部郎中
Kūkai (Jap.)		空海
Lanling	Lan-ling	蘭陵
Lantian	Lan-t'ien	藍田
Laolaizi	Lao-lai-tzu	老萊子
Laozi	Lao-tzu	老子
li (Truth)	li	理
Li (Master)	Li	李
Li (Mt.)	Li	驪

Pinyin	Wade-Giles	Characters
Li Bo	Li Po	李白
Li Changzhi	Li Ch'ang-chih	李長之
Li Guang	Li Kuang	李廣
Li Guangli	Li Kuang-li	李廣利
Li He	Li Ho	李郃
Li Linfu	Li Lin-fu	李林甫
Li Ping	Li P'ing	李平
Li Taibo ji	Li T'ai-po chi	李太白集
Li Xian	Li Hsien	李憲
Liangzhou	Liang-chou	涼州
Liao	Liao	遼
libu langzhong	li-pu lang-chung	吏部郎中
Lidai shihua	Li-tai shih-hua	歷代詩話
Lie xian zhuan	Lieh-hsien chuan	列仙傳
Liezi	Lieh-tzu	列子
liu chun	liu-ch'un	留春
Liu Shenxu	Liu Shen-hsü	劉愼虛
Liu Song	Liu Sung	劉宋
Liu Weichong	Liu Wei-ch'ung	劉維崇
Liu Xie	Liu Hsieh	劉勰
Liu Xu	Liu Hsü	劉昫
Liuxia Hui	Liu-hsia Hui	柳下惠
Liuyi shihua	Liu-i shih-hua	六一詩話
Long	Lung	隴
Lu (Mt.)	Lu	廬
Lu (kingdom)	Lu	魯
Lu Gong	Lu Kung	魯恭
Lu Huaixuan	Lu Huai-hsüan	盧懷萱
Lu Ji	Lu Chi	陸機

Pinyin	Wade-Giles	Characters
Lu Tong (Jieyu)	Lu T'ung (Chieh-yü)	陸通（接輿）
Lun wen yi	Lun wen-i	論文意
Lun yu	Lun-yü	論語
Luo	Lo	洛
Luoyang	Lo-yang	洛陽
Lü An	Lü An	呂安
Lü Qiuxiao	Lü Ch'iu-hsiao	閭丘曉
Lü Wang	Lü Wang	呂望
lüshi	lü-shih	律詩
Mei Yaochen	Mei Yao-ch'en	梅堯臣
Meng Chang (Bozhou)	Meng Ch'ang (Po-chou)	孟嘗（伯周）
Meng Haoran (Xiangyang)	Meng Hao-jan (Hsiangyang)	孟浩然（襄陽）
Meng Qi	Meng Ch'i	孟棨
menxia sheng	men-hsia sheng	門下省
Ming (dynasty; emperor)	Ming	明
ming (name)	ming	名
Mingdai lunzhu congkan	Ming-tai lun-chu ts'ung-k'an	明代論著叢刊
Ming shi	Ming shih	明詩
Mingguang	Ming-kuang	明光
Minghuang zalu	Ming-huang tsa-lu	明皇雜錄
Nan shi	Nan shih	南史
Ni Heng (Zhengping)	Ni Heng (Cheng-p'ing)	禰衡（正平）
Ning	Ning	寧
Niutou Fayong	Niu-t'ou Fa-yung	牛頭法容
Ouyang Xiu	Ou-yang Hsiu	歐陽修
pailü	p'ai-lü	排律
Pei Di	P'ei Ti	裴迪

Pinyin	Wade-Giles	Characters
Pei Yaoqing	P'ei Yao-ch'ing	裴耀卿
Penglai	P'eng-lai	蓬萊
Pian	P'ien	扁
piaoji	p'iao-chi	驃騎
ping	p'ing	平
Ping Danran	P'ing Tan-jan	平淡然
Pushi	P'u-shih	普施
Puti	P'u-t'i	菩提
Puyang	P'u-yang	濮陽
Qi (district)	Ch'i	祁
Qi (prince)	Ch'i	岐
Qi (river)	Ch'i	淇
Qian Qi	Ch'ien Ch'i	錢起
Qian Zhongshu	Ch'ien Chung-shu	錢鍾書
Qiang	Ch'iang	羌
Qianyuan	Ch'ien-yüan	乾元
Qin	Ch'in	秦
Qing (dynasty)	Ch'ing	清
qing	ch'ing	情
Qinghe	Ch'ing-ho	清河
Qingming	Ch'ing-ming	清明
qingqi	ch'ing-ch'i	清奇
qingtan	ch'ing-t'an	清談
Qingyuan	Ch'ing-yüan	清源
Qiu feng ci	Ch'iu-feng tz'u	秋風辭
Qiu Wei	Ch'iu Wei	邱爲
Qiwu Qian (Xiaotong)	Ch'i-wu Ch'ien (Hsiao-t'ung)	綦毋潛（孝通）
qiyuan li	ch'i-yüan li	漆園吏

Pinyin	Wade-Giles	Characters
Qizhou	Ch'i-chou	齊州
Qu Yuan	Ch'ü Yüan	屈原
Quan Han Sanguo Jin Nan Bei Chao shi	Ch'üan Han San-kuo Chin Nan-bei-ch'ao shih	全漢三國晉南北朝詩
Rang wang	Jang wang	讓王
Rao Chao	Jao Ch'ao	繞朝
Ren jian shi	Jen-chien shih	人間世
ren yi	jen-i	仁義
Ruan Fu	Juan Fu	阮孚
Ruan Ji	Juan Chi	阮籍
Runan	Ju-nan	汝南
Sanguo zhi	San-kuo chih	三國志
Sengzhao	Seng-chao	曾肇
Shan gui	Shan kuei	山鬼
Shan Jian (Jilun)	Shan Chien (Chi-lun)	山簡 (季倫)
Shang (dynasty; Mt.)	Shang	商
Shang (Xiang) Chang	Shan (Hsiang) Ch'ang	尚長
shangshu sheng	shang-shu sheng	尚書省
shangshu youcheng	shang-shu yu-ch'eng	尚書右丞
shangshu zuopuye	shang-shu tso-p'u-yeh	尚書左僕射
Shangyuan	Shang-yüan	上元
Shen Deqian	Shen Te-ch'ien	沈德潛
Shen si	Shen-ssu	神思
Shen xian zhuan	Shen-hsien chuan	神仙傳
Shen yi zhuan	Shen-i chuan	神異傳
Shen Zifu	Shen Tzu-fu	沈子福
shengwen	sheng-wen	聲聞
shenyun	shen-yün	神韻
Shi Chong (Jilun)	Shih Ch'ung (Chi-lun)	石崇 (季倫)
shi fa	shih-fa	詩法

Pinyin	Wade-Giles	Characters
shi fo pai	shih-fo p'ai	詩佛派
Shi Gao	Shih Kao	史高
Shi ji	Shih-chi	史記
Shi jing	Shih-ching	詩經
Shi pin	Shih-p'in	詩品
Shi shi	Shih-shih	詩式
Shi Xuanchao	Shih Hsüan-ch'ao	史絃超
Shi yi	Shih-i	詩議
Shishuo xinyu	Shih-shuo hsin-yü	世說新語
Shitou	Shih-t'ou	石頭
Shixing	Shih-hsing	始興
shiyushi	shih-yü-shih	侍御史
Shouyang	Shouyang	首陽
Shu	Shu	蜀
Shu Qi	Shu Ch'i	叔齊
Shu zheng ji	Shu cheng chi	述征記
Shui jing	Shui-ching	水經
Shun	Shun	舜
Sibu beiyao	Ssu-pu pei-yao	四部備要
sicang canjun	ssu-ts'ang ts'an-chün	司倉參軍
Sikong Tu	Ssu-k'ung T'u	司空圖
Sima Guang	Ssu-ma Kuang	司馬光
Sima Qian	Ssu-ma Ch'ien	司馬遷
Sima Xiangru	Ssu-ma Hsiang-ju	司馬相如
Siming shihua	Ssu-ming shih-hua	四溟詩話
Song (dynasty)	Sung	宋
Song (Mt.)	Sung	嵩
Song Qi	Sung Ch'i	宋祁

Pinyin	Wade-Giles	Characters
Song shu	Sung shu	宋書
Song Zhiwen	Sung Chih-wen	宋之問
songbie	sung-pieh	送別
Sou shen ji	Sou-shen chi	搜神記
Su Dan	Su Tan	蘇耽
Su Shi (Dongpo)	Su Shih (Tung-p'o)	蘇軾（東坡）
Su Wu (Ziqing)	Su Wu (Tzu-ch'ing)	蘇武（子卿）
Sui (dynasty)	Sui	隋
sui (year)	sui	歲
Sui Hui	Sui Hui	隨會
Suizhou	Sui-chou	隨州
Sumen	Su-men	蘇門
Sun Chuo	Sun Ch'o	孫綽
Sun Deng	Sun Teng	孫登
Sun Wu	Sun Wu	孫武
Suzong	Su-tsung	肅宗
Taibo	T'ai-po	太白
Taihang	T'ai-hang	太行
Taishō shinshū dai-zōkyō (Jap.)		大正新脩大藏經
Taiyi	T'ai-i	太乙
Taiyuan	T'ai-yüan	太元
taizi zhongshuzi	t'ai-tzu chung-shu-tzu	太子中庶子
taizi zhongyun	t'ai-tzu chung-yün	太子中允
Taizong	T'ai-tsung	太宗
Tan yi lu	T'an-i lu	談藝錄
Tanbi	T'an-pi	曇壁
Tang (dynasty)	T'ang	唐
Tang (emperor)	T'ang	湯

Pinyin	Wade-Giles	Characters
Tang Ju	T'ang Chü	唐舉
Tang shi yanjiu lun-wenji	T'ang shih yen-chiu lunwen-chi	唐詩研究論文集
Tang xian sanmei ji	T'ang-hsien san-mei chi	唐賢三昧集
Tangzhou	T'ang-chou	唐州
Tanxing	T'an-hsing	曇興
Tao hua yuan ji	T'ao-hua-yüan chi	桃花源記
Tao Qian (Yuan-ming)	T'ao Ch'ien (Yüan-ming)	陶潛（淵明）
Ti xing	T'i hsing	體性
Tian dao	T'ien-tao	天道
tian nü	t'ien-nü	天女
Tian wen	T'ien wen	天問
Tian xia	T'ien-hsia	天下
Tian yun	T'ien-yün	天運
Tianbao	T'ien-pao	天寶
Tiantai	T'ien-t'ai	天台
Tingting	T'ing-t'ing	亭亭
Wai wu	Wai wu	外物
Wan	Wan	宛
Wang (river)	Wang	輞
Wang Can	Wang Ts'an	王粲
Wang Changling (Shao-bo, Jiangning)	Wang Ch'ang-ling (Shao-po, Chiang-ning)	王昌齡（少伯，江寧）
Wang Chulian	Wang Ch'u-lien	王處廉
Wang Huizhi	Wang Hui-chih	王徽之
Wang Ji	Wang Chi	汪極
Wang Jia	Wang Chia	王駕
Wang Jin	Wang Chin	王縉
Wang Kai	Wang K'ai	王愷

Pinyin	Wade-Giles	Characters
Wang Shizhen (1526-90)	Wang Shih-chen	王世貞
Wang Shizhen (1634-1711)	Wang Shih-chen	王士禎
Wang Wei (Mojie, Youcheng)	Wang Wei (Mo-chieh, Yu-ch'eng)	王維（摩詰，右丞）
Wang Wei pingzhuan	Wang Wei p'ing-chuan	王維評傳
Wang Wei shixuan	Wang Wei shih-hsüan	王維詩選
Wang Wei xiaozu	Wang Wei hsiao-tsu	王維小組
Wang Wei yanjiu	Wang Wei yen-chiu	王維研究
Wang Xizhi	Wang Hsi-chih	王義之
Wang Youcheng jizhu	Wang Yu-ch'eng chi-chu	王右丞集注
Wang Yunxi	Wang Yün-hsi	王運熙
Wangzi Qiao	Wang-tzu Ch'iao	王子喬
Wei	Wei	魏
Wei Jin Nan Bei Chao wenxueshi can-kao ziliao	Wei Chin Nan-pei-ch'ao wenhsüeh-shih ts'an-k'ao tzu-liao	魏晉南北朝文學史參考資料
Wei Mu	Wei Mu	韋穆
Wei Qing	Wei Ch'ing	霡青
Wei Yingwu	Wei Ying-wu	韋應物
Weilu shihua	Wei-lu shih-hua	圍爐詩話
Weiyang	Wei-yang	未央
wen	wen	文
Wen fu	Wen-fu	文賦
Wen Weng	Wen Weng	文翁
Wen xuan	Wen-hsüan	文選
Wenxin diaolong	Wen-hsin tiao-lung	文心雕龍
Wenxue yichan	Wen-hsüeh i-ch'an	文學遺產
Wu (emperor)	Wu	武
Wu (kingdom)	Wu	吳

Pinyin	Wade-Giles	Characters
wu (nothingness)	wu	無
wu (realize)	wu	悟
Wu daifu	Wu tai-fu	五大夫
Wu Ke	Wu K'o	吳可
Wu liu xiansheng	Wu-liu hsien-sheng	五柳先生
Wu Qi	Wu Ch'i	吳起
Wu Qiao	Wu Ch'iao	吳喬
wu wei	wu-wei	無爲
wu xin	wu-hsin	無心
Wu Yue chun qiu	Wu Yüeh ch'un-ch'iu	吳越春秋
Wu Zhongyi	Wu Chung-i	吳中一
Wuling	Wu-ling	武陵
xi	hsi	兮
Xi ci	Hsi-tz'u	繫辭
Xi Kang	Hsi K'ang	嵇康
Xi wang mu	Hsi-wang-mu	西王母
Xi Xi	Hsi Hsi	嵇喜
Xia	Hsia	夏
xian	hsien	縣
Xiang	Hsiang	湘
Xiang (Shang) Chang (Ziping)	Hsiang (Shang) Ch'ang (Tzu-p'ing)	向長（子平）
Xiang jun	Hsiang-chün	湘君
Xiangyang	Hsiang-yang	襄陽
Xiannong	Hsien-nung	纖穠
Xiao (pass)	Hsiao	蕭
xiao (whistle)	hsiao	嘯
Xiao Difei	Hsiao Ti-fei	蕭滌非
Xiao Tong	Hsiao T'ung	蕭統

Pinyin	Wade-Giles	Characters
xiao ya	hsiao ya	小雅
Xie An	Hsieh An	謝安
Xie Huilian	Hsieh Hui-lien	謝惠連
Xie Lingyun	Hsieh Ling-yün	謝靈運
Xie Zhen	Hsieh Chen	謝榛
xin	hsin	心
Xin Tang shu	Hsin T'ang shu	新唐書
Xinbian zhuzi ji- cheng	Hsin-pien chu-tzu chi- cheng	新編朱子集成
Xinchang	Hsin-ch'ang	新昌
Xinfeng	Hsin-feng	新豐
xing	hsing	興
xingbu shilang	hsing-pu shih-lang	刑部侍郎
Xingqing	Hsing-ch'ing	興慶
Xingrong	Hsing-jung	形容
Xionghun	Hsiung-hun	雄渾
Xiongnu	Hsiung-nu	匈奴
xiucai	hsiu-ts'ai	秀才
Xu Bo	Hsü Po	許伯
Xu Wugui	Hsü Wu-kuei	徐无鬼
Xuan	Hsüan	宣
Xuancheng	Hsüan-ch'eng	宣城
Xuanzong	Hsüan-tsung	玄宗
Xulüquanqu	Hsü-lü-ch'üan-ch'ü	虛閭權渠
Yan	Yen	燕
Yan Hui (Yuan)	Yen Hui (Yüan)	顏回（淵）
Yan Yu (Canglang)	Yen Yü (Ts'ang-lang)	嚴羽（滄浪）
Yang	Yang	陽
Yang Ji	Yang Chi	楊濟

Pinyin	Wade-Giles	Characters
Yang Wanli	Yang Wan-li	楊萬里
Yang Zhu	Yang Chu	楊朱
Yangzhou	Yang-chou	揚州
Yanran	Yen-jan	燕然
Yanzhou shanren si bu gao	Yen-chou shan-jen ssu-pu-kao	弇州山人四部稿
Yao	Yao	堯
Ye	Yeh	鄴
Yi Yin	I Yin	伊尹
Yijing	I-ching	易經
Yin	Yin	殷
Yin Yao	Yin Yao	殷遙
Yin Zhongwen	Yin Chung-wen	殷仲文
Ying	Ying	郢
Yingzhou	Ying-chou	瀛洲
Yiyuan zhiyan	I-yüan chih-yen	藝苑卮言
Yongjia Xuanjue	Yung-chia Hsüan-chüeh	永嘉玄覺
you shiyi	yu shih-i	右拾遺
You Tiantaishan fu	Yu T'ien-t'ai-shan fu	遊天台山賦
You xian shi qi shou	Yu-hsien shih ch'i shou	遊仙詩七首
Youloupinluojiaye	Yu-lou-p'in-lo-chia-yeh	優樓頻螺迦葉
Youxian	Yu-hsien	右賢
Yu	Yü	禹
Yu Boya	Yü Poya	俞伯牙
Yu fu	Yü-fu	漁夫
Yu Jipu shu	Yü Chi-p'u shu	與極浦書
Yu Qing	Yü Ch'ing	虞卿
Yu yan	Yü-yen	寓言
Yuan An	Yüan An	袁安

Pinyin	Wade-Giles	Characters
Yuan Xian	Yüan Hsien	袁憲
Yuan you	Yüan-yu	遠遊
Yue	Yüeh	越
yuefu	yüeh-fu	樂府
Yuefu shiji	Yüeh-fu shih-chi	樂府詩集
Yuezhi	Yüeh-chih	月支
Yulin	Yü-lin	榆林
Yun	Yün	鄖
Yunyun	Yün-yün	云云
Yuwen	Yü-wen	宇文
Yuyang	Yü-yang	漁陽
Zai you	Tsai-yu	在宥
ze	tse	仄
Zhang Heng (Pingzi)	Chang Heng (P'ing-tzu)	張衡（平子）
Zhang Hua	Chang Hua	張華
Zhang Jiuling	Chang Chiu-ling	張九齡
Zhang Lu	Chang Lu	張魯
Zhang Yin	Chang Yin	張諲
Zhang Yue	Chang Yüeh	張說
Zhang Zhi	Chang Chih	張芝
Zhang Zhiyue	Chang Chih-yüeh	張志岳
Zhao	Chao	趙
Zhao Diancheng	Chao Tien-ch'eng	趙殿成
Zhao Feiyan	Chao Fei-yen	趙飛燕
Zhao yinshi	Chao yin-shih	招隱士
Zhaoming Wen xuan	Chao-ming Wen-hsüan	昭明文選
Zheng Pu (Zizhen)	Cheng P'u (Tzu-chen)	鄭樸（子眞）
Zhi bei you	Chih pei-yu	知北遊
Zhi le	Chih-le	至樂

Pinyin	Wade-Giles	Characters
zhi nanxuan	chih nan-hsüan	知南選
zhi yin	chih-yin	知音
Zhiman	Chih-man	智滿
Zhiqiong	Chih-ch'iung	智瓊
Zhong Hong	Chung Hung	鍾嶸
Zhong Shanfu	Chung Shan-fu	仲山甫
Zhong Ziqi	Chung Tzu-ch'i	鍾子期
Zhongguo wenxue piping shi	Chung-kuo wen-hsüeh p'i-p'ing-shih	中國文學批評史
Zhongnan	Chung-nan	終南
zhongshu ling	chung-shu-ling	中書令
zhongshu sheng	chung-shu sheng	中書省
zhongshu sheren	chung-shu she-jen	中書舍人
Zhou	Chou	周
Zhou Weide	Chou Wei-te	周維德
Zhou yi yinde	Chou-i yin-te	周易引得
Zhu Daosheng	Chu Tao-sheng	竺道生
Zhuang Shen	Chuang Shen	莊申
Zhuangzi	Chuang-tzu	莊子
Zhuangzi yinde	Chuang-tzu yin-te	莊子引得
Zhuo Wenjun	Cho Wen-chün	卓文君
zi (cognomen)	tzu	字
zi (naturally)	tzu	自
Zilu	Tzu-lu	子路
Ziran	Tzu-jan	自然
Zixu fu	Tzu-hsü fu	子虛賦
Zizhi tongjian	Tzu-chih t'ung-chien	資治通鑑
Zizhou	Tzu-chou	梓州
zong	tsung	宗

Pinyin	Wade-Giles	Characters
Zou	Tsou	鄒
Zu Baoquan	Tsu Pao-ch'üan	祖保泉
Zu Yong	Tsu Yung	祖詠
Zu Zixu	Tsu Tzu-hsü	祖自虛
zuo buque	tso pu-ch'üeh	左補闕
Zuo zhuan	Tso chuan	左傳

Selected Bibliography

I. WANG WEI

A. Collections of Wang Wei's Poetry

Chen Yixin, ed. *Wang Wei shixuan.* Peking: Renmin, 1959.
Fu Donghua, ed. *Wang Wei shixuan.* Hong Kong: Daguang, 1973.
Zhao Diancheng, ed. *Wang Youcheng ji zhu. Sibu beiyao,* 2 vols. 1736; rpt. Taipei: Zhonghua, 1966.
————. *Wang Youcheng ji jianzhu.* Punctuated ed., 2 vols. Peking: Zhonghua, 1961.

B. Translations and Secondary Sources

Chang Yin-nan and Lewis C. Walmsley. *Poems by Wang Wei.* Rutland, Vt.: Charles E. Tuttle Company, 1958.
Chen Yixin. "Lun Wang Wei di shi," *Wenxue yichan cengkan,* No. 3 (1956), pp. 79–95.
————. "Wang Wei di zhengzhi shenghuo he ta di sixiang," in *Tang shi yanjiu lunwenji,* No. 2, Pt. 1. Peking: Zhongguo yuwenxue shebian, 1969, pp. 12–20.
————. "Wang Wei shengping shiji chutan," *Wenxue yichan cengkan,* No. 6 (1958), pp. 137–47.
————. (Ch'en Yi-hsin.) "Wang Wei, the Nature Poet," *Chinese Literature,* No. 7 (July 1962), pp. 12–22.
Ch'eng Hsi and Henry W. Wells. *An Album of Wang Wei.* Hong Kong: Lingchao, 1974.
Daudin, Pierre. "L'Idéalisme bouddhique chez Wang Wei," *Bulletin de la Société des Etudes Indochinoises,* Nouvelle Série, Vol. XLIII, No. 2 (1968).
Deng Kuiying. "Wang Wei shi jianlun," in *Tang shi yanjiu lunwenji.* Peking: Renmin, 1959, pp. 37–45.
Gong Shu. "The Function of Space and Time as Compositional Elements in Wang Wei's Poetry: A Study of Five Poems," *Literature East and West,* Vol. XVI, No. 4 (April 1975), pp. 1168–93.
Graham, A. C. Review of *Poems of Wang Wei* [by G. W. Robinson], *Bulletin of the School of Oriental and African Studies,* Vol. XXXVII, Pt. 3 (1974), pp. 711–14.
Guo Bogong. *Geyong ziran zhi liang da shihao.* Taipei: Shangwu, 1964.
Han Weijun. "Wang Wei xiancun shige zhiyi," *Wenxue yichan cengkan,* No. 13 (1963), pp. 177–84.

Jin Ding. "Wang Wei dingyou shijian zhiyi," *Wenxue yichan cengkan*, No. 13 (1963), pp. 172–76.

Juhl, R. A. "Patterns of Assonance and Vowel Melody in Wang Wei's Yüeh-fu Poems," *Journal of the Chinese Language Teachers Association*, Vol. XII, No. 2 (May 1977), pp. 95–110.

Li Changzhi. "Lun Wang Wei di liang shou shi," *Yuwen xuexi*, No. 2 (1957), pp. 5–7.

Liou Kin-ling. *Wang Wei le poète*. Paris: Jouve et Cie, 1941.

Liu Weichong. *Wang Wei pingzhuan*. Taipei: Zhengzhong, 1972.

Lu Huaixuan. "Wang Wei di yinju yu chushi," *Wenxue yichan cengkan*, No. 13 (1963), pp. 161–71.

Luk, Thomas Yuntong. "A Cinematic Interpretation of Wang Wei's Nature Poetry," *New Asia Academic Bulletin*, Vol. I (1978), pp. 151–61.

Luk, Yuntong. "Wang Wei's Perception of Space and His Attitude Towards Mountains," *Tamkang Review*, Vol. VIII, No. 1 (April 1977), pp. 89–110.

Robinson, G. W. *Poems of Wang Wei*. Baltimore: Penguin, 1973.

Wagner, Marsha L. "From Image to Metaphor: Wang Wei's Use of Light and Color," *Journal of the Chinese Language Teachers Association*, Vol. XII, No. 2 (May 1977), pp. 111–17.

Walmsley, Lewis C. and Dorothy B. *Wang Wei the Painter-Poet*. Rutland, Vt.: Charles E. Tuttle Co., 1968.

Wang Wei xiaozu (Wang Wei Study Group). "Lun Wang Wei shige di pingjia," in *Wenxue yanjiu yu pipan zhuankan*, No. 1. Peking: Renmin, 1958, pp. 59–75.

Wang Yunxi. "Wang Wei he ta di shi," introduction to Zhao Diancheng, ed., *Wang Youcheng ji jianzhu*, pp. 1–16.

Xiao Difei. "Guanyu Wang Wei di shanshui shi," in *Tang shi yanjiu lunwenji*, No. 2, Pt. 1. Peking: Zhongguo yuwenxue shebian, 1969, pp. 68–74.

Yip, Wai-lim. *Hiding the Universe: Poems by Wang Wei*. New York: Grossman, 1972.

———. "Wang Wei and the Aesthetic of Pure Experience," *Tamkang Review*, Vol. II, No. 2 and Vol. III, No. 1 (October 1971–April 1972), pp. 199–209. Reprinted as "Wang Wei and Pure Experience," introduction to *Hiding the Universe*, pp. v–xv.

Yu, Pauline R. "Wang Wei: Seven Poems," *The Denver Quarterly*, Vol. 12, No. 2 (Summer 1977), pp. 353–55.

———. "Wang Wei's Journeys in Ignorance," *Tamkang Review*, Vol. VIII, No. 1 (April 1977), pp. 73–87.

———. "Wang Wei: Recent Studies and Translations," *Chinese Literature: Essays, Articles, Reviews*, Vol. I, No. 2 (July 1979), pp. 219–40.

Zhang Zhiyue. "'Shi zhong you hua': Taolun Wang Wei shi di yishu tedian," *Wenxue yichan cengkan*, No. 13 (1963), pp. 147–60.

Zhuang Shen. *Wang Wei yanjiu*, Vol. I. Hong Kong: Wanyou, 1971.

II. POETRY AND LITERARY CRITICISM

A. Primary Sources in Chinese

Anthology of Literature. See Xiao Tong.

Complete Poems of the Han, Three Kingdoms, Jin, Northern and Southern Dynasties. See Ding Fubao, *Quan Han Sanguo Jin Nan Bei Chao shi.*

Ding Fubao, ed. *Lidai shihua xubian.* 5 vols. Rpt. Taipei: Yiwen, n.d.

————. *Quan Han Sanguo Jin Nan Bei Chao shi.* 6 vols. Rpt. Taipei: Yiwen, n.d.

Fan Wenlan, ed. *Wenxin diaolong zhu.* Rpt. Taipei: Daming, 1965.

Fountain of Ancient Poetry. See Shen Deqian.

Guo Maoqian (ca. 1100). *Yuefu shiji.* Rpt. Shanghai: Zhonghua, 1930.

Guo Shaoyu. *Canglang shihua jiaoshi.* Peking: Renmin, 1961.

————. *Zhongguo wenxue piping shi.* Rpt. Hong Kong: Hongzhi, n.d.

He Wenhuan, ed. *Lidai shihua.* 1740; rpt. Taipei: Yiwen, 1974.

Henzō Kinkō (Kūkai [774–835]), ed. *Bunkyō hifuron (Wenjing mifu lun).* Ed. Zhou Weide. Peking: Renmin, 1975.

Hong Xingzu, ed. *Chu ci buzhu.* Rpt. Taipei: Yiwen, 1973.

Jiang Kui (ca. 1155–1221). *Baishi daoren shishuo,* in He Wenhuan, pp. 439–41.

Jiaoran (ca. 760). *Shi shi,* in He Wenhuan, pp. 18–28.

————. *Shi yi,* in Henzō Kinkō, pp. 141–49.

Lidai shihua. See He Wenhuan.

Li Taibo ji. Rpt. Taipei: Heluo, 1975.

Liu Xie (ca. 485–523). See Fan Wenlan.

Lu Ji (261–303). *Wen fu,* in *Wei Jin Nan Bei Chao wenxueshi cankao ziliao.* Peking, 1961; rpt. Hong Kong: Hongzhi, n.d.

Meng Qi (9th cent.). *Ben shi shi,* in Ding Fubao, ed., *Lidai shihua xubian,* I, 1a–12b.

Ouyang Xiu (1007–72). *Liuyi shihua,* in He Wenhuan, pp. 156–62.

Qian Zhongshu. *Tan yi lu.* Shanghai: Kaiming, 1948.

Shen Deqian (1673–1769). *Gu shi yuan jianzhu.* Rpt. Taipei: Guting, 1970.

Sikong Tu (837–908). See Zu Baoquan.

Songs of Chu. See Hong Xingzu.

Wang Changling (698–757). *Lun wen yi,* in Henzō Kinkō, pp. 127–41.

Wang Shizhen (1526–90). *Yiyuan zhiyan,* in *Yanzhou shanren si bu gao.* 15 vols. *Mingdai lunzhu congkan.* Rpt. Taipei: Weiwen, 1976, XIII (entire); appendix: XIV, 6875–7942.

Wang Shizhen (1634–1711). *Daijingtang shihua.* 2 vols. Rpt. Taipei: Qingliu, 1976.

Wu Qiao (ca. 1660). *Weilu shihua. Congshu jicheng,* vol. 2609. Shanghai: Shangwu, 1935.

Xiao Tong (Prince Zhaoming of Liang [501–31]). *Zhaoming Wen xuan.* Rpt. Taipei: Wenhua, 1969.

Xie Zhen (1495–1575). *Siming shihua. Congshu jicheng,* vol. 2581. Shanghai: Shangwu, 1935.

Yan Yu (fl. 1180–1235). See Guo Shaoyu, *Canglang shihua jiaoshi.*

Zhong Hong (fl. 483–513). *Shi pin,* in He Wenhuan, pp. 7–17.

Zu Baoquan, ed. *Sikong Tu shi pin zhushi ji yiwen.* Hong Kong: Shangwu, 1966.

B. *Western Primary and Secondary Sources*

Abrams, M. H. *The Mirror and the Lamp: Romantic Theory and the Tradition.* New York: Oxford University Press, 1953.

Auerbach, Erich. *Mimesis: The Representation of Reality in Western Literature.* Trans. Willard R. Trask. Princeton: Princeton University Press, 1963.

Bate, Walter Jackson, ed. *Criticism: The Major Texts*. Enlarged ed. New York: Harcourt Brace Jovanovich, 1970.

Baudelaire, Charles. *Oeuvres complètes*. Ed. Y.-G. Le Dantec. Tours: Gallimard, 1958.

Benn, Gottfried. *Probleme der Lyrik*. Wiesbaden: Limes Verlag, 1951.

Dufrenne, Mikel. *The Phenomenology of Aesthetic Experience*. Trans. Edward S. Casey et al. Evanston: Northwestern University Press, 1973.

_____. *Le Poétique*. Paris: Presses universitaires de France, 1963.

Eliot, T. S. *Four Quartets*. New York: Harcourt Brace and World, 1943.

_____. "From Poe to Valéry," in *To Criticize the Critic*. New York: Farrar, Straus and Giroux, 1968, pp. 27–43.

_____. "Tradition and the Individual Talent," in *The Sacred Wood*. Rpt. London: Methuen and Co., 1972, pp. 47–59.

Fenollosa, Ernest. "The Chinese Written Character as a Medium for Poetry," rpt. in Ezra Pound, *Instigations*. Freeport, N.Y.: Books for Libraries Press, 1969, pp. 357–88.

Friedrich, Hugo. *Die Struktur der modernen Lyrik*. Hamburg: Rowohlt, 1956.

Frye, Northrop. "Three Meanings of Symbolism," *Yale French Studies*, No. 9 (1952), pp. 11–19.

Gras, Vernon L., ed. *European Literary Theory and Practice: From Existential Phenomenology to Structuralism*. New York: Dell, 1972.

Grimm, Reinhold, ed. *Zur Lyrik-Diskussion*. Darmstadt: Wissenschaftliche Buchgesellschaft, 1966.

Halliburton, David. *Edgar Allan Poe: A Phenomenological Study*. Princeton: Princeton University Press, 1974.

Heidegger, Martin. "Georg Trakl: Eine Erörterung seines Gedichtes," in *Unterwegs zur Sprache*. Pfullingen: Verlag Günther Neske, 1959. First published in *Merkur*, 7 (1953), pp. 226–58.

_____. "Hölderlin and the Essence of Poetry," in *Existence and Being*. Trans. D. Scott. Chicago: H. Regnery and Co., 1949. Rpt. in Gras, pp. 27–41.

Hofmannsthal, Hugo von. "Ein Brief," in *Gesammelte Werke, Prosa* II. Ed. Herbert Steiner. Frankfurt: Fischer, 1951, pp. 7–22.

Ingarden, Roman. *The Literary Work of Art*. Trans. George G. Grabowicz. Evanston: Northwestern University Press, 1973.

Longinus. "On the Sublime," excerpted in Bate, pp. 62–75.

MacLeish, Archibald. *Poetry and Experience*. Baltimore: Penguin, 1960.

Magliola, Robert. "The Phenomenological Approach to Literature: Its Theory and Methodology," *Language and Style*, Vol. V, No. 2 (Spring 1972), pp. 79–99.

Mallarmé, Stéphane. *Oeuvres complètes*. Ed. H. Mondor and G. Jean-Aubry. Paris: Gallimard, 1945.

Merleau-Ponty, Maurice. Preface to *Phenomenology of Perception*. Trans. Colin Smith. London: Routledge and Kegan Paul, 1962. Rpt. as "What is Phenomenology?" in Gras, pp. 69–85.

Miller, J. Hillis. *Poets of Reality*. New York: Atheneum, 1969.

Nietzsche, Friedrich. *The Birth of Tragedy and the Genealogy of Morals*. Trans. Francis Golffing. Garden City: Doubleday, 1956.

Poe, Edgar Allan. "The Philosophy of Composition," in *The Complete Works of Edgar Allan Poe*. Ed. James A. Harrison. 17 vols. New York: AMS Press Inc., 1965, XIV, 193–265.

———. "The Poetic Principle," in *The Complete Works*, XIV, 266–96.

Pound, Ezra. "A Few Don'ts," *Poetry*, Vol. 1, No. 6 (March 1913). Rpt. in *Literary Essays of Ezra Pound*. New York: New Directions, 1968, pp. 4–7.

Poulet, Georges. "Criticism and the Experience of Interiority," in *The Structuralist Controversy: The Languages of Criticism and the Sciences of Man*. Ed. R. Macksey and E. Donato. Baltimore: Johns Hopkins University Press, 1970, pp. 67–72.

———. *Etudes sur le temps humain*. Paris: Plon, 1956.

Rilke, Rainer Maria. *Ausgewählte Gedichte*. Selected by Erich Heller. Frankfurt: Suhrkamp Verlag, 1966.

———. *Briefe*. Ed. Ruth Sieber-Rilke and Karl Altheim. 2 vols. Wiesbaden: Insel-Verlag, 1950.

Richard, Jean-Pierre. *L'Univers imaginaire de Mallarmé*. Paris: Editions du Seuil, 1961.

Rimbaud, Arthur. *Oeuvres*. Ed. Suzanne Bernard. Paris: Garnier, 1960.

Sidney, Sir Philip. "An Apology for Poetry," in Bate, pp. 82–106.

Stevens, Wallace. "Adagia," in *Opus Posthumous*. Ed. Samuel French Morse. New York: Alfred A. Knopf, 1957, pp. 157–80.

———. *The Necessary Angel*. New York: Vintage, 1951.

Valéry, Paul. *Oeuvres*. Ed. Jean Hytier. 2 vols. Tours: Gallimard, 1959.

Verlaine, Paul. *Oeuvres complètes*. Ed. Charles Morice. 2 vols. Paris: Albert Messein, 1919.

III. OTHER SECONDARY SOURCES AND TRANSLATIONS

Bodde, Derk. *Festivals in Classical China: New Year and Other Annual Observances During the Han Dynasty 206 B.C.–A.D. 220*. Princeton: Princeton University Press, 1975.

Bodman, Richard W. "Poetics and Prosody in Early Mediaeval China: A Study and Translation of Kūkai's *Bunkyō hifuron*." Ph.D. dissertation, Cornell University, 1978.

Boodberg, Peter A. "Cedules from a Berkeley Workshop in Asiatic Philology," *Ts'ing Hua Journal of Chinese Studies*, Vol. VII, No. 2 (August 1969), pp. 1–69.

Buxbaum, David and Fritz Mote, ed. *Transition and Permanence: Chinese History and Culture*. Hong Kong: Cathay Press, 1972.

Chang Chung-yüan. *Original Teachings of Ch'an Buddhism*. New York: Vintage, 1971.

Chang, Garma C. C. *The Buddhist Teaching of Totality: The Philosophy of Hwa-Yen Buddhism*. University Park, Pa.: Pennsylvania State University Press, 1971.

Chaves, Jonathan. *Mei Yao-ch'en and the Development of Early Sung Poetry*. New York: Columbia University Press, 1976.

Ch'en, Kenneth K. S. *Buddhism in China: A Historical Survey*. Princeton: Princeton University Press, 1964.

———. *The Chinese Transformation of Buddhism*. Princeton: Princeton University Press, 1973.

Conze, Edward. *Buddhism: Its Essence and Development*. New York: Harper and Row, 1959.

_____, trans. *Buddhist Wisdom Books*. New York: Harper and Row, 1972.

Davis, A. R. "The Double Ninth Festival in Chinese Poetry: A Study of Variations upon a Theme," in *Wen-lin: Studies in the Chinese Humanities*. Ed. Chow Tse-tsung. Madison: University of Wisconsin Press, 1968, pp. 45–64.

Debon, Günther, trans. *Ts'ang-lang's Gespräche über die Dichtung*. Wiesbaden: Otto Harrassowitz, 1962.

Dumoulin, Heinrich. *A History of Zen Buddhism*. Boston: Beacon, 1971.

Eoyang, Eugene. "The Solitary Boat: Images of Self in Chinese Nature Poetry," *Journal of Asian Studies*, Vol. XXXII, No. 4 (August 1973), pp. 593–621.

Fang, Achilles, trans. "Rhymeprose on Literature" [Lu Ji's *Wen fu*], *Harvard Journal of Asiatic Studies*, Vol. 14 (1951), pp. 527–66. Rpt. in John L. Bishop, ed., *Studies in Chinese Literature*. Cambridge, Ma.: Harvard University Press, 1966, pp. 3–42.

Frankel, Hans. "The Contemplation of the Past in T'ang Poetry," in Twitchett and Wright, pp. 345–65.

_____. *The Flowering Plum and the Palace Lady: Interpretations of Chinese Poetry*. New Haven: Yale University Press, 1976.

_____. "*Yüeh-fu* Poetry," in *Studies in Chinese Literary Genres*. Ed. Cyril Birch. Berkeley: University of California Press, 1971, pp. 69–107.

Fung Yu-lan. *A History of Chinese Philosophy*. Trans. Derk Bodde. 2 vols. Princeton: Princeton University Press, 1953.

_____. *A Short History of Chinese Philosophy*. Ed. Derk Bodde. New York: The Free Press, 1948.

Hawkes, David. *Ch'u Tz'u: The Songs of the South*. Oxford: Clarendon Press, 1959.

Hightower, James Robert. *The Poetry of T'ao Ch'ien*. Oxford: Clarendon Press, 1970.

Holzman, Donald. *Poetry and Politics: The Life and Works of Juan Chi (A.D. 210–263)*. Cambridge: Cambridge University Press, 1976.

Hurvitz, Leon, trans. *Scripture of the Lotus Blossom of the Fine Dharma (The Lotus Sūtra)*. New York: Columbia University Press, 1976.

Kao Yu-kung and Tsu-lin Mei. "Syntax, Diction and Imagery in T'ang Poetry," *Harvard Journal of Asiatic Studies*, No. 31 (1971), pp. 49–136.

Karlgren, Bernhard, trans. *The Book of Odes*. Stockholm: Museum of Far Eastern Antiquities, 1974.

Lattimore, David. "Allusion and T'ang Poetry," in Twitchett and Wright, pp. 405–439.

Lau, D. C., trans. *Tao Te Ching*. Baltimore: Penguin, 1963.

Legge, James, trans. *The Chinese Classics*. Vol. V: *The Ch'un Ts'ew with the Tso Chuen*. Rpt. Taipei: Wenxing, 1966.

Liu, James J. Y. *The Art of Chinese Poetry*. Chicago: University of Chicago Press, 1962.

_____. *The Chinese Knight-Errant*. Chicago: University of Chicago Press, 1967.

_____. *Chinese Theories of Literature*. Chicago: University of Chicago Press, 1975.

Liu Wu-chi and Irving Y. Lo, eds. *Sunflower Splendor: Three Thousand Years of Chinese Poetry*. New York: Doubleday Anchor, 1975.

Luk, Charles, trans. *The Vimalakīrti Nirdeśa Sūtra*. Berkeley: Shambala, 1972.

Lynn, Richard John. "Orthodoxy and Enlightenment: Wang Shih-chen's

Theory of Poetry and Its Antecedents," in *The Unfolding of Neo-Confucian-ism*. Ed. William Theodore deBary. New York: Columbia University Press, 1975, pp. 218–59.

Mather, Richard B. "The Landscape Buddhism of the Fifth-Century Poet Hsieh Ling-yün," *Journal of Asian Studies*, Vol. XVIII, No. 1 (November 1958), pp. 67–79.

———. "Vimalakīrti and Gentry Buddhism," *History of Religions*, Vol. 8, No. 1 (August 1968), pp. 60–73.

Miller, James Whipple. "English Romanticism and Chinese Nature Poetry," *Comparative Literature*, Vol. XXIV, No. 3 (Summer 1972), pp. 216–36.

Mote, Frederick. "The Cosmological Gulf Between China and the West," in Buxbaum and Mote, pp. 3–21.

———. *Intellectual Foundations of China*. New York: Alfred A. Knopf, 1971.

Murti, T.R.V. *The Central Philosophy of Buddhism: A Study of the Mādhyamika System*. London: Allen and Unwin, 1955.

Needham, Joseph and Wang Ling. *Science and Civilisation in China*. Vol. II: *History of Scientific Thought*. Cambridge: Cambridge University Press, 1951.

Owen, Stephen. *The Poetry of the Early T'ang*. New Haven: Yale University Press, 1977.

Pulleyblank, E. G. *The Background of the Rebellion of An Lu-shan*. Oxford: Oxford University Press, 1966.

Rickett, Adele Austin, ed. *Chinese Approaches to Literature from Confucius to Liang Ch'i-ch'ao*. Princeton: Princeton University Press, 1978.

Robertson, Maureen. " . . . To Convey What Is Precious": Ssu-K'ung T'u's Poetics and the Erh-shih-ssu Shih P'in," in Buxbaum and Mote, pp. 323–57.

Soothill, William Edward and L. Hodous. *A Dictionary of Chinese Buddhist Terms*. Rpt. Taipei: Chengwen, 1972.

T'ang Chün-i. "The Individual and the World in Chinese Methodology," in *The Chinese Mind: Essentials of Chinese Philosophy and Culture*. Ed. Charles A. Moore. Honolulu: East–West Center Press, 1967, pp. 264–85.

Twitchett, Denis and Arthur F. Wright, eds. *Perspectives on the T'ang*. New Haven: Yale University Press, 1973.

Waley, Arthur. *The Nine Songs: A Study of Shamanism in Ancient China*. San Francisco: City Lights Books, 1973.

Watson, Burton. *Chinese Lyricism: Shih Poetry from the Second to the Twelfth Century*. New York: Columbia University Press, 1971.

———. *Chinese Rhyme-Prose: Poems in the Fu Form from the Han and Six Dynasties Period*. New York: Columbia University Press, 1971.

———, trans. *The Complete Works of Chuang Tzu*. New York: Columbia University Press, 1970.

Yampolsky, Philip B., trans. *The Platform Sutra of the Sixth Patriarch*. New York: Columbia University Press, 1967.

Yip, Wai-lim. *Chinese Poetry: Major Modes and Genres*. Berkeley: University of California Press, 1976.

Yu, Pauline. "Chinese and Symbolist Poetic Theories," *Comparative Literature*, Vol. XXX, No. 4 (Fall 1978), pp. 291–312.

———. "The Poetics of Discontinuity: East–West Correspondences in Lyric Poetry," *PMLA*, Vol. 94, No. 2 (March 1979), pp. 261–74.

_____. "Ssu-k'ung T'u's *Shih-p'in*: Poetic Theory in Poetic Form," in *Studies in Chinese Poetry and Poetics*, Vol. I. Ed. Ronald Miao. San Francisco: Chinese Materials Center, 1978, pp. 81–103.

Zürcher, E. "Buddhism in China," in *The Legacy of China*. Ed. Raymond Dawson. Oxford: Oxford University Press, 1964, pp. 56–79.

_____. *The Buddhist Conquest of China: The Spread and Adaptation of Buddhism in Early Medieval China*. Leiden: E. J. Brill, 1959.

IV. OTHER SOURCES IN CHINESE

Han shu. 8 vols. Peking: Zhonghua, 1975.

Hou Han shu. 12 vols. Peking: Zhonghua, 1973.

Jin shu. 10 vols. Peking: Zhonghua, 1974.

Jingde chuan deng lu. *Taishō shinshū daizōkyō*, Vol. 51, No. 2076, pp. 196–467. Rpt. Tokyo: The Taisho Shinshu Daizokyo Kanko Kai, 1973.

Jiu Tang shu. 16 vols. Peking: Zhonghua, 1975.

Nan shi. 6 vols. Peking: Zhonghua, 1975.

Sanguo zhi. 4 vols. Peking: Zhonghua, 1973.

Shi ji. 10 vols. Peking: Zhonghua, 1974.

Song shu. 8 vols. Peking: Zhonghua, 1974.

Xin bian zhuzi jicheng. 8 vols. Taipei: Shijie, 1974.

Xin Tang shu. 20 vols. Peking: Zhonghua, 1975.

Zhou yi yinde. Harvard-Yenching Institute Sinological Index Series Supplement 10. Rpt. Taipei: Chengwen, 1966.

Zhuangzi yinde. Harvard-Yenching Institute Sinological Index Series Supplement 20. Cambridge, Mass.: Harvard University Press, 1956.

Index of Poem Titles

(Page numbers of poems are in italics)

Index of Proper Names and Terms

(Page numbers in italics refer to poems)